BEARS

BEARS

MAJESTIC CREATURES OF THE WILD

CONSULTING EDITOR
Ian Stirling, Ph.D.

ILLUSTRATIONS
David Kirshner, Ph.D.
Frank Knight

RODALE PRESS
EMMAUS, PENNSYLVANIA

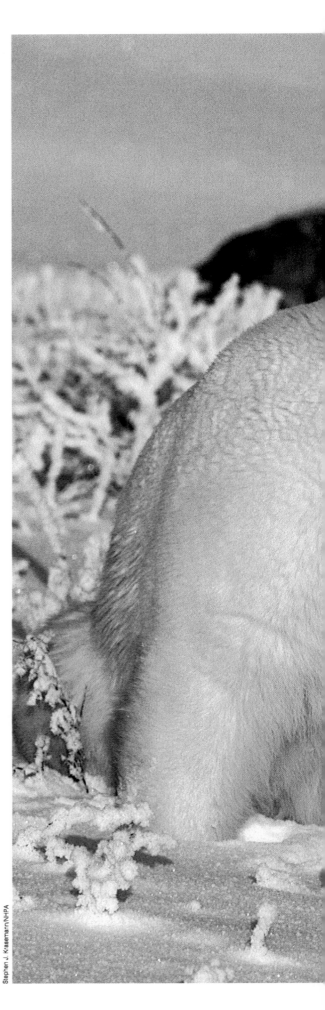

Published 1993 by Rodale Press, Inc.
33 East Minor Street, Emmaus, PA 18098, USA

By arrangement with Weldon Owen
Produced by Weldon Owen Pty Limited
43 Victoria Street, McMahons Point NSW 2060, Australia
Fax (02) 929 8352
A member of the Weldon International Group of Companies
Sydney • San Francisco • London
Chairman: Kevin Weldon
President: John Owen
General Manager: Stuart Laurence

Publisher: Sheena Coupe
Project Coordinator: Lu Sierra
Editor: Gillian Hewitt
Picture Editor: Jenny Mills
Captions: Ian Stirling
Series Design: Sue Burk

Design and Art Direction:
Andi Cole, Andi Cole Design
Index: Dianne Regtop
Coeditions Director: Derek Barton
Production Director: Mick Bagnato
Production Coordinator: Simone Perryman

Copyright © 1993 Weldon Owen Pty Limited

Library of Congress Cataloging-in-Publication Data
Bears/consulting editor, Ian Stirling: illustrations, David Kirshner, Frank Knight.
p. cm. — (Majestic creatures of the wild)
Includes bibliographical references and index.
ISBN 0–87596–552–0 (hardcover)
1. Bears. I. Stirling, Ian. II. Kirshner, David. III. Knight, Frank. IV. Series.
QL737.C27B4 1993
599.74'446—dc20
92–40717
CIP

If you have any questions or comments concerning this book, please write to:
Rodale Press
Book Readers' Service
33 East Minor Street
Emmaus, PA 18098

Printed by Kyodo Printing Co. (S'pore) Pte Ltd
Printed in Singapore

10 9 8 7 6 5 4 3 2 1

Distributed in the book trade by St. Martin's Press

A Weldon Owen Production

Front cover: To most people, the polar bear (*Ursus maritimus*), largest of all the bears, symbolizes the Arctic. No animal is more at home in the polar sea–ice habitat. Photo by Stan Osolinski/The Stock Market/Stock Photos.
Back cover: A female brown bear (*Ursus arctos*) and her cub look for berries in the fall. Photo by Daniel J. Cox/Oxford Scientific Films
Endpapers: American black bears (*Ursus americanus*) enjoy swimming, particularly on hot summer days. Photo by Erwin and Peggy Bauer/Bruce Coleman Ltd
Page 1: A brown bear hauls a salmon from the clear waters of an Alaskan lake.
Page 2: A sleeping cinnamon-phase American black bear, safe from disturbance or potential danger.
Page 3: In Sichuan, China, a giant panda (*Ailuropoda melanoleuca*) surveys the treetops.
Page 7: Two young grizzlies playfight in McNeil River, Alaska, where large numbers of bears congregate during the salmon run. This area is a popular site with tourists wishing to view these animals in their natural habitat.
Pages 8–9: Glistening drops of water create a halo around a grizzly bear cub as it shakes itself.
Pages 10–11: An approaching boat at Wager Bay, Northwest Territories, Canada, frightens away a polar bear and her two yearling cubs.

▶ In the icy beauty of the Canadian Arctic, a mother polar bear affectionately nuzzles her young cub.

Stephen J. Krasemann/NHPA

CONSULTING EDITOR
Dr. Ian Stirling
Senior Research Scientist, Canadian Wildlife Service, Canadian Department of the Environment; Adjunct Professor of Zoology, University of Alberta, Edmonton, Alberta, Canada

CONTRIBUTORS

Ms. Alison Ames
Senior Officer for the Universities Federation for Animal Welfare, Potters Bar, England

Dr. Fred. L. Bunnell
Professor of Forest Wildlife Ecology and Management, University of British Columbia, Vancouver, British Columbia, Canada

Ms. Wendy Calvert
Biologist with the Canadian Wildlife Service, Canadian Department of the Environment, Edmonton, Alberta, Canada

Dr. Joseph D. Clark
Assistant Chief (Research), Arkansas Game and Fish Commission, Little Rock, Arkansas, USA

Mr. Peter L. Clarkson
Wolf and Brown Bear Biologist, Department of Renewable Resources, Goverment of NW Territories, Inuvik, NW Territories, Canada

Ms. Shelley M. Cox
Curatorial Assistant and Laboratory Supervisor, George C. Page Museum, California, USA

Dr. Andrew E. Derocher
Research Biologist, Canadian Wildlife Service Polar Bear Project, Canadian Department of the Environment, Edmonton, Alberta, Canada

Dr. David L. Garshelis
Bear Project Leader, Minnesota Department of Natural Resources, Grand Rapids, Minnesota, USA

Dr. Valerius Geist
Professor of Environmental Sciences and Programme Director for Environmental Sciences, The University of Calgary, Alberta, Canada

Dr. Stephen Herrero
Professor of Environmental Science and Biology, The University of Calgary, Alberta, Canada

Dr. Robert S. Hoffmann
Assistant Secretary for Research, Smithsonian Institution, Washington, DC, USA

Mr. Fred W. Hovey
Department of Biological Sciences, Simon Fraser University, Burnaby, British Columbia, Canada

Mr. Jack W. Lentfer
Independent wildlife consultant specializing in marine mammals; member of the Alaska Board of Game

Mr. Robert K. McCann
The Center for Applied Conservation Biology, Faculty of Forestry, University of British Columbia, Vancouver, Canada

Ms. Judy A. Mills
Research Associate, IUCN/SCC Bear Specialist Group, US Fish and Wildlife Service, University of Montana, Missoula, Montana, USA

Dr. Stephen J. O'Brien
Chief, Laboratory of Viral Carcinogenesis, National Cancer Institute, Frederick, Maryland, USA

Dr. Michael R. Pelton
Professor of Wildlife Science, Department of Forestry, Wildlife, and Fisheries, University of Tennessee, Knoxville, Tennessee, USA

Dr. Malcolm A. Ramsay
Associate Professor, Department of Biology, University of Saskatchewan, Saskatoon, Saskatchewan, Canada

Mr. Donald G. Reid
Department of Zoology, University of British Columbia, Vancouver, Canada

Dr. Lynn L. Rogers
Wildlife Research Biologist, US Forest Service's North Central Forest Experiment Station, Ely, Minnesota, USA

Dr. Barry Sanders
Peter and Gloria Gold Professor, English and the History of Ideas, Pitzer College, Claremont, California, USA

Dr. John Seidensticker
Curator of Mammals, National Zoological Park, Smithsonian Institution, Washington, DC, USA

Dr. Christopher Servheen
Grizzly Bear Recovery Coordinator, US Fish and Wildlife Service; Co-chairman, IUCN/SSC Bear Specialist Group; Adjunct Research Professor, School of Forestry, University of Montana, Missoula, Montana, USA

Mr. Christopher A. Shaw
Collection Manager, George C. Page Museum, California, USA

Mr. Scott D. Shull
Research Assistant, Arkansas Cooperative Fish and Wildlife Research Unit, University of Arkansas, Fayetteville, Arkansas, USA

Dr. Kimberly G. Smith
Professor of Biological Sciences, University of Arkansas, Fayetteville, Arkansas, USA

Dr. Blaire Van Valkenburgh
Associate Professor, Department of Biology, University of California, Los Angeles, California, USA

Mr. Alasdair M. Veitch
Department of Zoology, University of Alberta, Edmonton, Alberta, Canada

Ms. Diana L. Weinhardt
Zoologist, Lincoln Park Zoological Gardens, Chicago, Illinois, USA; Editor, International Spectacled Bear Studbook

Mr. Wenshi Pan
Professor of Zoology, Beijing University, Beijing, China

Dr. W. Chris Wozencraft
Research Assistant, Winrock International Institute for Agricultural Development, Arlington, Virginia.

Dr. Zhi Lü
Department of Zoology, Beijing University, Beijing, China

8

CONTENTS

FOREWORD

Bears will have fascinated most of us at one time or another, whether we met them in zoos or in the wild. Bears, in general, are large animals—nearly the size of a human for the smallest species and four or five times that size for the largest—and are therefore long-lived. In common with humans, a bear of some 30 years of age will have accumulated a fair bit of experience in dealing with the world, and a female will pass on some of the knowledge she has acquired to her offspring.

Bears remind us of ourselves. If startled they will stand upright and look at us, and we feel an affinity with them. Their eyesight is probably comparable to our own, but their hearing is acute, and they rely on their highly developed olfactory sense for identifying strange objects. Aboriginal people who have grown up with bears have a great respect for them, and bears are woven frequently into their mythology; there are even legends of bears that have mated with humans and created a separate race. Above all, the largest species of bears command respect because they are life threatening if provoked.

In 1968 I was at a field camp in Sri Lanka in an area frequented by sloth bears. One night as I was on my way to the river to fetch water, I encountered a bear. It would have been difficult to say which of us was the more surprised. This was not the first time I had encountered a bear in the wild, but there in the darkness, I was extremely startled. The bear stood on its hind legs and roared, then both of us fled. This is typical of human encounters with bears. The two species are an even match, and I love bears very much.

A distinguished set of authors has put together this fine volume dealing with the biology, behavior, and conservation of bears. I hope readers will be inspired to actively participate in making the world a safer place for these magnificent animals.

John F. Eisenberg
Katharine Ordway Professor of Ecosystem Conservation
University of Florida

INTRODUCTION

Only those able to see the pageant of evolution can be expected to value its theatre, the wilderness, or its outstanding achievement, the grizzly.

Aldo Leopold

The eight living species of bears exhibit extraordinary variation in everything from body size and distribution to their adaptations for survival in habitats that range from tropical forests to polar ice fields. The largest species is ten times heavier than the smallest. Although most bears are omnivores—they will eat almost anything—some have evolved specialized roles as carnivores and herbivores. Even so, giant pandas, which normally eat only bamboo, will still eat meat, while polar bears, which specialize in hunting seals, also eat berries. One species, the sloth bear, mainly eats termites.

As wonderful as bears are, it is not our fascination with unraveling their scientific secrets that must now be our highest priority. Our primary concern must be to ensure their very survival. Large numbers of bears are being killed illegally to support traditional medical practices, and the burgeoning human population is competing with them for habitat. Bears live at low densities over large areas. The home ranges of terrestrial bear species range from less than 10 square kilometers (4 square miles) to over 2,000 square kilometers (770 square miles). The home ranges of polar bears in some areas of drifting pack ice can exceed 300,000 square kilometers (116,000 square miles). To maintain healthy populations of bears, it is critical to conserve large areas of natural habitat, a commodity which is becoming scarcer by the day. Protecting areas large enough for wild bear populations will also maximize our chances of preserving whole ecosystems and the natural relationships of all the animals and plants that live within them. Wilderness areas that retain their wild bear populations will provide us with hope for the future.

Ian Stirling
Consulting Editor

▲ Standing on the bank of a river in Alaska, a subadult brown bear paws at salmon swimming by.

EVOLUTION

AND BIOLOGY

HOW THE BEARS CAME TO BE

W. CHRIS WOZENCRAFT AND ROBERT S. HOFFMANN

The largest terrestrial carnivores on Earth today are two closely related species of the Ursidae, the bear family, in the order Carnivora. Adult male polar bears (*Ursus maritimus*) may tip the scales anywhere between 400 and 800 kilograms (880 and 1,760 pounds) and some northern populations of brown bears (*Ursus arctos*) may weigh from 525 to nearly 700 kilograms (1,150 to 1,550 pounds). As impressive as these bears may seem today, one of their ancestors would have exceeded even today's record sizes.

▼ Even when simply play-fighting, over 1,000 kilograms (2,200 pounds) weighs in behind the teeth and claws of these two adult male polar bears, representing enormous potential for damage.

The extinct giant short-faced bear (*Arctodus simus*) was at least twice the size of the Kodiak bear, and probably weighed in at between 600 and 1,000 kilograms (1,320 and 2,200 pounds).

A wide diversity of sizes and adaptations make up the bear family, the Ursidae, whose substantial fossil record can be traced back to a small fox-like ancestor, *Cephalogale*, in the Oligocene epoch of Europe, nearly 40 million years ago. Bears are, or were, widely distributed in the Northern Hemisphere, though there are few in the Southern Hemisphere. They feature prominently in the

folklore and history of many cultures. Today, they are represented by eight species, and are found on every continent except Antarctica and Australia. In most places they are nowhere near as abundant as they were in prehistoric and early historic times; in fact, six species are listed by CITES as endangered.

DISTINGUISHING FEATURES

A variety of physical features distinguishes bears from other carnivores, such as cats, dogs, raccoons, badgers, and weasels, and it is principally these features that enable paleontologists to identify the

▼ In an Alaskan ice-age refugium about 12,000 years ago—a geographical area unaffected by the surrounding climatic change—most mammal species, both prey and predator, were larger than their present-day descendants. In this assemblage are the bison, the wooly mammoth, the giant short-faced bear, the wolverine, the brown bear, and the yak.

Modern bears have six to seven post-canine teeth, two molars in the upper and three in the lower jaw, and four premolars, as well as their large canines, and six upper and six lower incisors. This is close to the primitive arrangement for most carnivores. The premolars, important for holding onto prey in meat eaters, are not as significant in plant-eating bears and therefore are usually reduced in this family, and in some are lost in adulthood. In most families of carnivores, the dominant set of teeth are the fourth upper premolar and the first lower molar, which are the principal teeth that cut meat. The development of these teeth stimulated the divergence of the carnivores from their ancestors. In bears, these teeth are smaller than the molars that follow them, which indicates a shift from a cutting to a crushing function.

The ear region of bear skulls is unique, and bears can easily be distinguished from other carnivores on this feature alone. In most carnivores, such as cats, dogs, raccoons, and weasels, the middle ear consists of a balloon-shaped bony structure that forms a resonating chamber surrounding the ear drum. Known as auditory bullae, these inflated structures, which increase hearing sensitivity, are formed by the fusion of two bones, the entotympanic and the ectotympanic. In most families of carnivores, the inflated chamber is predominately entotympanic bone, with the ectotympanic forming only a small portion of the total chamber walls. In bears, however, the entotympanic is reduced, does not form a significant part of the chamber walls, and is hidden from external view. Looking at the undersurface of the ear region of a bear skull, only the flat, uninflated ectotympanic can be seen.

All bears have five toes on each foot with non-retractile claws, as in most carnivores, but unlike cats. Their posture is plantigrade—like humans, they walk on the soles of their hindfeet. Although bears have a reduced or absent clavicle or collar bone, as is typical of large non-primate mammals, most species can climb trees adeptly, but their ability to swing by their front limbs is inhibited.

▲ The small carnivore *Ursavus* appeared about 20 million years ago. Descendants of this genus are thought to have given rise to most of the living species of bears.

Ken Lucas/Planet Earth Pictures

▲ The skull of the American black bear (*Ursus americanus*) has a low forehead and is much lighter boned than that of the brown bear.

rich fossil diversity. Although many species of the Carnivora diverged early from their more herbivorous ancestors and specialized in eating meat (for example, the cat family, Felidae), bears represent a trend to a more generalized diet, concentrating on plants and vegetables rather than meat, but usually with a year-round diet that includes both. To survive on plants, bears need to crush the plant cells and release the food material within. They are well adapted to do this, since they have the most enlarged, cusped teeth of any carnivore. Their ability to digest large amounts of vegetation during favorable times, and switch to animal material during others, has enabled them to evolve a herbivory/predatory niche that is uniquely bear-like and successful, especially in temperate climates. The "explosion" in the diversity of bears which occurred during the Pliocene and Pleistocene, between 5 million and 10,000 years ago, coincided with a period of increasing seasonality of vegetation and climate.

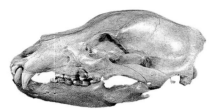

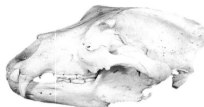

Ken Lucas/Planet Earth Pictures

▲ Brown bear skulls have a high degree of variability. Because of this, one taxonomist went to the extreme of describing no less than 232 different species of extinct and living brown bears. Shown here are skulls of a currently recognized subspecies, the Kodiak bear (*Ursus arctos middendorffi*), at the top, the extinct Californian brown bear (*Ursus arctos californicus*), in the middle, and a brown bear (*Ursus arctos horribilis*), at the bottom, from Yellowstone National Park in the United States.

◄ In close proximity, the open mouth threat is a powerful display of weaponry, and it may end an encounter. Sometimes large males lock jaws and twist, pushing aggressively, resulting in broken canine teeth.

▼ The size of the giant short-faced bear (*Arctodus simus*) is dramatically illustrated by comparing a fossilized skull (right) with the skull of a present-day brown bear.

FOSSIL BEARS

Widespread during the Miocene epoch (24 to 5 million years ago), *Cephalogale* was similar to a dog, and was originally placed in a canid subfamily called the Hemicyoninae ("hemi" meaning half, and "cyon" meaning dog), which exhibited characteristics shared by both dogs and bears.

From this small dog-like ancestor came the first truly bear-like carnivore, *Ursavus*, from which were derived nearly all other bears. It is likely that *Ursavus depereti*, or a similar species, gave rise to the Agriotherinae, best represented by the extinct *Agriotherium* and *Indarctos*. These bears were present in the Pliocene (5 to 2 million years ago) and Pleistocene (2 million to 10,000 years ago) and had much shorter muzzles than the bears

known today. They had a rather prominent upper fourth premolar, which is reduced in present bears. Examinations of their teeth show that *Agriotherium* and *Indarctos* went in two different evolutionary directions. *Agriotherium* became more of a predator, whereas *Indarctos* became more herbivorous and eventually gave rise to one of the few highly herbivorous modern carnivores, the giant panda (*Ailuropoda melanoleuca*).

In the late Pliocene, two more branches on the bear tree diverged from this *Ursavus*-like ancestor. The short-faced bears first appeared during this time and produced the largest known terrestrial carnivore, *Arctodus simus*, which had long legs and was evidently highly mobile and carnivorous in its habits. There was also the much smaller *Plionarctos*, which gave rise to one of the most primitive bears

THE CAVE BEAR

VALERIUS GEIST

The cave bear (*Ursus spelaeus*) was a large, apparently herbivorous bear, the largest of which would have been equal in size to the huge brown bears of the Alaska Peninsula. Like its predecessor, the smaller Deninger's cave bear (*Ursus deningeri*), which lived 700,000 to 300,000 years ago, it was confined to western Europe.

The cave bear had a large head with massive canine teeth: its premolars were reduced or absent. The third molar reached the largest size ever for bears and was severely worn, indicating powerful mastication, and its broad, high-domed skull provided attachment for the large chewing muscles. The cave bear's face was more dish-like than that of the grizzly and its muzzle was large and well supplied with nerves. The cave bear's front legs were massive, with huge front paws and big, broad claws similar to those of the grizzly bear, while its pelvis and hind legs were comparatively small.

A drawing in the cave Le Colombier in Ain, France, from the Upper Paleolithic (35,000 to 15,000 years ago) shows the cave bear to have had short ears and a pig-like face. It was a huge "teddy"—the most bear-like of bears ever.

Male cave bears were about twice the weight of females, and body size varied considerably from region to region. Together with its small geographic range this indicates that, unlike its relative the brown bear, the cave bear roamed little.

Bears become large wherever they have access to rich protein sources, such as spawning salmon or the carcasses of buffalo that drown after falling through the ice of major rivers. It is likely that, despite being herbivorous, the cave bear was also carnivorous at times. Its large paws and claws, and its powerful front legs and shoulders suggest that it dug for much of its food. It may have fed on the root-beds of plants growing in deep glacial silt, much as grizzly bears dig out tangles of thick, sweet *Hedysarum* at the base of large glaciers in the western Yukon. For protein it might have dug out large colonies of the big plains marmot (*Marmota boback*).

Competition between males for breeding females and also for food resources is suggested by the cave bear's large canine teeth. Evidence suggests that numerous subadult bears failed to survive winter sleep, probably because they were unable to fatten adequately in fall because rich local food spots were defended by mature adults.

During periods when the huge glaciers that covered much of Europe had melted away, the size of cave bears reduced somewhat and they tended to live at high elevations. This may have been linked to low glacial silt production, resulting in a limited number of root beds.

In the late Pleistocene, with the number of brown bears increasing in Europe, the range of the cave bear began to shrink and its numbers declined. They vanished at the end of the glaciation, about 10,000 years ago, but the finding of unfossilized bones of a few cave bears indicates that some may have lived into more recent times.

The most outstanding feature of this bear is the thousands upon thousands of its bones that have been found in caves throughout Europe, from France to Russia. These bones were trampled and moved about by thousands of denning bears over the years, and so articulated skeletons—those which have the bones still joined together—are scarce. Cave bear bones have seldom been found in fossil beds with those of other large mammals, as have the remains of brown bears.

Cave bears used caves for winter sleep and the females probably also gave birth in caves. The bears left their tracks in the mud on the floors, made claw marks on the walls, and in narrow passages their coats polished the walls. There is evidence that early humans hunted the smaller brown bear, but none to indicate they hunted the cave bear.

► Cave bears were so named because they denned in caves during the winter. The bones of large numbers of bears accumulated in some caves, indicating that they were used over many generations. It is estimated that 30,000 to 50,000 bears died in the Dragon Cave near Mixnitz in Austria.

Field Museum/Photo Researchers Inc.

still alive today, the spectacled bear (*Tremarctos ornatus*) of northwestern South America. This bear has a short muzzle, more primitive auditory bullae than other modern bears and teeth that are intermediate between the primitive *Ursavus* and the more herbivorous *Ursus*. The second branch that evolved at this time gave rise to what are known as the true bears, subfamily Ursinae.

The dawn bear (*Ursavus elmensis*), of the Miocene, was not much larger than a raccoon but in form it resembled the ancestors of modern bears. It was not until the late Pliocene, during a period of widespread, relatively rapid, climatic change, that the first truly identifiable species of the genus *Ursus* appeared—*U. minimus*. During this time, as in short-faced bears, there was a general increase in body size in *Ursus* which would have helped with temperature regulation in an increasingly seasonal climate. It was at the beginning of the ice ages, about 2.5 million years ago, that *Ursus minimus* gave rise to a new species, *Ursus etruscus*. This large bear, perhaps similar to the Asiatic black bear (*Ursus thibetanus*), ultimately gave rise to the present diversity of Northern Hemisphere bears. The cave bear (*Ursus spelaeus*), which appeared about 300,000 years ago, and whose extinction was witnessed by early humans, is considered closely related to modern brown bears. It is unique in that

▲ *Agriotherium* was a short lived but widely spread genus of primitive bear that evolved in Europe during the Miocene, and in the course of the Pliocene spread to North America, Asia and Africa.

many of its physical features resemble those of the distantly related short-faced bears.

TO WHAT ARE THE BEARS RELATED?

Systematic analysis of morphological characteristics suggests that among the living species of carnivores, bears are the closest relatives of the sea lions and walruses, while this group is closely related to the raccoon, dog, and weasel families. Sea lion and polar bear skulls are quite similar in appearance—both have long muzzles, teeth in nearly parallel rows, and flattened

▲ A Romanian postage stamp from 1966 showing the extinct cave bear.

▼ The relatively small and shy spectacled bear of South America is the only living relative of the ferocious giant short-faced bear which roamed southern North America up to about 10,000 years ago.

19

Peter Johnson/NHPA

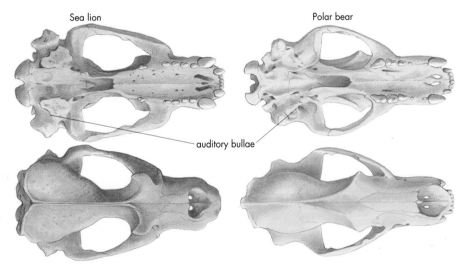

Sea lion

Polar bear

auditory bullae

▲ (Top) Hooker's sea lion (*Phocarctos hookeri*), of the subantarctic islands south of New Zealand, is a member of the family Otariidae, the fur seals and sea lions. The skeletal morphology of the Otariidae more closely resembles that of bears than those of any other groups of living carnivores.

▲ There are several similarities between the skulls of sea lions and bears. In particular, both have long muzzles, parallel rows of teeth, and flattened auditory bullae.

auditory bullae. The early sealers used to call sea lions "sea bears," because when they make their way over the rocks they move in a way that resembles the way bears move.

Taking the family tree an additional branch further back, this group of animals is part of the group of carnivores that is known as the Arctoidea, a group that includes seals (Phocidae), dogs and foxes (Canidae), weasels and otters (Mustelidae), and raccoons (Procyonidae). Their closest ancestors among the fossil species are members of the Amphicyonidae, which are sometimes referred to as the "bear-dogs." The greatest radiation of amphicyonids was during the Oligocene and Miocene, between 36 and 5 million years ago, when they were among the dominant carnivores of Eurasia.

THE TWO PANDAS

Whereas the relationship of the family of bears to other families of carnivores appears to be widely agreed upon, some differences of opinion remain about the relationships of the species within the family. The greatest controversy surrounds the giant panda and the enigmatic red panda (*Ailurus fulgens*). The red panda was first introduced to Western naturalists in 1825, and the name "panda" is derived from a French attempt to spell a Nepalese name for the cat-like animal. Some time later, when the larger animal, first described as the "black and white bear," was discovered by Europeans, its reliance on bamboo (like the red panda) and some similar feeding adaptations were pointed out by early anatomists, who suggested that it was in many respects a "giant" panda. Tied together by the name "panda" ever since, their unique bamboo-eating adaptations have masked the usual clues used by evolutionary biologists to discern relationships among species.

Biochemists, molecular biologists, and paleontologists have traced the evolutionary history of the giant panda back to the extinct subfamily Agriotherinae, represented by the fossil *Indarctos* and *Agriotherium*. The red panda, however, has remained problematical. Although it resembles the North American raccoon, biologists have recently pointed out that it does not share features that all other members of the raccoon family have in common. Some have suggested that it may be most closely related to the extinct bear subfamily, the Amphicyondontines, which were common in Eurasia in the Oligocene. Detailed studies have given conflicting results, with some biologists placing the red panda closer to the raccoon family, others placing it closer to the bear family, and still others placing it squarely between the two. An intermediate between the giant and the red panda may be the extinct *Parailurus*, found in Eurasia and North America, bringing further support to a central Asiatic place of origin for the pandas.

SCHEMES FOR THE REMAINING BEARS

Among the remaining bears, it is agreed that the South American spectacled bear is the most primitive—the next branch on the tree above the pandas. However, this is where agreement ends, for as many schemes have been proposed as there are species for the remaining six bears, all of which appear to be closely related and to represent a burst of evolution in the last 5 million years. This confusion is compounded by the great variety of forms found within some of the widely distributed species. For example, there have been as many as 232 species and subspecies described for the brown bear (*Ursus arctos*), which is now recognized as one variable species. This diversity in size and form may reflect the large degree of adaptability in the brown bear that has enabled it

Dan Guravich

to exploit subtle differences in ecological niches throughout the northern temperate zone.

The only living bear to have returned to a more predatory habit is the polar bear, believed to be most closely related to the brown bear. Of the four species of *Ursus*, the brown, the American black (*Ursus americanus*), the Asiatic black (*Ursus thibetanus*) and the polar bear (*Ursus maritimus*) are considered most closely related to each other. There is considerable

▶ The skull of the giant panda has undergone significant morphological change in response to its diet. Its round face and head result from the large muscles between the top of the skull and the jaws that are needed to grind up bamboo.

▶ (Far right) As with the giant panda, the heavy appearance of the skull of the red panda (*Ailurus fulgens*) is an adaptation to its diet. This similarity led some anatomists to conclude that the two species were closely related. Ken Lucas/Planet Earth Pictures

Jean-Paul Ferrero/AUSCAPE International

▲ An adult male polar bear swimming among ice floes. The skulls of polar bears closely resemble those of sea lions, the two animals being closely related through a common ancestor.

disagreement as to the proper genera for the sloth bear and the sun bear. At different times they have been placed in separate genera (*Melursus* and *Helarctos* respectively) and in the same genus (*Melursus*). More recently, they have been included in the genus *Ursus*, even though some of their characteristics differ from those of other ursine bears.

The Ursidae was the last carnivore family to appear in the fossil record during the Oligocene. Most of its present diversity only goes back 5 million years and is attributable mainly to increasing fluctuations in climate. During this time bears have diversified into mainly herbivorous and omnivorous niches. The giant panda may be the most herbivorous carnivore, whereas the polar bear is predominantly a meat eater. With the exception of the sun bear, bears represent the largest terrestrial mammalian carnivores, both now and in the fossil record.

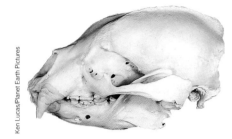

▲ The skulls of the sloth bear (*Melursus ursinus*) (top) and the sun bear (*Ursus malayanus*) (bottom) are strikingly similar in general appearance to those of other ursine bears, such as the American black bear (see page 16), and indicate their close taxonomic relationship.

THE GIANT SHORT-FACED BEAR

CHRISTOPHER A. SHAW AND SHELLEY M. COX

During the Pleistocene epoch, between about 2 million and 10,000 years ago, the bear family was much more diverse in the Americas than it is today. In addition to the three extant species of Ursus, the subfamily Tremarctinae was represented in North America and included one extinct species of spectacled bear (*Tremarctos floridanus*) and two of short-faced bears (*Arctodus simus* and *A. pristinus*). At that time, closely related species of the living spectacled bear (*Tremarctos ornatus*) and three extinct species of short-faced bears (*Arctodus bonariensis*, *A. pamparus*, and *A. brasiliensis*) lived in South America. The giant short-faced bear (*Arctodus simus*), was the largest and probably the most powerful Pleistocene predator in the world.

The skull proportions of the giant short-faced bear most closely resemble those of today's spectacled bear. However, the structure of the face in the former would have been cat-like in profile, with a long, high-vaulted skull, a short, broad muzzle and wide palate, and similarly shaped cheek bones, above which the eyes would have been set far forward, just ahead of a low forehead. The last upper premolar and lower first molar formed opposing blades, for shearing meat, and were more prominently developed than in any living bear. The large, conical canine teeth (as in large cats) were wide apart and capable of delivering an exceptionally strong bite. In addition, this bear possessed a premasseteric fossa, a paired indentation on the lower jaw (lacking in all living bears except Tremarctos), that is related to the attachment of powerful biting muscles. These adaptations imply that the giant short-faced bear may have been more carnivorous than living bears, with the exception of the polar bear.

Relative to other bears, the giant short-faced bear had long, slender legs. Its upper limbs were proportionally longer than the lower limbs and the front legs were shorter than the hind. The animal walked flat-footed, with the paws turned forward, in contrast to the "toed-in" position of most bears. This unusual limb structure, combined with its relatively short body, implies that the giant short-faced bear could run more swiftly than other bears. Perhaps these structural features also made it easier for the bear to look over tall grass or other vegetation. In any case, the adaptations of the skull and limbs for speed were better suited than those of other bears to preying upon the large herbivores, such as camels, bison, and horses, that inhabited North America during the Pleistocene.

Sexual dimorphism in giant short-faced bears was marked, with males' skeletal dimensions averaging 25 percent larger than females'. The average male weighed about 610 kilograms (1,345 pounds), but

Ken Lucas/Planet Earth Pictures

▲ In this re-creation, a giant short-faced bear is shown walking beside a brown bear, to indicate their difference in size.

◄ The extinct giant short-faced bear (*Arctodus simus*) was the largest terrestrial mammalian carnivore the world has ever known. Its long legs, compared with those of present-day species, suggest it chased down some of its prey.

the largest specimen ever recovered is estimated to have weighed 1,000 kilograms (2,200 pounds) or more. The prevalence of females found in some cave deposits suggests that such sites may have been favored for winter denning and for giving birth.

The giant short-faced bear inhabited North America along with a smaller and more primitive species, the lesser short-faced bear (*A. pristinus*), but their distributions do not appear to have overlapped. The lesser short-faced bear is known only from the southeastern United States as far north as southeastern Pennsylvania. The giant short-faced bear, however, was widespread over North America, from Alaska through western Canada and the United States,

to central Mexico, and lived in a variety of habitats from steppe tundra and boreal forest to open savanna. While the origin of the giant short-faced bear is not fully understood, it is thought that the lesser short-faced bear may have been its ancestor. The other Tremarctine bear found in North America, the extinct Florida spectacled bear, also known as the Florida "cave bear" (*Tremarctos floridanus*), was restricted to the southern United States and Mexico and appears to share more skeletal features and habits with the living spectacled bears of South America than with the short-faced bears.

The recovery of some giant short-faced bear remains in deposits containing human artifacts suggests that Paleoindians coexisted with this species shortly before its extinction. Dramatic changes in climate and vegetational patterns toward the end of the last ice age, perhaps aggravated by the influx in North America of new predators —humans—caused the extinction of the large prey preferred by the giant short-faced bears, and thus brought about their demise.

BEARS AND EARLY HUMANS

VALERIUS GEIST

Europeans of the last ice age, the Neanderthal and Cro-Magnon people, were lucky that the great bear of Europe, the cave bear (*Ursus spelaeus*), was largely herbivorous and spent much of its life in winter sleep in deep caves. For reasons unknown, the bears of Europe did not become as large as the giant short-faced bear (*Arctodus simus*) of North America, or the polar bear (*Ursus maritimus*) of the Arctic. The brown bear, or grizzly (*Ursus arctos*), which came to lower North America after the carnivorous giant short-faced bear died out at the end of the ice age, is not a specialized carnivore. It occupied the great plains, as had the giant short-faced bear before it, but unlike the latter, the cold-adapted grizzly never went into South America. The mountains of northern Mexico remain its southern limit.

European people met the cave bear and the smaller brown bear, and probably benefited from the relationship between these two animals. The cave bear's huge canine teeth and powerful build insured that brown bears acted cautiously lest they were killed by cave bears, which probably defended pockets of rich plant food and had a nasty disposition. To this day brown bears seldom den in natural caves, as did cave bears, but dig individual dens in secluded spots and occupy them warily, as if afraid of being discovered. Where two species of bears coexist, one plays the underdog, as do black bears to brown bears in North America. The brown bear in ice-age Alaska lived with the giant short-faced bear, so the grizzly may have evolved to live as a subordinate, acting cautiously and avoiding confrontations.

With cave bears largely ignoring them, and brown bears avoiding trouble, humans, even without effective weapons and domestic dogs, could live as hunters in ice-age Europe. Research shows that ice-age people killed brown bears, but not cave bears. The reasons for this are found in historical accounts of bear hunting with primitive weapons. Only with difficulty, and providing they had dogs, could hunters kill brown and polar bears, which suggests that cave and giant short-faced bears would have been too large and dangerous to hunt in such a way.

Bears are fearsome opponents and are hard to kill with primitive weapons. There are records from later times of mounted men with lances attacking grizzly bears in North America. Cavalry lances have narrow blades that can be freed quickly from a pierced body, but with multiple lances through their bodies, grizzlies counter-attacked, maiming or killing several cavalrymen and horses before being dispatched. In these instances dogs were not used to distract the bears, as was the case with medieval European hunters, who used broad-bladed boar spears for bear hunting. The Inuit people of the Arctic also used dogs and broad-bladed lances.

Native Americans of the plains would go in groups to hunt grizzlies, prepared as if for war, and expecting casualties. The natives of California were forced by the presence of grizzlies to abandon their richest lands, and eulogized the musket-bearing Spaniards who destroyed the animals, enabling the native people to return home.

Because it is likely that cave and giant short-faced bears were beyond the capacity of ice-age hunters to kill safely, in Europe this probably meant that humans avoided cave bears and focused on plains game, primarily reindeer, for food. The Neanderthals were carnivorous, and while the Cro-Magnon people who succeeded them were more diverse in their food habits, apparently they did not depend on plant food. The cave bear probably did. Thus it would have been prudent for humans to avoid places where there were concentrations of plants on which cave bears fed, just as today humans living along the Arctic coast generally avoid areas that are favored by polar bears.

In North America, human occupation began when that of the giant short-faced bear ended, but there are tantalizing records of earlier human occupation of South America. It appears that large carnivores, plus many ecologically specialized large herbivores, made human life in North America impossible. Only when this fauna

24

collapsed did humans make inroads. Between 13,000 and 8,000 BC, the number of fireplaces per 1,000 years of occupation increased slowly as the number of megafauna species declined.

The greatest obstacle for humans in North America must have been the huge carnivores, especially the giant short-faced bear. No kill by hunters would have been defensible against this beast; no hut would have been safe at night; no human would have been able to outrun this bear; and few trees would have been present or tall enough to climb for safety in the open country where it roamed. The smell of broiling meat and fat would have been irresistible to the bear. Skeletons of giant short-faced bears fill natural cave traps and tar pits, while those of grizzly bears do not. This indicates that the former went heedlessly after tempting prey. Fragile, narrow spear blades would have been useless against its 550 to 700 kilogram (1,200 to 1,540 pound) bulk. The only sane response from humans would have been to stay away.

The end of the giant short-faced bear coincided with a cold snap about 12,500 years ago, during which time prey numbers probably declined sharply. Shortly after the giant short-faced bear's demise, the number of plant-eating animals increased, and they became the prey of Paleoindians. As the number of North American species of mammals declined, so Siberian species moved in, including the brown bear, timber wolf, moose, elk, and bison. Brown bears became numerous in North America, but the black bear adjusted well to their arrival and flourished, as did humans.

◀ A carving of a bear found in northern Europe. It dates from between 12,000 and 17,000 years ago. Ronald Sheridan / Ancient Art and Architecture Collection

▼ This late nineteenth-century oil painting by Emmanuel Benner gives a highly romantic view of how stone-age people might have defended themselves against a scavenging brown bear.

THE MOLECULAR EVOLUTION OF THE BEARS

STEPHEN J. O'BRIEN

The bear family has provided a particular challenge to students of evolutionary biology and taxonomy (biological classification). The fossil record of bears is incomplete and leaves unanswered a considerable number of questions about the ancestral relationships between the eight species that are living today.

Dan Guravich

▶ In profile, the characteristic shoulder hump and dished face make it easy to identify a brown bear from a distance.

▼ Analogous traits are those that are similar in structure and function but have independent evolutionary origins, such as the wings of a fly and a bat. The fact that both insects and bats can fly does not indicate that they are related. Homologous traits are those that are similar in structure as a result of shared ancestry. The forepaw of a bear and the flipper of a whale appear unalike, being adapted for different environments, but the bones of both are similar in number and structure. This is because the skeletons of both these mammals are modifications of the same basic plan.

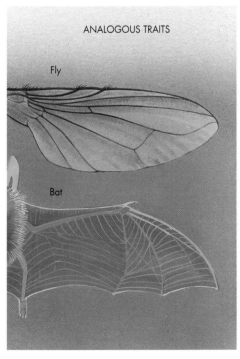

ANALOGOUS TRAITS

Fly

Bat

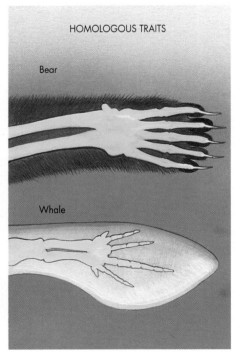

HOMOLOGOUS TRAITS

Bear

Whale

Biological classification depends heavily upon reconstructing the evolutionary history of a group of species. Taxonomists attempt to deduce ancestral relationships by comparing individual specimens from related species. For example, bears are large and stockily built, and most are adept at climbing trees. They share several unique dental and skeletal characteristics, and they all have a keen sense of smell. These common features form the basis for their being grouped together in the family Ursidae.

TRAITS IN COMMON

Classification among the bear species based on their form and behavior has been problematical and often controversial. Difficulties stem from the need to select the correct traits upon which to base evolutionary inferences. Ideally, only homologous traits should be considered, that is, traits that have arisen in closely related species because they inherited them from a common ancestor. All members of the class Mammalia, for example, have body hair, young that are nourished by the mammary glands of females, and four-chambered hearts. All members of the cat family have retractable claws, four toes on their hind feet, and pupils that contract. The degree of evolutionary relationship is determined by counting the number of homologous characteristics shared by particular species; the greater the number of shared traits, the more closely they are related.

However, interspersed in every species comparison are analogous traits, traits that have arisen as a result of unrelated organisms evolving similar structures in response to living in the same environment. The wings of birds, bats, and insects are examples of analogous traits, as is the acquisition of an opposable "thumb" in hominoid primates and in the giant panda. Analogous traits perform identical functions but have arisen independently. They may confound the deductive process and mislead the naturalist.

Another complication that arises when selecting homologous traits is that their genetic basis is seldom understood. For example, a small change in

Divergent evolution

Parallel evolution

Convergent evolution

▲ There are three basic patterns which describe how species have evolved in response to evolutionary pressures. In divergent evolution two or more groups from the same stock evolve differently, usually because they become isolated geographically from one another and develop in response to differing environmental pressures. In parallel evolution genetically related groups become isolated but evolve in similar ways, in response to similar selective pressures. In convergent evolution, completely unrelated animals evolve similar structures in response to similar environmental pressures.

Art Wolfe

◄ Widely distributed throughout forested areas, there are thought to be about half a million black bears in North America.

▲ The spectacled bear is the only living representative of the Tremarctine bears, several species of which once ranged over northern regions of South America and southern North America.

▼ The evolutionary relationships of the bears, as determined by molecular methods, suggest that the raccoon and bear families diverged about 30 million years ago. This analysis places the panda in the family Ursidae (the bears) and not in the Procyonidae (the raccoons). However, the panda and the spectacled bear differ sufficiently from the other bears to warrant their own subfamilies.

an animal's anatomy could result from a major genetic reorganization or, conversely, an apparently large anatomical change (like the panda's "thumb") could be the consequence of a minor genetic change.

When researchers gather up groups of useful traits to compare between species, the number of genetic changes should be equivalent for each trait, to eliminate biases; this is rarely possible with anatomical traits. Bearing in mind that there are 135,135 different ways to connect eight species in an evolutionary tree, it is easy to see why the search for correct relationships between species can be both treacherous and tumultuous.

THE MOLECULAR APPROACH

In the last decades a new way of deducing evolutionary history and taxonomic relationships has been developed. The idea is to examine homologous gene sequences and protein gene products (amino acid sequences) of particular species and to construct evolutionary relationships from the DNA molecules that encode the information for making, say, a brown bear, a giant panda, or a spectacled bear. The molecular approach goes to the genetic source code that is transmitted from generation to generation through gametes. The genetic information determines not only the form and function of the animal, but it is also the raw material that evolves and adapts as new species originate over time.

Establishing gene homology is a relatively straightforward process since homologous genes share high amounts of DNA sequence identity, and also the "weight" of different gene or DNA changes is known because the sizes of different genes can be measured. Finally, the number of genes available for study is virtually unlimited. The bear genetic complement is over 3 billion DNA base pairs and encodes some 100,000 gene units, each on the average 1,000 base pairs long. When researchers are in doubt, they can always go back for further information!

Constructing an evolutionary tree with molecular data requires an understanding of an important conceptual advance—the molecular clock. This hypothesis is based on the notion that as species diverge from a common ancestor, they accumulate mutations in their chromosomal DNA framework in a random but steady manner. The longer two species have been separated, the greater the amount of divergence. The amount of difference (termed the genetic distance) between two species would be roughly proportionate to the time elapsed since their ancestors diverged from their presumed "missing link." Working backwards with a matrix of genetic distances

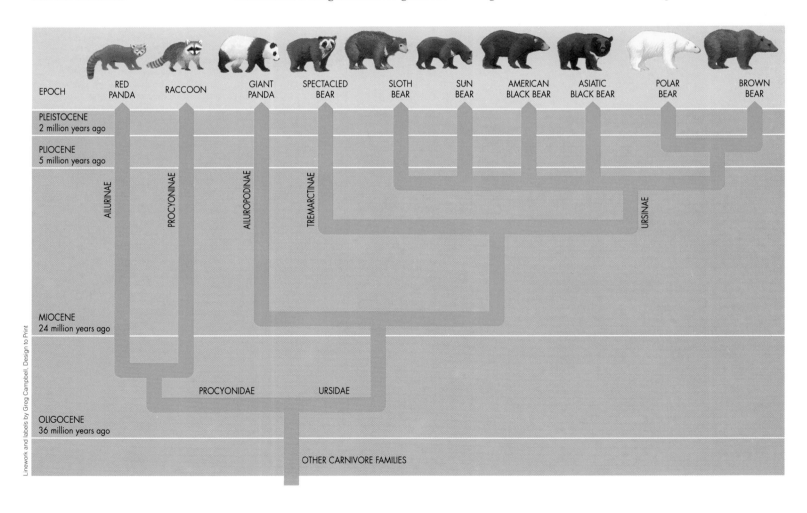

between species, sophisticated mathematical methods can be used to construct an evolutionary tree that best accommodates the data. In fact, there are now three theoretical methods (termed distance based, parsimony, and likelihood) that are used to build evolutionary trees. If the same results are achieved with each method, particularly with several different DNA stretches, one can be reasonably confident about the relationships that have been worked out.

The molecular clock hypothesis has met with a certain amount of controversy. Critics point out that the accumulations of mutations do not occur precisely in proportion with time, resulting in the clock producing evolutionary trees with errors in limb lengths. These criticisms are troubling, but they do not invalidate the approach for determining relationships. Instead they emphasize the need to repeat the analyses with different genes or DNA stretches. In practice, the molecular methods have stood the test of time.

MOLECULAR METHODS USED WITH BEARS

The application of molecular methods to the evolutionary history and taxonomy of the bears has proved persuasive and illuminating. Several molecular methods have been applied to determine the relationships between bear species using blood and skin cell cultures. Three of these methods—allozyme genetic distance, 2DE genetic distance,

and albumin immunological distance—measure differences in protein (gene product) sequences between species.

Another method, DNA-DNA hybridization, estimates similarity of the entire DNA complement by separating DNA strands (DNA being a ladder-like structure with complementary strands) of a species and measuring their ability to anneal, or reassociate, with complementary DNA from a different species. The number of hybrid DNA molecules that are formed in the experiment depends on the amount of DNA sequence matches that exist between DNA fragments from the two species. Since DNA similarity in homologous DNA segments of different species declines as a function of time elapsed since the compared species diverged from a common ancestor, this measurement provides an estimate of evolutionary time, or genetic distance.

The fifth molecular method examines the intricate banding (or stripes) of extended chromosomes using special techniques. Chromosomes of each species exhibit different inherited patterns and these can be compared in order to reconstruct the chromosome breakage, exchange, and rearrangement that occurred during the course of the bear's evolution.

▲ In the warm climate of the tropical rainforests, the sun bear evolved a less shaggy coat than those of bears in more northerly areas.

▼ The light colored hair on the backs of some brown bears gives them a grizzled appearance, especially when they are back lit. The name "grizzly" is derived from this characteristic.

ESTABLISHING THE ANCESTRY OF THE RED PANDA

STEPHEN J. O'BRIEN

The red or lesser panda (*Ailurus fulgens*) was first introduced to Western naturalists in 1825 by Frédéric Cuvier, who described this shy, tree-dwelling animal with a deep crimson coat as arguably "the most handsome mammal in existence." For 44 years it was the only panda that was known to the West, and both the animal itself and its curious herbivorous diet were described at length.

Nearly all the nineteenth-century taxonomists and mammalogists, including Milne-Edwards, Gervais, and Mivart, considered the red panda to be descended from the ancestors of today's procyonids (the family that includes raccoons, coatis, olingos, and so on), with the divergence having taken place around 20 million years ago.

Certain experts disagreed, however. R.I. Pocock, the British naturalist, argued that the red panda and the giant panda differed sufficiently from the procyonids and from one another to each merit being placed in a separate family, and he placed the red panda in a single-species family, the Ailuridae. After studying the animal in some detail, Thenius and Eisenberg both agreed with him.

Molecular studies carried out in 1973 by Vincent Sarich hinted that red pandas were closer to bears than to procyonids, which lent support to Segall's suggestion, made in 1943, that the red panda was, in fact, a primitive form of bear. Schaller and his Chinese colleagues Jinchu Hu, Wenshi Pan, and Zhu Jing, subsequently argued that similarities both in form and behavior between the giant panda and the red panda supported placing both of the animals in the Ailuridae family.

Recent detailed research by Wozencraft, using the principles of Hennigian cladistics (an approach that emphasizes shared derivative characteristics for the construction of evolutionary trees) also supports associating the red panda with bears (including the giant panda) rather than with the procyonids.

When three different molecular methods (DNA hybridization, allozyme genetic distance, and 2DE genetic distance) were applied, however, each supported, albeit weakly, the placement of the red panda with the procyonids. Because the protein analysis involved such a large number of DNA base pairs (approximately 7,400), and because both cladistic and genetic distance analyses supported the association of red panda and raccoons, it is not possible to dismiss the suggestion that the red panda has a procyonid ancestor, even though some authors have done so.

While it will be difficult—perhaps impossible—to establish the point at which the red panda branched from the evolutionary tree (whether from the bears, the procyonids, or somewhere in between) because it took place so many millions of years ago, it is hoped that additional research will help to establish further details of the history of this remarkable species.

▲ The red panda, also known as the lesser panda, lives in mountain forests and bamboo thickets from the Himalayas through south-central China. One female that was radio-tracked for nine months had a home range of about 3.5 square kilometers (1.3 square miles). Red pandas are adept climbers.

Gérard Lacz/NHPA

Each of these methods provides an independent estimate of the pattern of historic divergence between the species, and researchers using each one reached at the same conclusions. The data revealed that around 30 million years ago, during the Oligocene epoch, the ancestors of the ursids and the procyonids (the raccoon family) diverged from each other. Within 10 million years of that event, the red panda (*Ailurus fulgens*) diverged from the procyonid lineage. There are 19 species of modern procyonids, and all but the red panda are found in the Americas. On the ursid line, between 25 and 18 million years ago, well after the split from the procyonids, the giant panda (*Ailuropoda melanoleuca*) diverged from the other bears.

The next divergence was between the spectacled bear (*Tremarctos ornatus*) and the ursine bears, which occurred between 15 and 12 million years ago. The lineages leading to the remaining ursine species—the sun bear (*Ursus malayanus*), the sloth bear (*U. ursinus*), the American black bear (*U. americanus*), the Asiatic black bear (*U. thibetanus*), the brown bear (*U. arctos*), and the polar bear (*U. maritimus*)—first became distinct between 7 and 5 million years ago.

From the molecular data it has so far been impossible to discern the branching pattern among the ursine bears, because their splits appear to have been almost simultaneous. The single exception to this multi-species divergence involves the brown bear and the polar bear. These two species apparently diverged from a common ancestor more recently than other species diverged from the ancestor of ursine bears.

CHECKING THE DATES OF DIVERGENCE

Although molecular results can produce conclusive relative relationships, the dates of points of divergence have to be checked against the fossil record of the ursid ancestors. Fortunately, there are several fossil specimens that are consistent not only with the molecular tree but, because of their geological dating, supply a time scale. For example, *Agriarctos* is generally believed to be an early ancestor of the giant panda line and occurred during the Miocene, about 15 million years old. The common ancestor or "missing link" for the non-panda ursids is *Ursavus*, dated at 20 to 18 million years old. *Plionarctos* is a suspected ancestor of spectacled bears from the late Miocene, some 6 million years ago, while *Ursus minimus* (about 5 million years old) is thought to be a primitive ursine ancestor.

The rates of molecular changes in the bears can also be compared with changes in the same genes during the evolution of primates, where the fossil dates are more precise. Since the genes of bears and primates appear to evolve at similar rates, primate dates can be used to infer ursid dates. Both ursid fossil dates and primate dates were checked against molecular results from the

John Shaw/NHPA

▲ The raccoons are members of the procyonids, a family that is closely related to the bears. Like this common North American raccoon (*Procyon lotor*), they are all excellent climbers.

Norman Tomalin/Bruce Coleman Ltd

◀ The red panda (*Ailurus fulgens*), also known as the lesser panda, was once thought to be the closest living relative of the giant panda. Red pandas are found from Nepal through Burma and south central China.

TAXONOMY OF BEARS AND PANDAS

Order Procyonidae

I.   Subfamily Procyoninae—New World procyonids

    Ring tails (2 species)
    Raccoons (7 species)
    Coatis (3 species)
    Kinkajou (1 species)
    Olingos (5 species)

II. Subfamily Ailurinae—Old World procyonids

    Red panda (*Ailurus fulgens*)

Order Ursidae

I.   Subfamily Ailuropodinae

    Giant panda (*Ailuropoda melanoleuca*)

II. Subfamily Tremarctinae

    Spectacled bear (*Tremarctos ornatus*)

III. Subfamily Ursinae

    Sun bear (*Ursus malayanus*)
    Sloth bear (*Ursus ursinus*)
    American black bear (*Ursus americanus*)
    Asiatic black bear (*Ursus thibetanus*)
    Brown bear (*Ursus arctos*)
    Polar bear (*Ursus maritimus*)

Art Wolfe

bears and there was considerable, though not universal, agreement. Clearly, paleontological and molecular approaches, when considered together, provide the insight that is needed to resolve this puzzling history.

ESTABLISHING THE TAXONOMY

While there is still considerable uncertainty about the details of the split among the six ursine bear species, and there is controversy over whether the red panda belongs with the ursids or the procyonids, the major features of the evolutionary tree of the bears are consistent with most of what is known so far about bear evolution. Using the results of molecular research, combined with dated fossils and the results of studies in paleontology, morphology, and behavior, the following taxonomic convention has been recommended. The Oligocene divergence of Procyonidae and Ursidae supports their designation as orders within the class Mammalia. The relatively ancient divergence of New World procyonids (raccoons, coatis, olingos, and so on) and the Old World procyonid red panda merits subfamily designation for both the red panda (Ailurinae) and the other species (Procyoninae). The divergence of the giant panda's ancestor from the ursid line 10 million years after ursids split from procyonids is sufficiently recent to classify that species within the Ursidae (and not as a separate family, or in the Procyonidae). However, the giant panda's more ancient divergence from other bears would also justify assigning the giant panda

subfamily status (Ailuropodinae). Similarly the less ancient but still primitive divergence of the spectacled bear from ursine bears was the basis for placing this species in its own subfamily (Tremarctinae) as well. Both the giant panda and the spectacled bear differ markedly in morphology and in chromosomal makeup from the ursine bears, which supports this scheme.

The ursine bears form the third ursid subfamily, Ursinae, consisting of six species, all in the genus *Ursus*. While the six ursine bear species were historically classified as five distinct genera, their relatively recent divergence shows that they

are closely related and it is now thought more consistent to place them within a single genus.

In summary, the recent Ursidae are a heterogeneous family that is made up of eight species, six of which are the result of a recent, contemporaneous radiation. The remaining ursids—the spectacled bear and the giant panda—are the sole surviving representatives of their lineages. The former branched from the main line of ursids 15 to 10 million years ago and is now restricted to South America; the latter is endemic to China and is the living relict of an isolated bear lineage that extends back 22 to 18 million years.

▲ The polar bear's white coat, so important for camouflage in the Arctic, probably arose from light color phase brown bears that were living on the Asian coast of the Arctic Ocean.

FUZZY THINKING ABOUT THE GIANT PANDA'S ANCESTRY

STEPHEN J. O'BRIEN

So the question has stood for many years, with the bear proponents and the raccoon adherents and the middle-of-the-road group advancing their several arguments with the clearest of logic, while in the meantime the giant panda lives serenely in the mountains of Szechuan with never a thought about the zoological controversies he is causing by just being himself.

Edwin Colbert, 1938

The shy and gentle giant panda, *Ailuropoda melanoleuca*, lives a nomadic life high in the alpine bamboo forest on the edge of the Tibetan plateau in western China. With its alluring eyespots, Mickey Mouse ears, and playful appearance, it has become a symbol for all the world's endangered species.

From an evolutionary viewpoint, the giant panda has been a major puzzlement. For nearly 130 years, from the time it was introduced to Western scientists, it was at the center of one of the most vigorous debates in the history of taxonomy (biological classification).

The giant panda was first described to the West by the French missionary-naturalist Père David in 1869. He sent a description of the animal, which he called *Ursus melanoleuca* (meaning black and white bear), to his mentor Alphonse Milne-Edwards, son of (and later successor to) the Director of the Paris Museum of Natural History. The following year, after examining skins and skeletal material sent him by David, Milne-Edwards decided that some of the animal's bones and teeth more closely resembled those of the red panda, *Ailurus fulgens*, than those of other bears. Since the red panda had been placed in the raccoon family, Procyonidae, Milne-Edwards concluded that the giant panda was really a procyonid in which certain bearlike traits had evolved.

Although the giant panda certainly looks like a bear, it has some unique characteristics and habits. First, like the red panda, it is largely herbivorous, living mainly on a diet of bamboo shoots, stems, and leaves. This bamboo diet has led to specialized adaptations, some of which are apparent in the panda's Miocene progenitors of at least 8 million years ago. The giant panda's skull and jaw are massive, its jaw muscles are powerful, and its teeth are suited to crushing and grinding. The animal also has a sixth digit on its forepaws, resulting from an evolutionary adaptation of the wrist bone to form a "thumb." All these characteristics suggest that the giant panda is specialized for sitting on its hindquarters for long periods, eating bamboo!

The giant panda has several other features that are atypical for bears. The male genitalia are tiny and backward-pointing, in a manner similar to the raccoons. The panda does not really behave like a bear either. Most bear species of the temperate and arctic regions of North America and Eurasia have a period of winter sleep, whereas the panda does not. This might be because pandas are unable to store enough energy from bamboo, a relatively inefficient source of energy. Bears roar or growl, whereas the giant panda bleats, rather like a sheep or a goat.

Conflicting conclusions

Over the past century, more than 50 treatises have been published relating to the scientific classification of the two pandas, some of them containing new information, but many reinterpreting earlier data. With almost equal frequency, it has been concluded that the giant panda is a specialized member of the bear family, the Ursidae; a specialized member of the raccoon family, the Procyonidae; or that it constitutes a separate carnivore family, the Ailuropodinae, either on its own, or along with the red panda.

In 1869, the year that Milne-Edwards opted for the giant panda being a procyonid, Gervais examined the animal's brain and joined the bear camp. In 1885, Mivart reviewed the classification of arctoid (bear- and dog-like) carnivores and placed the giant panda in the Procyonidae. Mivart's conclusions were supported by the work of an impressive collection of British and American naturalists over the next century. The noted British taxonomist, R.I. Pocock, suggested that the giant panda deserved separate ranking and placed it in a separate family, the Ailuropodidae.

In 1964 D. Dwight Davis, then curator of mammals at Chicago's Field Museum of Natural History, published an extraordinary monograph based upon the anatomy of Su Li, a male panda that died in 1938 at the Brookfield Zoo. Davis' opus, recently described by Stephen Jay Gould as "our century's greatest work of comparative anatomy," described some 50 organ systems. Davis' taxonomic conclusions were resounding: "the giant panda is a bear and very few genetic mechanisms—perhaps no more than half a dozen—were involved in the primary adaptive shift from *Ursus* to *Ailuropoda*."

Davis' view was quickly accepted by such authorities as Gould and Ernst Mayr. Others disagreed with him, pointing out that his analysis was largely anatomical and did not follow standard taxonomic principles. These critics also noted that many of his findings were irrelevant from an evolutionary point of view, since traits shared by bears and pandas were found in many other carnivores as well. On the first page of his monograph, Davis admitted that he had been convinced, a priori, that the giant panda was a bear, and had assumed this throughout his text, making no attempt to present comparative data because "this became so difficult, I gave up." Gould recently remarked that "Davis' personal tragedy must reside in his failure to persuade his colleagues."

R.F. Ewer, in her excellent monograph on the carnivores, published in 1973, agreed with a comprehensive review of the giant panda's ancestry published in 1966 by Ramona and Desmond Morris, mammal curators at the London Zoo. Having studied both the animal's anatomy and behavior, the Morrises concluded that it was a procyonid. More recently, ethologists John Eisenberg and George Schaller independently argued in favor of separate family status, as did a number of paleontologists (C. Chu, T. Wang, W.C. Pei, and E. Thenius) who examined the meager fossil record of the ursids and procyonids. The first banded chromosomal study lent support to this view, since giant pandas have 42 largely metacentric (biarmed) chromosomes while most of the bears have 74 largely acrocentric (single-armed) chromosomes. This constituted a dramatic difference.

In 1986 a 600-page text on the anatomy of the giant panda was published in China. Written by a group of zoologists from the Beijing Zoological Gardens and associated universities, it presented data based on 27 specimens. These scientists came to the conclusion that the giant panda differed from the bear and favored assigning it to a separate family.

Genetic studies

Studies using molecular genetic methods eventually resolved the question. Five separate approaches were applied to the genes and gene products of the giant panda, the red panda, bears, and raccoons. In each case, evolutionary trees were drawn up following the research, and they were all in accord. It now seems clear that the ancestors of the giant panda diverged from the ursid lineage around 20 million years ago, 10 to 15 million years after the ursids split from procyonids. The red panda represents a primitive split from the New World procyonids that took place less than 10 million years after the ursid– procyonid divergence. So the giant panda should indeed be classified with the bears, and the red panda with the raccoons.

What then, is to be made of material put forward by several authors as evidence of an evolutionary distinction between bears and the giant panda? First, it is important to emphasize that the meticulous details given in Dwight Davis' monograph affirmed the affinity of the giant panda with bears. Second, many of the characteristics that the giant panda shares with the red panda are related to the fact that both species are largely herbivorous. Most of these traits (for example, grinding teeth, a massive skull, a "thumb," behavioral similarities) could be seen as no more than adaptative responses to their diet. Other traits shared by the two pandas could simply be primitive carnivore characteristics retained in pandas but lost in bears and New World procyonids.

John Cancalosi/AUSCAPE International

The question of the giant panda's ancestry has provided excellent opportunities for scientists to test the effectiveness of a range of biological characteristics in providing information about how various organisms are related. The lessons learned as a result of this great taxonomic controversy have shown how the combined interpretation of

▲ In earlier studies, researchers thought giant pandas were bears because they shared similarities in body proportions and anatomical details such as the structure of the brain, the ear ossicles, and the respiratory tract.

molecular, morphological, and paleontological findings can be used to establish the evolutionary histories of other groups. The answer can be found in the genes, in the anatomy, and in the functional adaptations; but clues that are sometimes far from obvious have to be recognized.

THE LIVING BEARS

IAN STIRLING

Although similar in general appearance, bears have evolved a significant diversity of adaptations. As a group, they exploit a wide range of environments, from tropical rainforests through temperate mountains and plains, to the drifting ice of the Arctic Ocean.

Bears are medium to large mammals, ranging from only about 27 kilograms (60 pounds) for the female sun bear to over 800 kilograms (1,760 pounds) for an exceptionally large male polar bear. Even when the smaller species are included, the bears are, on average, significantly heavier than all other species of terrestrial carnivores. The degree of difference in size between males and females—known as sexual dimorphism—ranges from marginal to about double.

There are eight species of living bears in three subfamilies, predominantly resident in the northern hemisphere. So far as is known, there have never been any bears in Australia. Fossil bears have been found in southern Africa but the absence of living species in what is one of the richest ecological areas of the world today remains a puzzle. In historical times, at least, only a small population of brown bears remained in the mountains of northwestern Africa, and these animals had been exterminated by about the mid-1800s. There were several species of bears in South America during the Pleistocene (up to about 1 million years ago), of which the spectacled bear is the lone survivor.

Even though there are only a few living species of bears, there has been a surprising amount of debate over their taxonomy, or classification. For several years, scientists argued over whether the giant panda should be classified with the bears or the raccoons, although modern genetic analysis suggests quite clearly that it is a bear.

As recently as 1953, after evaluating the large degree of structural variability in the skulls of brown bears, one scientist subdivided them into 232 recent and 39 fossil species and subspecies! Today, the Convention on International Trade in Endandered Species (CITES) recognizes only one species of brown bear (*Ursus arctos*), with several geographically separate populations in Europe, eastern Asia, and western North America in Appendix II, and two subspecies (Tibetan and Himalayan) in Appendix I. Although consensus has been reached on how many species of bears there are, there is still some discussion about the naming of genera and recognition of subspecies. In the following, the taxonomy used is that given in the fifth edition (1991) of *Walker's Mammals of the World*.

FAMILY URSIDAE

INTERNATIONAL RANKINGS OF THE STATUS OF BEAR SPECIES

CLASSIFICATION	CONVENTION ON INTERNATIONAL TRADE IN ENDANGERED SPECIES (CITES)[1]	IUCN RED BOOK LISTING[2]	
SUBFAMILY AILUROPODINAE			
Giant panda			
Ailuropoda melanoleuca	Appendix I	endangered	
SUBFAMILY TREMARCTINAE			
Spectacled bear			
Tremarctos ornatus	Appendix I	endangered	
SUBFAMILY URSINAE			
Sun bear			
Ursus malayanus	Appendix I	endangered	
Sloth bear			
Ursus ursinus	Appendix I	endangered	
American black bear			
Ursus americanus	Appendix II	unclassified	
Asiatic black bear			
Ursus thibetanus	Appendix I	vulnerable	
Brown bear			
Ursus arctos	Appendix I	unclassified	
Polar bear			
Ursus maritimus	Appendix II	vulnerable	

[1] Definitions for CITES classifications

Appendix I: Species are rare or endangered, and trade will not be permitted for primarily commercial purposes; trade allowed for scientific or educational purposes; captive bred animals or those captured before listing may be traded; permits are required by both the exporting and importing nations.

Appendix II: Species are not rare or endangered at present but could become so if trade is not regulated. Export permits are required from the country of origin and the Scientific Advisory Body to CITES must approve.

[2] Definitions for IUCN classifications

Endangered: in danger of extinction, and survival is unlikely if the causal factors continue operating.

Vulnerable: believed likely to move into the endangered category in the near future if the causal factors continue operating; may include species with populations that are still abundant but could be threatened by adverse factors.

SUBFAMILY TREMARCTINAE
Tremarctos ornatus
Spectacled bear

APPEARANCE The spectacled bear is small and dark, ranging in color from black to brown, and a few have a reddish tinge. It has distinctive circular or semicircular creamy white markings on the face around the eyes, reminiscent of spectacles. Lines and patches of white usually extend onto the throat and chest as well. The amount and pattern of the white markings can be quite variable.

SIZE There are few measurements available for this bear. However, the body length of adults is about 150 to 180 centimeters (60 to 72 inches) and males may be 30 to 40 percent larger than females. Males weigh 100 to 155 kilograms (220 to 340 pounds) and females weigh 64 to 82 kilograms (140 to 180 pounds). At birth, cubs weigh from 300 to 360 grams (10 to 11½ ounces).

HABITAT Spectacled bears are highly adaptable and are found in a wide range of habitats, including rainforest, cloud forest, dry forest, steppe lands, and coastal scrub desert. Possibly because of loss of habitat and persecution by humans, they appear to be more common in heavy forest. They have been reported at altitudes ranging from 180 to 4,200 meters (600 to 13,800 feet) but prefer moist forests between about 1,800 and 2,700 meters (6,000 and 8,800 feet). No populations have been documented from areas that lack bromeliads and fruits.

DISTRIBUTION Spectacled bears are found mainly in or near forested mountains from Venezuela and Colombia south through Ecuador, Peru, and into Bolivia.

REPRODUCTION Females reach sexual maturity between four and seven years of age. Mating occurs in April, May, and June, and pairs stay together for a week or two, with copulation occurring numerous times. Litters of one, two, or occasionally three cubs are born from November to February.

SOCIAL SYSTEM Nothing is known of the social organization of spectacled bears in the wild. In captivity, females and their cubs regularly vocalize to communicate, using two and five types of calls respectively.

DIET Spectacled bears eat a wide variety of foods, including rabbits, mice, birds, berries, grasses, and orchid bulbs, but have a strong preference for the leaves, bases, and hearts of plants of the Bromeliaceae family and the fruits of other plant groups. They will sometimes climb cacti to feed on fruit at the top. Tree nests are often constructed as a platform to feed from fruit-laden branches and to sleep in.

SUBFAMILY URSINAE
Ursus malayanus
Sun bear

APPEARANCE The sun bear has a short, sleek, black coat. The muzzle is short, and gray to faint orange in color. The crescent-shaped chest patch is yellowish or white. The muzzle is shorter and lighter colored than that of a black bear and in most cases the white area extends above the eyes. The ears are small and round. The paws are large and the soles are naked, which is thought to be an adaptation for climbing trees. The claws are large, curved, and pointed.

SIZE This is the smallest of the bears. Adults are about 120 to 150 centimeters (48 to 60 inches) long and weigh 27 to 65 kilograms (60 to 145 pounds). Males are 10 to 20 percent larger than females.

HABITAT Sun bears live in lowland tropical rainforests. They are excellent climbers and are thought to sleep in trees.

DISTRIBUTION The range of this species is not well documented but it is known throughout Southeast Asia from northern Burma and Bangladesh, south and east across Laos, Cambodia, Vietnam, and Thailand, and south to peninsular Malaysia and the islands of Sumatra and Borneo. Because of large-scale habitat destruction and poaching, it is likely that its range has recently been reduced in northern and western regions.

REPRODUCTION There is little information about reproductive behavior in the wild but cubs are apparently born throughout the year. The gestation period for six births at the East Berlin Zoo was reported to be 95 to 96 days, suggesting there was no delayed implantation. Conversely, three pregnancies at the zoo in Fort Worth, Texas, lasted 174 to 240 days, suggesting delayed implantation. Litters consisted of either one or two cubs, weighing about 325 grams (10 ounces) each. Cubs are reported to remain with their mothers until they are fully grown.

SOCIAL SYSTEM Nothing is known of the social organization of sun bears in the wild.

DIET Sun bears are omnivorous. They have been reported to eat termites, small mammals, birds, and growing tips of palm trees, and the nests of wild bees. At times they cause considerable damage to agricultural crops, such as oil palms.

SUBFAMILY URSINAE
Ursus maritimus
Polar bear

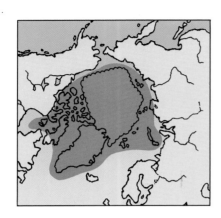

APPEARANCE The polar bear is immediately recognizable from the distinctive white color of its fur. The neck of the polar bear is longer than in other species of bears. The head is elongated but the ears are relatively small. The front paws are large and are used like paddles for swimming while the hind legs trail behind. The nose, and the skin underneath the white fur, are black. The soles of the feet have small papillae and vacuoles like suction cups to make them less likely to slip on the ice.

The polar bear is the largest land carnivore alive in the world today. Adult males weigh from 400 to 600 kilograms (880 to 1,320 pounds) and occasionally exceed 800 kilograms (1,760 pounds). Females are about half the size of males and normally weigh 200 to 300 kilograms (440 to 660 pounds). Immediately before entering the maternity den in the fall, the weight of a pregnant adult female can exceed 500 kilograms (1,100 pounds) because of the enormous amount of stored fat. Adult males measure 240 to 260 centimeters (95 to 105 inches) and females 190 to 210 centimeters (75 to 85 inches). At birth, cubs weigh 600 to 700 grams (1 pound 3 ounces to 1 pound 6 ounces).

HABITAT The preferred habitat of polar bears is the annual ice adjacent to the shorelines of the continents and archipelagos throughout the circumpolar Arctic. Wind and currents create cracks in the ice that concentrate the seals they hunt. Although polar bears have been recorded as far north as 88°, they rarely enter the zone of heavy multiyear ice of the central polar basin because it is unproductive biologically and there is little to eat. In areas such as Hudson Bay, where the ice melts completely for a few months in the late summer and fall, bears spend the summer on land, resting to conserve energy and waiting for freeze-up. Males tend to remain along the coast, while family groups and subadults go further inland.

DISTRIBUTION Polar bears are found throughout the circumpolar Arctic. The farthest south that polar bears live all year round is James Bay in Canada, which is about the same latitude as London, England. During winter, when the polar ice pack extends further south, polar bears move as far south as Newfoundland and into the northern Bering Sea. They then move back north as the southern edge of the pack ice recedes throughout the summer.

REPRODUCTION Polar bears mate from late March to late May. Implantation of the fertilized egg is delayed until late September to early October and the cubs are born between late November and early January. A little under 70 percent of the litters consist of two cubs, 25 to 30 percent are singletons, and there are a small number of triplet litters. Litters of four cubs have been reported, but are extremely rare and it would be unlikely for all the cubs to survive. Cubs remain with their mothers until they are two-and-a-half years of age, so the most often that females normally breed is once every three years.

SOCIAL SYSTEM Throughout most of the year, polar bears are distributed as solitary individuals, except for females accompanied by their cubs. They have large overlapping home ranges but do not defend territories. The adult sex ratio is 1:1 but since most females reproduce only once every three years, only a third of them are available in each breeding season. This results in intense competition between males for mates, which is probably one of the reasons why males are twice the size of females.

DIET Polar bears are the most carnivorous of all the bears and live almost entirely on ringed seals, and to a lesser degree, on bearded seals. They are also known to prey on young walruses and occasionally even capture narwhals and belugas. In summer, if they are along the coast, they may eat some grass, kelp, or berries, and scavenge on the carcasses of terrestrial or marine mammals.

SUBFAMILY URSINAE
Ursus ursinus
Sloth bear

APPEARANCE The sloth bear is small and usually black, with a long shaggy coat, especially over the shoulders. Brown and gray hairs may be mixed in with the dark coat, and cinnamon and reddish individuals have also been reported. It has a distinctive whitish or yellowish chest patch in the shape of a wide U, or sometimes a Y if the lower part of the white hairs extend down the chest. The snout is light colored and mobile. The nostrils can be closed voluntarily. It is thought that the reduced hair on the muzzle may be an adaptation for coping with the defensive secretions of termites.

SIZE Adults are 150 to 190 centimeters (60 to 75 inches) long. Males weigh 80 to 140 kilograms (175 to 310 pounds), and females weigh 55 to 95 kilograms (120 to 210 pounds).

HABITAT Sloth bears are found in forested areas and in grasslands, predominantly at lower elevations. They apparently favor drier forests and have been reported to prefer areas with rocky outcrops.

DISTRIBUTION Most sloth bears are found in India and Sri Lanka, but they have also been reported from Bangladesh, Nepal, and Bhutan.

REPRODUCTION Mating occurs in May, June, and July. In captivity, mating pairs come together for only one or two days during which time there may be considerable vocalizing and fighting. Gestation lasts from six to seven months. Most litters consist of either one or two cubs, but litters of three cubs have been reported. Cubs are born in earth dens and apparently do not leave them until they are two to three months old. The cubs stay with their mothers until they are nearly adult, at two or more years of age.

SOCIAL SYSTEM There is little information on social organization, but observations in the wild suggest sloth bears live as solitary individuals, except for females with cubs. Limited observations suggest sloth bears may have small home ranges. They give several vocalizations, but their functions are not understood.

DIET Sloth bears feed extensively on termites and have special adaptations for doing this: The naked lips are capable of protruding, and the inner pair of upper incisors are missing, which forms a gap through which termites can be sucked. The sucking noises made by feeding in this manner can apparently be heard from over 100 meters (330 feet) away. They also eat eggs, other insects, honeycombs, carrion, and various kinds of vegetation. In Nepal, they eat fruits extensively when in season, from March to June.

SUBFAMILY URSINAE
Ursus thibetanus
Asiatic black bear

APPEARANCE This medium-sized, black-colored bear has a lightish muzzle and ears which appear large in proportion to the rest of its head, especially when compared with other species of bears. There is a distinct white patch on the chest, which is sometimes in the shape of a V, and white on the chin. A brown color phase also occurs.

SIZE There is limited information available on these bears, but total length of adults is 130 to 190 centimeters (50 to 75 inches). Adult males range from 100 to 200 kilograms (220 to 440 pounds) and adult females from 50 to 125 kilograms (110 to 275 pounds).

HABITAT Asiatic black bears live predominantly in forested areas, especially in hills and mountainous areas. In summer, they have been reported at altitudes over 3,000 meters (9,900 feet), descending to lower elevations during winter. Apparently, they den for winter sleep in the northern parts of their range. It has been suggested that in the southern limits of their range, where it is quite hot, they do not undergo winter sleep, but this has not been confirmed.

DISTRIBUTION Asiatic black bears are found over a wide area of southern Asia. They occur along the mountains from Afghanistan, through Pakistan and northern India, Nepal, Sikkim, Bhutan, into Burma and northeastern China. They are also found in southeastern Russia, and on Taiwan and the Japanese islands of Honshu and Shikoku.

REPRODUCTION There is little detailed information on reproduction in Asiatic black bears, but there seem to be differences between populations in southwestern and southeastern Asia. Sexual maturity of females is thought to occur at three to four years of age. In Russia, mating is reported to occur in June and July, with births occurring between December and March. In Pakistan, mating has been reported to occur in October, with young being born in February. Cubs are weaned at less than six months old, but may stay with their mothers for two to three years. Females have sometimes been reported with cubs of different ages.

SOCIAL SYSTEM In Russia, the home range is reported to be 10 to 20 square kilometers (4 to 8 square miles). Little information is available on social organization. The bears are reported to be mainly nocturnal, sleeping in trees or caves during the day.

DIET Asiatic black bears have been reported to feed on a wide range of foods, including fruits, bees' nests, insects, invertebrates, small vertebrates, and carrion. They occasionally kill domestic livestock, but the degree to which they prey on wild hoofed mammals is unknown. In fall they frequently make crude leafy feeding platforms in nut-bearing trees.

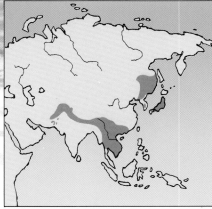

SUBFAMILY URSINAE
Ursus americanus
American black bear

APPEARANCE This medium-sized bear is usually black with a brown muzzle, lacks a shoulder hump, and often has a white patch on the chest. Although black is the predominant color, chocolate and cinnamon brown color phases are also common, which often results in people confusing them with brown bears. Black bears with white and pale-blue coats (known respectively as Kermode and glacier bears) also occur in small numbers. Kermode bears are found along the north-central coast of British Columbia, and glacier bears are found in Alaska, northwestern British Columbia, and the Yukon Territory, Canada. Black bears have strong, highly curved claws and the profile of the face is convex when compared with the more concave profile of a brown bear.

SIZE Adult male black bears range from about 130 to 190 centimeters (50 to 75 inches) in length and weigh 60 to 300 kilograms (130 to 660 pounds). Females measure from 130 to 190 centimeters (50 to 75 inches) and weigh 40 to 80 kilograms (90 to 175 pounds). Black bears vary considerably in size, depending on the quality of the food available. Males may be from about 20 to 60 percent larger than females. At birth, cubs weigh 225 to 330 grams (7 to 11 ounces).

HABITAT Black bears are normally found only in forested areas, but within such habitat they are highly adaptable. They live in both arid and moist forests, from sea level to over 2,000 meters (6,560 feet). Historically, black bears are thought to have stayed away from open habitat because of the risk of predation by brown bears. Black bears have become established in the tundra of northern Labrador, a region where there are no brown bears.

DISTRIBUTION Black bears are widely distributed throughout the forested areas of North America although they have been totally driven out from some of their original range. They are presently found in northern Mexico, 32 states of the United States, and all the provinces and territories of Canada except Prince Edward Island.

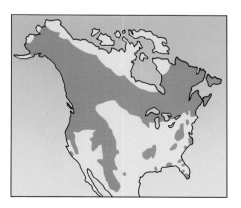

REPRODUCTION Females reach sexual maturity at three to four years of age and males a year or so later. Mating takes place in June, July, and August, and pairs may remain together for only a few hours or for several days. Pregnancy lasts about 220 days, and the cubs are born in a maternity den in January and February. Litter size ranges from one to five, but two is the average. Cubs may be weaned at six to eight months, but they remain with their mothers for a year and a half. Consequently, the most often that female black bears can mate, unless they lose their cubs prematurely, is every two years. Longevity in the wild is 20 to 25 years.

SOCIAL SYSTEM Except for females with cubs, black bears spend most of their time alone. During the breeding season, a male and female may remain together for several days at a time and groups of bears may feed in close proximity to each other if food is abundant, such as in berry patches or at dumps. Female home ranges are 3 to 40 square kilometers (1 to 15 square miles). While the home ranges of individual bears are usually exclusive from those of other bears of the same sex, male home ranges are larger and may overlap those of several females. A young adult female is often allowed to establish her territory within that of her mother, while subadult males must disperse.

DIET Black bears are omnivorous and feed on a wide range of foods, depending on what is available. Insects (particularly ants), nuts, berries, acorns, grasses, roots, and other vegetation form the bulk of their diet in most areas. Black bears can also be efficient predators of deer fawns and moose calves. In some areas of coastal British Columbia and Alaska they also feed on spawning salmon.

SUBFAMILY URSINAE
Ursus arctos
Brown bear

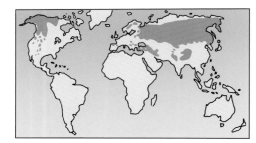

APPEARANCE The brown bear (sometimes called a grizzly in North America) is a large animal, usually dark brown in color, though it can vary from a light creamy shade through to black. The long guard hairs over the shoulders and back are often tipped with white which, from a distance, gives a grizzled appearance. The brown bear is characterized by a distinctive hump on the shoulders, a slightly dished profile to the face, and long claws on the front paws.

SIZE There is considerable variability in the size of brown bears from different populations, depending on the food available. Determining representative weights of specific populations is also difficult as there are seasonal considerations to take into account—for instance, some bears can weigh twice as much in fall as they might weigh in spring. Adult males may weigh 135 to 390 kilograms (300 to 860 pounds) compared with 95 to 205 kilograms (205 to 455 pounds) for females. At birth, cubs weigh 340 to 680 grams (11 ounces to 1 pound 6 ounces).The largest bears are found on the west coast of British Columbia and Alaska, and on offshore islands along coastal Alaska, such as Kodiak and Admiralty. There, males average over 300 kilograms (660 pounds) and females over 200 kilograms (440 pounds). Brown bears from the interior ranges of North America, Europe, and the subArctic are roughly two-thirds the size of their Alaskan and Kamchatkan cousins.

HABITAT Brown bears occupy a wide range of habitats including dense forests, subalpine mountain areas, and tundra. They were once abundant on the central plains of North America, but have since been exterminated.

DISTRIBUTION The range of the brown bear is the widest of any species of bear in the world. They are found in localized populations in eastern and western Europe, across northern Asia and in Japan. In North America, brown bears are found in western Canada, Alaska, and in the states of Wyoming, Montana, Idaho, and Washington.

REPRODUCTION Female brown bears reach sexual maturity at four-and-a-half to seven years of age. Males may become sexually mature at a similar age but are probably not large enough to be able to enter the breeding population until they are eight to ten years old. Mating takes place from early May to the middle of July but implantation does not occur until about October or November. The young are born from about January to March. The litter size ranges from one to four, but two is most common. Cubs remain with their mothers for at least two-and-a-half years, so the most frequently a female can breed is every three years. In some areas, such as near the Arctic coast, the breeding interval is considerably longer. Longevity in the wild is 20 to 25 years.

SOCIAL SYSTEM Under most circumstances, brown bears live as lone individuals, except for females accompanied by their cubs. During the breeding season, a male may attend a female for up to two weeks for mating. Brown bears are distributed in overlapping home ranges and male home ranges are larger than those occupied by females. Despite their propensity for a solitary existence, brown bears congregate at high densities where food is abundant, such as at salmon streams or garbage dumps. In such circumstances, adult males are the most dominant individuals.

DIET Brown bears mainly eat vegetation such as grasses, sedges, bulbs, and roots. They also eat insects such as ants, fish, and small mammals. In some areas they have become significant predators of large hoofed mammals such as moose, caribou, and elk.

SUBFAMILY AILUROPODINAE
Ailuropoda melanoleuca
Giant panda

APPEARANCE The sharply contrasting black and white coloration, added to the stocky characteristic shape of a bear, makes the giant panda one of the most recognizable animals in the world. The head, top of the neck, rump, and hind legs are white, while small patches of fur around the eyes, the ears, shoulders, and front legs are black. When compared with other bears, the head of the giant panda is large in relation to its body. The front paw has six digits as a result of the radial sesamoid, the wrist bone, becoming extended to form an awkward, but functional, opposable thumb. The male genitalia are small and pointed to the rear, which is more similar to the red panda (*Ailurus fulgens*) than to other bears.

SIZE Adult giant pandas range in body length from about 160 to 190 centimeters (64 to 76 inches). Males are slightly longer than females, have stronger forelegs, and are 10 to 20 percent heavier. In the wild males weigh from 85 to 125 kilograms (190 to 275 pounds), while females range between 70 and 100 kilograms (155 to 220 pounds). At birth, cubs weigh only 85 to 140 grams (3 to 5 ounces).

HABITAT Giant pandas live at an altitude of between 1,200 and 3,500 meters (4,000 and 11,500 feet) in mountain forests that are characterized by dense stands of bamboo. Home ranges average 8.5 square kilometers (3.3 square miles) for males and 4.6 square kilometers (1.8 square miles) for females.

DISTRIBUTION Pandas are found only in southwestern China, along the eastern edge of the Tibetan plateau. Although they were once more widespread, today they are limited to six small areas in Sichuan, Gansu, and Shaanzi provinces, totalling only 14,000 square kilometers (5,400 square miles).

REPRODUCTION Pandas reach sexual maturity from four-and-a-half to six-and-a-half years of age and mate during the spring, from March to May. Females are in estrus for one to three weeks, but peak receptiveness lasts for only a few days. Litters of one, two, or occasionally three cubs are born in August or September, usually in a hollow tree or cave. Normally, only one cub is raised. Although cubs are usually weaned at about nine months of age, they remain with their mothers for up to 18 months.

SOCIAL SYSTEM Except for females accompanied by cubs, giant pandas live a solitary existence. During the breeding season, several males may compete for access to a female. Home ranges of females are usually mutually exclusive, although they overlap occasionally, while the home range of each male may overlap those of several females. Pandas communicate by rubbing an acetic-smelling substance—secreted by glands surrounding the anogenital area—onto tree trunks and stones. They also scratch trees. Most territorial marking is thought to be done by males. Pandas are quite vocal and eleven distinct calls have been identified in the wild, although the function of each is not understood. In captivity, females vocalize during estrus as well.

DIET More than 99 percent of the food consumed by giant pandas consists of the branches, stems, and leaves of at least 30 species of bamboo, the species eaten varying from region to region. Adults consume 12 to 15 kilograms (26 to 33 pounds) of food per day when feeding on bamboo leaves and stems. However, when feeding on new bamboo shoots, they are capable of eating up to 38 kilograms (84 pounds) per day, which is about 40 percent of their average body weight. Although the proportion is small, pandas also feed to a limited degree on other plants and a small amount of meat. They feed mainly on the ground but are capable of climbing trees as well. They are active mainly at twilight and at night.

THE BIOLOGY OF BEARS

BLAIRE VAN VALKENBURGH

Many of the unusual features of bear biology relate to the animal's size and feeding habits: large size brings with it problems of temperature regulation and structural support, and plant matter is lower in energy content than meat and more difficult to digest. Bears have overcome these difficulties through a number of physical adaptations.

Bears are unusual members of the order Carnivora, an order which also includes cats, dogs, weasels, civets, and hyenas on land, and seals, sea lions, and walruses in the sea. With the exception of the highly predacious polar bear, bears tend to be the most herbivorous of the carnivores, feeding on fruits and tubers more often than prey. Moreover, all eight species are large, with the smallest of them, the sun bear, weighing more than the wolf, the largest of the canids. Indeed, the polar bear and Kodiak brown bear are currently the largest of all carnivores. Males of these species occasionally weigh in at up to 800 kilograms (1,760 pounds), nearly the size of an adult male bison. Surprisingly, the large size of bears is not achieved through the rapid growth of cubs. In comparison with other carnivores, newborn bear cubs are tiny relative to their mothers and grow slowly.

▲ Black bears fatten up for winter sleep by eating massive amounts of berries in the fall. They "strain" their intake so that it contains few leaves.

SPEED AND STRENGTH

All bears have a large head with small ears followed by massive shoulders and a short back and tail, all of which are supported on thick limbs and broad paws. Compared with big cats, bears have longer snouts and shorter, stiffer backs. Relative to large dogs, bears have bulky legs and much more spreading feet. Unlike these other carnivores, and more like humans, bears walk on the soles of their hindfeet, with their ankle joint positioned just above the ground. This condition is called plantigrade, and differs from the digitigrade posture of cats and dogs, in which the "soles" of the feet are elevated, along with the ankle, and only the toes touch the ground. To understand why bears are built so differently from cats and dogs, it is essential to explain the benefits of digitigrade feet.

Running around on your toes in a digitigrade posture is advantageous if speed is important. Speed is the product of stride length and stride frequency. Raising the ankle adds length to the part of the limb that determines stride length, that is from the shoulder or hip to the point of contact with the ground. Longer limbs take bigger strides, and digitigrade posture is therefore typical of mammals designed to run. Digitigrade animals also tend to

▼ A young brown bear feeding on succulent plants near the water where its visibility is limited, stands up to survey the area for potential danger.

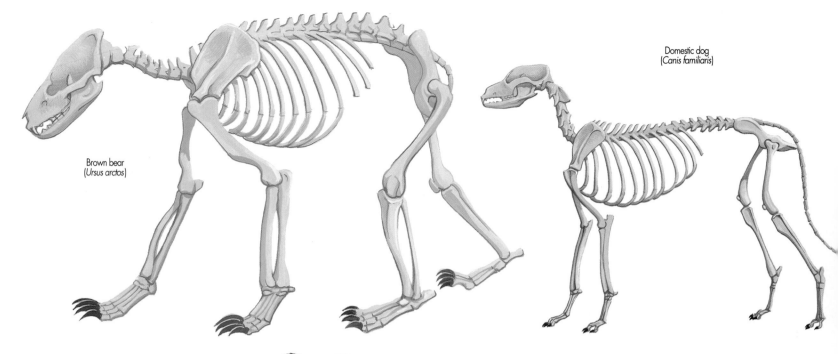

Brown bear
(*Ursus arctos*)

Domestic dog
(*Canis familiaris*)

▲ The skeletons of a bear and a domestic dog illustrate the difference between plantigrade and digitigrade postures. The dog is digitigrade, standing on its toes with the soles of its feet (metapodials) off the ground. By contrast, the soles of the bear's hindfeet are flat to the ground, as in humans, giving it a plantigrade posture. The forepaws of the bear are semi-digitigrade, with the metapodials in an intermediate position. Digitigrade animals tend to be faster than plantigrade animals, in part because their posture results in their limbs being relatively longer.

▼ Bears are threatened by few predators and capture few prey by chasing, so they seldom need to run at speed for any distance. Like this sloth bear, they tend to amble along on the flat surface of their feet.

have relatively long bones, or metapodials, making up the sole of the foot, adding further to total limb length. In addition, their limb muscles are much thicker close to the hip or shoulder joint, and taper towards the toes as long, elastic tendons. This construction reduces muscle mass near the ankles and feet, where the limb travels farthest during locomotion, and thus reduces inertial effects. If one

imagines the additional energy required to walk or run with ankle weights or heavy shoes, then the drawbacks of heavy feet become clear. There are yet further benefits to runners in having long tendinous muscle attachments. Tendons are elastic and act as energy-saving springs when running. They are stretched as the limb is flexed under the weight of the animal and then rebound, propelling the body forward and upward. So, digitigrade posture, long metapodials, and compact muscles with stretchy tendons are typical of carnivores built for speed.

Bears are clearly not built for speed. Although their forefeet are semi-digitigrade, their hind-feet are plantigrade. Moreover, their metapodials are short and their muscles thick throughout the length of the limb. In many ways, bears are built more like badgers than other similar-sized carnivores, such as tigers, and it shows in their speed. The top speed recorded for both black and brown bears is 50 kilometers (30 miles) per hour, whereas the range for the fully digitigrade lion and wolf is 55 to 65 kilometers (35 to 40 miles) per hour.

If bears are not built for speed, then what does the combination of massive limbs, plantigrade hind-feet, cumbersome paws, and a short back provide? Strength and mobility of limb movement are the answers. The stout limbs of bears are capable of producing large forces over a much greater range of motion than those of dogs or even cats. Bears use these capabilities when digging for food or shelter, fishing for salmon, climbing to escape danger, and battling with members of their own species as well as other predators. Imagine a wolf trying to perform a bear hug or climb a tree. Dogs have forfeited these abilities in favor of speed. Cats are more like bears in their range of possible movements, but lack strength. Bears may not be able to outrun danger, but can successfully defend themselves through brute force.

Black bear
(*Ursus americanus*)

Giant panda
(*Ailuropoda melanoleuca*)

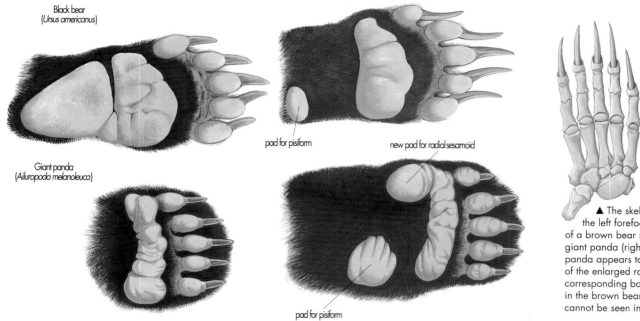

pad for pisiform

new pad for radial sesamoid

pad for pisiform

▲ A view of the soles of the left hindfeet (left) and forefeet (right) of a black bear and a giant panda. The panda's "thumb" is apparent as the bottom of the "L" in the L-shaped pad of the panda's foot. The isolated pads below the major pad on the forepaws of both bears protect a large wrist bone, the pisiform. The black bear, which often digs for its food, has much longer claws than the panda, which digs rarely.

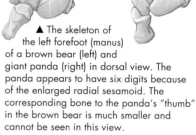

enlarged radial sesamoid

▲ The skeleton of the left forefoot (manus) of a brown bear (left) and giant panda (right) in dorsal view. The panda appears to have six digits because of the enlarged radial sesamoid. The corresponding bone to the panda's "thumb" in the brown bear is much smaller and cannot be seen in this view.

▼ Over 99 percent of the panda's diet consists of bamboo stems, branches, and leaves. The panda bites into the base of the stem with its incisor teeth and tears strips away from the sections being held by its paws.

PAWS AND CLAWS

Although all bears appear to have similar body builds, a closer look at their feet reveals differences among them that reflect their varied habits and abilities. Undoubtedly, the most remarkable bear paws are those of the giant panda. The panda has modified a wrist bone (sesamoid) of the forefoot to form a sixth digit that is used in a manner similar to the way we use our thumbs. Pandas grasp and manipulate their primary food, bamboo, bringing it to their mouths while they sit comfortably on their derrières. Although other ursids have the same bone, only the panda has enlarged it to form an extra digit. In the case of the polar bear, its feet have small papillae and vacuoles, like suction cups, to make them less likely to slip on the ice.

The claws of bears are not retractile, as they are in cats, but vary in size and shape according to their use. For example, the claws of species that frequently climb trees, such as the sun bear, the spectacled bear, and the black bear, are more curved and hook-like than those of the predominantly terrestrial brown and polar bears. The sloth bear, which feeds extensively on ants and termites, has large curved claws that it uses to rake open the nests of its insect prey. After ripping into such a nest, the sloth bear then places its flexible lips around the exposed tunnels and sucks out the angry occupants. The brown bear also has fairly long claws which are used mainly for digging up vegetation, but they are equally adapted for excavating ground squirrels from their subterranean homes or scooping migrating salmon out of a stream.

Ben Osborne/Ardea London

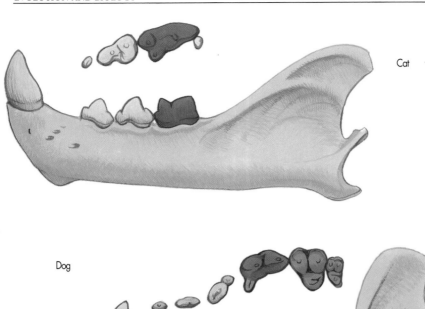

Cat

Dog

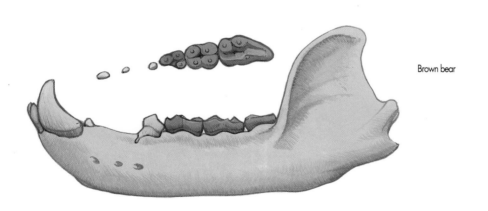

Brown bear

A comparison of dental adaptations among carnivores. Illustrated are lateral views of the lower dentition in the jaw, and occlusal views of the matching upper dentition above them. Teeth or portions of teeth adapted for slicing meat are shaded red and those adapted for grinding invertebrates and plant matter are shaded blue. The highly carnivorous cat is specialized for meat eating and has lost all grinding molars. The omnivorous dog and brown bear have a more generalized tooth row with some slicing and some grinding functions. The extremely herbivorous giant panda has expanded the grinding teeth relative to the slicing teeth so as to chew bamboo effectively.

Giant panda

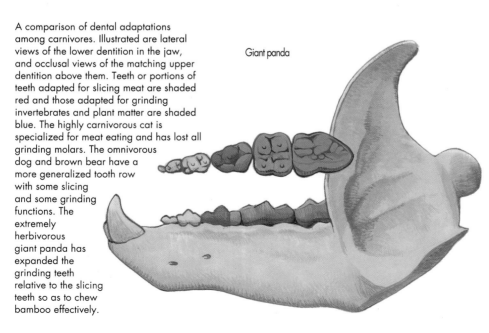

SKULLS AND TEETH

Skulls, and especially teeth, reveal much about a mammal's way of life because they reflect both the animal's diet and the way it goes about acquiring food. Meat-eaters face a very different set of problems from those of plant-eaters. Meat must be captured, killed, and butchered, whereas plant matter needs only to be found and consumed. However, it is a good deal more difficult to extract energy from plants than flesh, and thus herbivorous mammals are likely to show dental adaptations that improve digestive efficiency.

In many herbivores, the teeth are tall with complex surfaces made up of sharp crests separated by shallow valleys that serve to shred vegetation into small pieces which can be digested rapidly, Moreover, the teeth may be ever-growing, or nearly so, to resist the high rates of wear imposed by chewing up fibrous plant foods. As omnivores, most bears avoid the toughest of plant foods, such as grasses, and thus do not show such extreme dental adaptations. Nevertheless, there are differences among the ursids in tooth shape and size that reflect their varied diets.

The diets of bears range from almost entirely carnivorous, as in polar bears, to almost entirely herbivorous, as in the giant panda. There is even an ursid—the sloth bear—that specializes in insects. Nevertheless, most of the living species are mixed feeders that eat grubs, berries, and herbaceous plants more frequently than they eat squirrels, mice, and deer. Consequently, their teeth and skulls differ greatly from those of such meat specialists as cats. Relative to cats, bears have larger skulls and longer snouts that contain a greater number of molar teeth whose function is to mince up food and accelerate digestion. Typically, bears have from 32 to 42 teeth, the only variation being in the number of premolars present. The premolars in bears are reduced in size. They appear to have little functional importance and thus may be lost without negative consequences.

The upper and lower molar teeth of bears work as mortars and pestles, shredding and pulverizing food. The contrast in tooth function between a bear and a cat is dramatically clear in the shape of the first lower molar. This tooth usually has two functions in members of the order Carnivora. At the front, it is a slicing blade that works with its upper partner to form a set of scissors for cutting meat. The back of the tooth is basin-like and forms the mortar for a matching pestle above. Simply measuring the relative proportion of the first molar dedicated to slicing versus grinding functions provides an excellent estimate of diet in many species. Bears have very short blades and long basins, reflecting their omnivorous habits, while cats, the ultimate meat-eaters, have enlarged the bladed portion and lost the basin entirely. It follows that the most carnivorous bear, the polar bear, has increased the size of the meat-slicing blades of its teeth relative to other bears, although it does not approach the degree seen

J. M. Labat/AUSCAPE International

Norman Tomalin/Bruce Coleman Ltd

in cats. Similarly, the vegetarian panda has expanded the grinding surfaces of its teeth to deal with chopping up and crushing bamboo. In addition to simply being huge, panda molars have additional cusps to improve their crushing ability. The loss of two upper incisors and the reduced size of its remaining teeth enable the sloth bear to suck ants and termites, which make up most of its diet, into the mouth from where they can be swallowed.

Canine teeth are important in killing prey, and it is not surprising to find them reduced in size in all bears, including the polar bear. However, there is one species, the sun bear, which has remarkably long upper canine teeth for its size, rivalling those of lions and tigers. Unfortunately, so little is known of the ecology and behavior of the sun bear that the cause of its substantial canines remains a mystery. What little evidence there is suggests a largely vegetarian diet consisting of tree fruits and the growing tips of palms, neither of which are likely to require a stabbing bite. Because canine teeth are important in threat displays as well as attack behavior, the answer may lie in something other than diet.

Although teeth are the best indicators of diet, skulls also provide information about eating habits.

▲ The large canine teeth of a brown bear serve as a significant threat display, especially when the lower lip is extended. In this instance, the younger bear is lying down in submission.

◀ Even the sun bear, smallest of the world's bears, has well developed canine teeth which it uses as weapons or as tools for tearing trees apart to get at bees' nests.

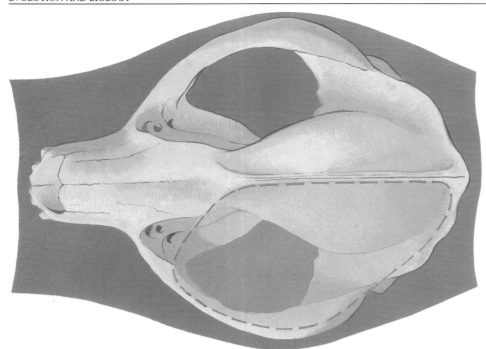

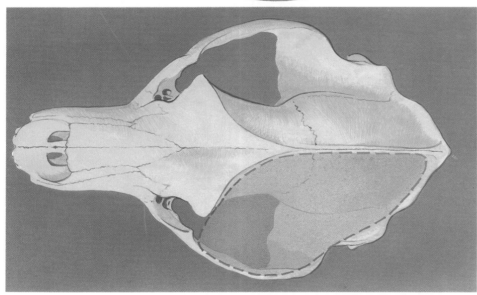

▲ The skull of a brown bear (bottom) exhibits a relatively smaller area for the jaw-closing muscles than that of a giant panda (top). Both skulls have been drawn to approximately the same length so as to highlight this difference. The area on the left side of the skull occupied by the major jaw-closing muscle, the temporalis, is shaded pink. The giant panda has large chewing muscles because bamboo must be chewed vigorously to break it into small pieces to speed digestion.

▶ Large canine teeth and long claws on the front feet are the tools used by a brown bear when catching migrating salmon from McNeil River in Alaska.

▶ (Opposite) One of the main reasons why the brown bears of coastal British Columbia, Alaska, and Kamchatka are huge is that they have reliable access each year to migrating salmon, an enormous and extremely rich food resource.

The muscles that close the jaws originate behind the orbit, the part of the skull which surrounds the eyeball, and their size varies among bears according to diet. Again it is the giant panda that is outstanding. Bamboo is extremely tough to chew, and the panda has evolved massive jaw muscles and a thick skull to handle the task. Whereas the skulls of most bears make up less than one-fifth of the total weight of their skeleton, that of the panda is closer to one-third. To resist the forceful pull of the major jaw-closing and bamboo-smashing muscles, a panda's skull roof is about twice as thick as that of a brown bear. Unlike more typical plant-eating mammals, such as horses and cows, which move their jaws from side to side, effectively shredding leaves and stems as the lower teeth slide across the uppers, pandas crush the bamboo with up-and-down jaw movements.

The absence of a more efficient side-to-side grinding behavior in the panda reflects its ancestry. The jaw joints of all species within the order Carnivora are designed to resist lateral movements (probably in response to struggling prey) and the panda has yet to overcome this inherited trait. Not surprisingly, the problem of such evolutionary "baggage" is not confined to the skeleton, but appears in aspects of soft-tissue anatomy as well.

OBTAINING NOURISHMENT

Like teeth, the digestive tracts of animals are designed for the foods they process. Many herbivorous mammals have enlarged a part of the gut to form a fermenting chamber where symbiotic micro-organisms work to break down the cellulose in plant cell walls, thus releasing the enclosed proteins and carbohydrates. No members of the order Carnivora have evolved such chambers, including the extremely herbivorous panda. In addition, because of the relative intractability of plant foods, herbivores usually have intestines that are much longer than those of carnivores. For example, the intestines of cows and deer are about 25 times longer than their body length, while those of dogs and cats are but four to five times their body length.

Bears, as omnivores, usually have a gut that is six to ten times their body length. However, the herbivorous bear that should have the longest intestine, the panda, has one that is only four to five times its body length. Given a diet of bamboo, an unimproved intestine, and the lack of a fermenting chamber, pandas digest no more than 21 percent of what they eat as opposed to the 60 percent efficiency achieved by a ruminating herbivore, such as a cow. Because of its inefficient digestion, the panda consumes 12 to 15 percent of its body weight in bamboo per day and must spend 12 to 14 hours a day feeding to survive and grow. By contrast lions often work only four hours a day to satisfy their energy needs. The foods of other omnivorous bears contain about three times the digestible energy of bamboo and therefore these species have less trouble acquiring their daily energy requirements.

WHY BEARS CUBS ARE SO SMALL AT BIRTH

MALCOLM A. RAMSAY

For placental mammals—mammals that are not marsupials, such as kangaroos and wombats, or monotremes, such as echidnas—the total weight of newborns in a litter is scaled precisely to the weight of the mother. From shrews to blue whales, this scaling pattern applies, with the sole exception of the bears.

Female bears give birth to litters of young that weigh 10 percent or less of the weight that would be predicted from the female's size. A 200 kilogram (440 pound) polar bear, for example, gives birth to a litter of cubs weighing about 800 grams (1 pound 8 ounces) each, rather than the 22 kilograms (48 pounds) predicted by the scaling relationship. Why is this?

Except for the tropical species, pregnant bears spend the time of active gestation and much of the early nursing period in a den, without food. All their nutritional requirements, as well as those of their developing offspring, must therefore be met entirely from stored body reserves, primarily fat. No other mammals, except some of the largest baleen whales, go without food and water for long periods during active gestation.

Fasting results in a marked change in the fuels used by a mammal to support its bodily processes, principally in a shift from dependence on glucose to a reliance on fatty acids released from stored fats. Mammalian fetuses, however, appear unable to use free fatty acids as an energy fuel, so a fasting pregnant female can only meet the demands of her developing fetuses for glucose through the breakdown of her own body proteins. Ultimately, this could put her life at risk.

Newborn mammals, however, can use free fatty acids almost exclusively to meet their energy requirements. By shortening the period of gestation and giving birth to very small offspring, the female can then incorporate the previously unavailable fatty acids from her fat stores into milk for her offspring. For pregnant females, such as bears, that are forced by environmental conditions to fast, there would have been strong selective pressure to shorten the gestation period and give birth as soon as possible.

A weakness in this argument relates to the tropical bears and the giant panda. These bears also give birth to tiny cubs, but they do not undertake prolonged fasts while pregnant. However, if the physiological and behavioral adaptations associated with the production of tiny young were established early in the evolution of the bears, then the tropical bears might still reflect this adaptation even though the direct causal pressure (the seasonal abundance of food) is no longer present. It is known, however, that denning itself arose in the ancestors of bears more than 10 million years ago, and was probably in response to seasonally fluctuating food supplies.

▼ At birth, brown bear cubs weigh only 340 to 680 grams (11 ounces to 1 pound 6 ounces) and their eyes are closed. Litter sizes range between two and four cubs. They are born in isolated earth dens in the middle of winter, and the mother keeps them cuddled close to her chest where they can nurse and keep warm.

Given their large size, all bears have substantial food requirements and these may be difficult to meet during the winter in cool temperate climates. Although vertebrate prey may still be available on occasion, the same cannot be said of succulent plants, fruits, tubers, and insect larvae. Bears in colder regions have solved the problem of food shortages by avoiding it through winter sleep. In temperate regions, brown, black, and female polar bears spend the winter in a deep sleep in which they may lose as much as 30 percent or more of their body mass. During this sleep, bears do not eat but survive by burning fat that was acquired in the fall. Upon emerging from their winter dens, bears rapidly return to normal mass, and have been recorded to gain weight at the rate of at least 1 kilogram (2 pounds) per day.

The fact that female and not male polar bears den in the winter is significant. Seals are the primary food of polar bears, and are not so rare in the winter that winter sleep is essential to avoid starvation. Thus male polar bears remain active throughout the year. Female polar bears den because of reproduction.

Polar bears, as well as brown and black bears, are born during the winter dormancy. The two or three tiny newborn cubs nurse and sleep, growing sufficiently during this period to be able to travel with their mother in the spring. Because it is essential for polar bears to be well insulated with fat, their milk is extremely high in fat relative to that of more tropical species such as the sun bear (46 percent versus 5 percent). The pattern of giving birth during winter sleep may be essential in cold climates. In all species of bears, the young are extremely small relative to those of other species of Carnivora and would probably die of exposure were they not kept warm by their mother in an insulated environment. Given that a bear must reach a certain size to survive the following winter without food, it is probably necessary for them to be born well before spring. The small size of newborn bears is remarkable relative to other species of Carnivora. For example, newborn bear cubs are typically only 1 to 3 percent of their mother's weight, whereas in dogs and cats, the same comparison would yield figures ranging from 10 to 20 percent.

▼ Brown bear cubs remain with their mother for at least two-and-a-half years before becoming independent, sometimes longer. Mother and cubs den together for winter sleep.

Dan Guravich

Norbert Rosing

Norbert Rosing

▲ (Top) By doing nothing more quickly than they have to, polar bears make efficient use of their energy, but when the need arises they can run at speeds exceeding 40 kilometers (25 miles) per hour for short distances.

▲ The sense of smell is highly developed in bears. Polar bears can smell the breathing holes of their principal prey species, the ringed seal, from at least a kilometer away, and a male can tell which way on the ice a breeding female is traveling just by sniffing her track.

Many, if not all, bears show a reproductive pattern known as delayed implantation, in which the development of the embryo is not continuous. Rather, it begins and then is arrested for a period of several months, allowing both mating and birth to occur during the most favorable seasons.

PREVENTING OVERHEATING

By and large, mammals find it more difficult to prevent overheating and dehydration than freezing. This is particularly true for large-bodied forms like bears because their low surface-area-to-volume ratio favors heat retention. Like all mammals, ursids have thin, convoluted sheets of bone called turbinates within their nasal passages. These fragile plates are covered with moist nasal mucosa and function to condition air as it is inhaled and

exhaled. Air is warmed and moistened on its way to the lungs and then cooled as it exits, causing water to condense within the nasal cavity. In this way water loss through respiration is minimized.

The turbinate bones of bears appear more complex and extensive in surface area than those of dogs and cats, and this is probably a result of their larger body size. As animals become larger, changes in volume outpace changes in area because volume increases as the cube of length, while area increases as the square. Anatomical structures, such as intestines or turbinates, whose function depends on surface area, are therefore likely to be larger relative to body size in heavier animals in order to preserve the necessary ratio of surface area to volume.

The brain is the organ most severely affected by a rise in temperature, and ursids appear to have

evolved a mechanism by which blood is cooled just before it enters the brain. A major supplier of blood to the brain, the internal carotid artery, loops back on itself and forms a flattened s-curve within a pocket of cooler venous blood at the base of the skull. The walls of the internal carotid are thinner within this venous pocket, thus assisting the transfer of heat from the arterial to the venous blood. Other large carnivores, such as lions, have similar counter-current heat exchangers imposed along the arteries supplying the brain, but they are positioned elsewhere on the skull.

Despite such adaptations, polar bears seem to overheat easily when running and may be incapable of traveling any distance at speeds greater than a walk. Their tendency to overheat is exacerbated by the layer of fat they carry which can be as much as 11 centimeters (4 1/2 inches) thick and is undoubtedly useful when swimming in frigid Arctic waters. Experimental studies of polar bears on treadmills suggest that locomotion is more costly in polar bears than in dogs, even at slow speeds. Clearly, as mentioned above, bears are built for strength rather than speed.

The sensory systems of ursids have been studied relatively little. Bears appear to rely heavily on their senses of smell and vision when foraging. Although the brains of bears are slightly larger for their body size than those of other carnivores, the portion devoted to the sense of smell, the olfactory bulbs, is average in size. Black bears are known to have color vision, and this is likely to be characteristic of all bears, enabling them to recognize edible plant matter, such as fruits and nuts.

▲ When polar bears on the sea ice try to capture ringed seals at their breathing holes beneath the hard wind-packed snow, they stand on their hind legs and pound straight down with their forepaws. Here a young polar bear practices his technique by trying to catch lemmings underneath the snow.

CYCLES OF FEASTING AND FASTING

MALCOLM A. RAMSAY

For most animals, fats, or lipids, represent a first-rate solution to the problem of storing large amounts of metabolic fuel within the body. Fats have a much higher energy density than other potential fuel, such as carbohydrates, and thus require less storage space. These storage fats are not spread uniformly throughout the body but are contained within specialized cells called adipocytes. These cells form discrete depots called white adipose tissue—generally referred to simply as fat.

Although fat is one of the most abundant tissues in the human body, the functional significance of its distribution is poorly understood and has received little scientific attention. The Western public, on the other hand, is much preoccupied with its distribution: millions of people devote themselves to weight-loss programs, and sizeable portions of the food budget in many households are spent on items that are low in fat and kilojoules. Anti-fat attitudes are reinforced by

▼ Brown bears in northern temperate areas spend up to six months in their winter dens surviving on stored fat reserves. In years when food is abundant in fall, they may cease feeding and become sluggish before entering the den. A bear's weight at the beginning of the winter may be double what it is in the spring.

J.M. Labat/AUSCAPE International

the media, which bombard their audiences with images of beautiful, but remarkably thin, models. The anatomical distribution of fat is big business.

FEEDING BINGES, THEN FASTING

It would seem there might well be cause for concern about the health of people who went on an annual feeding binge, doubled or even tripled their weight, then fasted. Yet this is exactly the dietary regimen that the temperate- and Arctic-zone bears undertake. In late summer, the high-latitude bears gorge themselves on foods such as berries, nuts, fish, insects, carrion, and prey, and this high-kilojoule diet causes a rapid increase

in body weight. The animals may become impressively obese, with large quantities of fat being stored under the skin and in the abdomen. As the winter advances, depending on local climatic conditions, the bears then enter dens for periods ranging from only a few weeks to more than six months.

While in their dens, bears go without food and use stored energy reserves to keep their bodies functioning. A bear's body weight falls continuously during the winter fast, with losses of more than 1 kilogram (2 pounds) per day recorded. On emerging from its den in spring a bear may weigh less than 50 percent of what it did in fall. By the end of the following summer, however, the bear will have regained its lost reserves and be ready to begin fasting once again.

The weight fluctuations displayed by bears are so impressive, and the ecological and physiological implications of their eating patterns so profound, that researchers have recently begun paying closer attention to this aspect of their lives.

EVOLUTIONARY OUTCOMES

Why do temperate-zone bears enter a den and go without food in winter rather than continuing to forage, as do the wolves and deer that live in the same habitats? Their behavior probably stems from their being primarily herbivorous but having evolved only relatively recently from a lineage of carnivorous mammals.

The ancestors of modern bears were meat eaters, so the digestive tract of a bear, unlike those of many herbivorous mammals, is not modified to contain a fermenting chamber where the cellulose in plant cell walls can be broken down to release proteins and carbohydrates. In addition, the teeth of bears are not well adapted to grind and break down fibrous plant materials in order to most efficiently extract their cell contents. Bears are thus restricted to feeding on plant foods that are relatively high in easily extractable nutrients. At high latitudes, however, foods such as these are highly seasonal and during the winter there is little or nothing for the bears to eat. Enforced periods of fasting are therefore the norm, and sizeable energy stores are required for survival.

POLAR BEARS

Polar bears are the most carnivorous of bears, and feed almost exclusively on seals. Nonetheless they, like their herbivorous relatives, also face a part of the year when there is little or nothing to eat, and they prepare for these fasts by laying up massive body stores when food is abundant. Their peak feeding period is in spring and summer, when recently weaned seal pups are available in large numbers. Seal pups can be so abundant that the polar bears sometimes consume only the layer of fat beneath the skin, known as the blubber, and leave the muscle mass untouched. At such times, polar bears may have the highest kilojoule intake of fat of any mammal, and they gain weight rapidly. In late summer, however, the melting of the sea ice limits the rate at which bears can capture seals. They then live on their stored fat for several months, until the sea freezes again or ice conditions improve and they can resume hunting. Pregnant females, however, must enter a den in order to have cubs. As they spend more than four months in their dens without access to food, abundant fat reserves are essential for survival.

COSTS OF BEING FAT

Storing fat is not a cost-free strategy, because fat animals are less agile and move more slowly than lean ones. For animals that must be able to escape rapidly from danger, or run to capture prey, agility and swiftness are indispensable. Being large omnivores, however, which do not usually chase down their food, and which have few predators, bears have less need of these traits than most mammals. As a consequence, putting on large amounts of weight does not place them at a disadvantage.

WHERE THE FAT IS STORED

The main function of adipose tissue is the uptake, storage, and controlled release of fats. The most efficient place for this tissue to be deposited is near an animal's center of mass, ideally in the abdominal cavity. In many mammals, however, and particularly in bears, most adipose tissue is stored subcutaneously (under the skin) and rather distant from the center of mass. In a bear there are many such deposits of fat, especially over the thighs and rump, and even in a relatively lean bear

such deposits may be many centimeters thick. One hypothesis to account for such deposits of fat in mammals is that it is an adaptation to provide thermal insulation.

For mammals living in cold environments, such as the high-latitude bears, and particularly the semi-aquatic polar bears living in the Arctic, this idea seems intuitively reasonable. In the fully aquatic mammals, such as seals and the smaller whales, subcutaneous fat deposits certainly provide thermal insulation and almost all fats are deposited there. However, most terrestrial mammals, including all the bears, store fat both subcutaneously and in the abdominal cavity—an inefficient arrangement if thermal insulation were a major goal. Furthermore, the abdominal stores of fat are not used up before the subcutaneous ones, as would be predicted by the thermal insulation hypothesis.

A more likely explanation for the thick subcutaneous fat found in bears is related to two factors. First, at certain times of the year, bears tend to store relatively more fat than do most mammals because of their need to survive long periods without food. Second, among mammals in general, the internal organs, and thus the abdominal cavities, of the larger species are proportionally smaller than those of the smaller species. For example, the abdominal organs of a weasel amount to more than 20 percent of its weight, whereas those of a

▼ A young brown bear without its mother has a hard time simply finding enough to eat, let alone enough to deposit fat for the winter. Subadults are inexperienced at finding food and are often displaced from the best sites by larger bears.

Stan Osolinski/Oxford Scientific Films

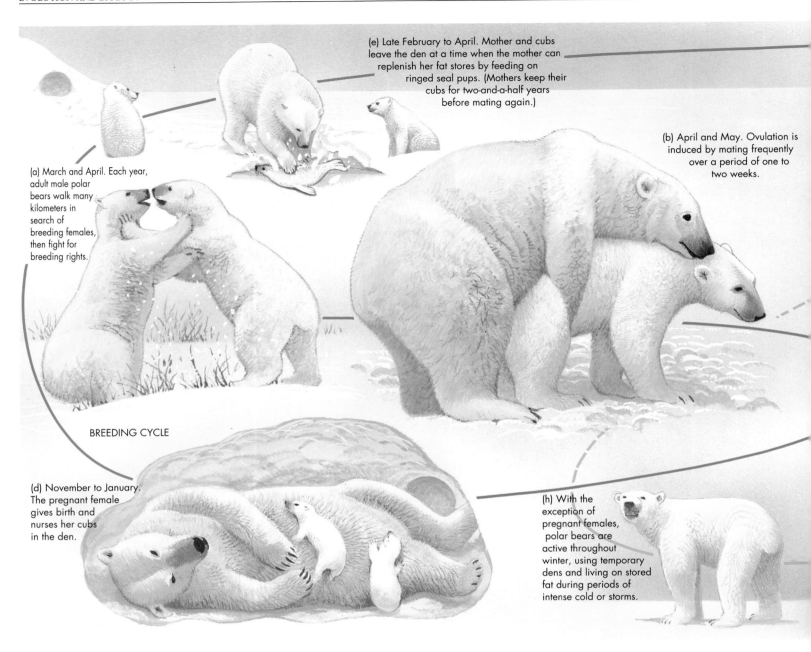

(e) Late February to April. Mother and cubs leave the den at a time when the mother can replenish her fat stores by feeding on ringed seal pups. (Mothers keep their cubs for two-and-a-half years before mating again.)

(b) April and May. Ovulation is induced by mating frequently over a period of one to two weeks.

(a) March and April. Each year, adult male polar bears walk many kilometers in search of breeding females, then fight for breeding rights.

BREEDING CYCLE

(d) November to January. The pregnant female gives birth and nurses her cubs in the den.

(h) With the exception of pregnant females, polar bears are active throughout winter, using temporary dens and living on stored fat during periods of intense cold or storms.

▲ Feeding and breeding cycles of the polar bear. Most bears fast only in winter, when denning, whereas polar bears can deposit fat or fast at any time of the year, depending on opportunity and need.

bear amount to less than 5 percent. Consequently, the abdominal cavities of large mammals can contain relatively less fat than those of smaller ones, so a large mammal would need to store relatively more fat under the skin than would a smaller one, even if each were carrying the same percentage of fat. The extensive subcutaneous fat in bears therefore probably results from packing constraints in the gut, rather than from thermal stress.

In human males, most fat is deposited in the abdominal cavity, whereas in females the greatest proportion is deposited on the hips and thighs. The former pattern is associated with a greater range of medical complications and a higher death rate than the latter. In bears the distribution of fat in both sexes is similar to the pattern seen in human females. Depositing fat in physiologically less harmful sites might be one of the means whereby bears can safely undergo periodic bouts of extreme obesity.

FAT CELLS AND BODY FATNESS

A recent finding stemming from the study of fat in bears relates to the properties of their adipocytes, the cells in which the fat is stored. Unlike those of many mammal species, the total number of fat cells in a bear remains relatively constant with age, but their volume can change more than tenfold, swelling or shrinking according to whether the bear is storing fat or using it up. The fat cells of pregnant females show the most extreme range in volume, which is perhaps an adaptation to their needs during pregnancy and lactation while fasting.

The adipocytes in most mammals, including humans, show nowhere near the same propensity to vary in volume as they do in bears, tending instead to multiply with increasing levels of fatness. Gaining a deeper understanding of the way bears limit the proliferation of adipocytes might offer a novel means of treating people prone to extreme obesity.

(f) April to July. Ringed seals, the polar bear's main prey, give birth in April, and the pups are weaned six weeks later. These fat, young pups are unwary and polar bears feed on them in large numbers.

(c) September. The fertilized egg is implanted in the uterus. In late October or early November the pregnant female digs her den.

(g) August to November. In late July the sea ice melts and polar bears come ashore, living on their stored fat until freeze-up, when they are able to hunt seals once again.

FEEDING CYCLE

CONTAMINANTS

Fat-soluble contaminants, such as polychlorinated biphenyls (PCBs) and other organochlorines, if ingested, become concentrated in fatty tissue. For female bears, the entire period of active gestation, and the first months of lactation, are undertaken while fasting. Consequently, all the nutrients for the developing fetuses and the newborn cubs come from the mother's body stores. The fat deposits of females may constitute more than 50 percent of their body weight at the start of fasting. Little research has been done in this area, but there is considerable concern that the sudden release during fasting of fat-soluble contaminants might interfere with fetal development and other critical physiological and developmental processes.

When fasting, all species of bears face the risk of being affected by fat-soluble contaminants, but the dangers are most marked for polar bears because of their place at the top of the Arctic marine food chain. The higher an animal's position in a food chain, the more it is at risk from high concentrations of contaminants in its tissues. For example, contaminants that affect the marine plankton community can subsequently be concentrated along the food chain by a multiple of two to three billion. Initial surveys have shown that levels of PCBs and various other contaminants have already reached high concentrations in the fat of some polar bears.

Other species of bears, being primarily herbivorous, feed lower on the food chain and therefore face less risk of being poisoned, but all bears that accumulate large fat reserves are vulnerable to contamination. Populations of bears that exploit seasonally spawning runs of fish are also feeding well up a food chain and therefore might also be at considerable risk.

BEAR MILK

ANDREW E. DEROCHER

Water, fat, protein, and sugar are the main ingredients in all mammal milk. Higher in fat and protein but lower in carbohydrates than milk from other terrestrial carnivores, bear milk has an energy content roughly three times greater than that of humans or cows. It closely resembles the milk of seals, whales, and dolphins.

Milk quality is especially important in bears because of the extremely small size of cubs at birth and their high growth rates. Until they leave the den, cubs are wholly nourished by their mother, who will not be feeding. Even after the cubs begin foraging, their mother will continue to nurse them, providing additional nutrition. Females of all species nurse their offspring until the dissolution of the family, meaning that a female brown or polar bear will nurse her cubs continuously for up to three years. It is thought that nursing assists in maintaining family bonds.

Bear milk is thick and viscous. The richest milk is found in polar bears, followed by brown and black bears. Sun bear and giant panda milk appears to be less rich. Since the female does not drink during hibernation, the high fat content may result from the milk being concentrated in order to conserve water.

In the relatively few samples of bear milk that have been analyzed, the fat content ranged from 5 to 46 percent. (Humans average 4.1 percent and cows 3.7 percent fat in their milk.) In polar bears, milk fat is high when the females are feeding on seals, and drops when they are fasting.

In comparison with other mammals, bear milk is high in protein, ranging from 4 to 19 percent. (Human milk is roughly 0.8 percent protein and cow milk 3.2 percent.) Protein content varies considerably between species and reflects differences in diet. Bear milk contains only 1 or 2 percent lactose (the most common milk sugar), whereas the mineral content is high, relative to other species. It is also moderately high in vitamins B6, B12, riboflavin, thiamin, nicotinic acid, and calcium pantothenate, and has more vitamin A and E than cow milk.

Researchers are concerned about milk being contaminated by toxins ingested by polar bears. Polychlorinated biphenyls (PCBs) polluting the marine environment are concentrated in the milk and the effects of these contaminants are unknown.

▼ From the time cubs are born to when they leave the maternity den several months later, they live entirely on their mother's milk. Brown bears and black bears have six functional nipples, while polar bears have only four.

Konrad Wothe/Oxford Scientific Films

BENEFITS TO HUMANS

So far, most studies of fatty tissue dynamics have been carried out on a limited range of mammal species—principally laboratory rodents, a few domestic species, and humans—none of which routinely become obese under normal circumstances. Animals living in highly seasonal environments often become seasonally obese, with no obvious ill effects. Bears, for example, display some of the most extreme examples of seasonal fatness known amongst mammals and clearly have evolved means of remaining physically fit while obese. The study of the dietary habits of bears will offer an insight into the fascinating phenomenon of a "feast and fast" lifestyle.

Carefully designed research programs on bears are likely to yield a considerable amount of information about the ways in which mammals conserve energy while fasting, how fats can be used safely by the body as its primary fuel, and how large fat loads can be tolerated without apparent ill effects. As well as having practical implications for the conservation and management of bear populations worldwide, these studies are relevant to several fields of human medicine. For example, much can be learned from bears regarding the alleviation of health hazards that are associated with extreme obesity and anorexia nervosa.

▲ A male brown bear leaves his den and begins to search for food.

▼ Feeding on salmon to deposit fat for the winter, brown bears leave carrion, providing food for scavengers like gulls.

Art Wolfe

WINTER SLEEP

MALCOLM A. RAMSAY

Much has been learned—and there is much yet to be learned—about the winter sleep of bears. The seemingly simple act of a bear entering a den in fall is underlaid by a marvelous suite of adaptations that allow it to survive in a surprisingly stressful environment.

Each fall, in the hardwood forests of eastern North America, black bears quietly enter dens and begin a winter sleep that will last until the following spring. All four species of bears that inhabit the temperate and Arctic regions of North America and Eurasia—the American and Asiatic black bears, the brown bear, and the polar bear—behave in a similar way. While humans have known that bears enter winter sleep since ancient times, a detailed understanding of why bears behave in this way, and what the physiological and ecological underpinnings of such behavior are, has been developed only recently. New technologies, such as remote monitoring of body temperature and activity patterns, methods of determining the metabolic rate of bears while in their dens, and satellite tracking of individual animals, are now enabling scientists to monitor bears in considerable detail.

Food shortages

Bears are driven to seek shelter in winter not as a result of thermal stress, but for nutritional reasons. Winter is a time of food scarcity for the animals that inhabit the temperate and Arctic regions of the Northern Hemisphere. For warm-blooded species, such as birds and mammals, seasonal food shortages are critical because they need to maintain their body temperature at a relatively high level. To do this they must have access to a great deal of food. Many species of birds are able to ensure continuous access to food by migrating to warmer regions during winter, whereas mammals, because most cannot fly, are unable to do this. Instead, they generally eke out a winter existence on limited supplies of relatively low-quality foods. For the terrestrial bears especially, winter is a time when food is absent, or in very short supply, so they disappear into shelters for lengthy periods. In their dens they do not eat, but live off their body reserves, awaiting the coming of plentiful food in spring.

Daniel J. Cox

▲ Black bears are extremely versatile in their choice of denning sites and have been recorded using culverts under highways and the airspace below houses without basements. Even a brush pile like this can be adequate once there is enough snow cover to provide insulation from the cold.

Adaptations to fasting

Bears are not alone among warm-blooded animals in undertaking lengthy fasts. For example, several species of small mammals, such as ground squirrels and some bats, undertake long bouts of hibernation in winter during which their body temperature, heartbeat rate, and metabolic rate are reduced to save energy. Emperor penguins and some breeding seals also fast for prodigiously long periods, although they do not hibernate, and they have developed some of the same specializations that are used by bears in order to do so.

Nevertheless, the winter sleep of bears is unique in several ways. Firstly, during the fast, which can exceed six months in some environments, bears do not eat, drink, urinate, or defecate. They do, however, undergo massive weight losses as body tissues are broken down to meet fuel requirements. Rather than starving, these animals are in a precisely regulated physiological state wherein more than 90 percent of their energy requirements are met from stored fats. To ensure sufficient energy supplies, bears eat large quantities of high-energy foods before the start of the winter fast and become obese, with fat reserves constituting more than 50 percent of their total body weight. Proteins, which break down as a normal part of daily wear and tear, are largely rebuilt during the fast, so the protein mass of bears remains constant or shows only a gradual decline. This is in marked contrast to the situation in most mammals, including humans, which show a continuous loss of protein when fasting. Without protein recycling, protein losses in winter-dormant bears would lead to reproductive failure and death.

Pregnancy and fasting

A second aspect of the winter sleep of bears is that gestation and early lactation, the most energy-costly portions of the mammalian reproductive cycle, are undertaken entirely while fasting. At the time she gives birth, a dormant female bear will have been without food and water for many weeks and, depending on the latitude and environment in which she lives, will continue to fast for several weeks more while nursing her newborn cubs. Except for some of the largest baleen whales, bears are the only mammals to go without food and water for protracted periods during active gestation; and only bears, some whales, and some seals fast during long portions of the lactation period. For most mammals, fasting while pregnant would be life-threatening, because of high energy demands and high levels of waste production. The balancing of pregnancy with fasting is an extraordinary metabolic feat that bears carry off routinely.

Bears show only a modest drop in body temperature and metabolic rate during winter dormancy, and are therefore easily aroused should they be disturbed in their den. Why do bears not drop their body-core temperature down close to freezing and thereby save energy, as do other hibernators? One reason has to do with the timing of birth. Most mammals living in seasonal environments give birth during the spring, near the start of the period when there is plenty of food. Newborns therefore have spring and summer in which to develop and build up their reserves of fat before having to face the rigors of winter. Body size, however, plays an all-important role in this strategy, for the length of gestation generally increases with adult body size among placental mammals. Thus, the largest species tend to have the longest periods of gestation.

To give birth in spring, therefore, large mammals, like bears, have to undertake gestation during winter, the period when food is most limited and hibernation is therefore most advantageous. However, a hibernating mammal, with a metabolic rate reduced appreciably below the normal level, would be unable to maintain normal fetal development. Bears, therefore, are constrained during winter sleep from dropping their metabolic rate because females are obliged to maintain pregnancy.

Smaller mammals are able to exploit the energy savings arising from greatly slowed metabolic processes because their relatively short gestation period allows them to forego fetal development during hibernation yet still give birth soon after emerging from hibernation. The largest mammals known to undertake hibernation with a significantly reduced metabolic rate are the marmots, which can weigh up to 7.5 kilograms (16 pounds).

Because bears maintain near-normal body temperature during their winter sleep, they wake easily if disturbed. Thus, if a predator such as a wolf discovers the den, the bear can defend itself. It is not clear, however, how likely bears are to abandon their dens if disturbed in midwinter by human activities. There are anecdotal accounts of bears overwintering in dens below occupied cabins, or next to busy roads, but there are also accounts of bears abandoning dens immediately after being disturbed by nearby humans. It is not clear what degree of disturbance is perceived as a threat by a bear. It is clear, however, that a bear that abandons its den in midwinter will greatly increase its energy expenditures and will thus risk starving to death. A female that abandons her den runs the additional risk of losing her litter. Determining how sensitive denned bears are to outside activity may be of significance in determining conservation strategies for threatened populations of bears.

Bears and human health

One of the products of protein breakdown is a mildly toxic substance known as urea. In humans about 25 percent of this urea is recycled back into proteins by bacteria in our intestines. The rest is filtered by our kidneys and excreted in urine. For people with malfunctioning kidneys, urea build-up is life-threatening, and their blood usually needs to be filtered through an artificial kidney (dialysis). A bear in winter sleep also produces urea continuously, but the bear recycles virtually all of it back into amino acids, the building blocks of proteins. Researchers are trying to understand how bears do this. If the feat could be duplicated in humans with kidney failure, dialysis would not be needed.

Scientific insights gathered from bears in winter sleep might also improve the lives of people as dissimilar as bed-ridden invalids and astronauts in space. The bones of such people carry little weight and, consequently, lose calcium steadily. Such losses can be so significant that an astronaut returning to Earth from a protracted stay in space is in danger of breaking bones just by walking. Yet bears emerge from their winter dens with no detectable bone loss. Like urea build-up, the secret appears to lie in recycling. Bears in winter sleep recycle lost calcium into newly deposited bone layers. Thus bone production balances bone loss during the long weeks of inactivity in a winter den. If scientists could duplicate what bears do to stimulate new bone growth, they might well have a novel way to treat bone loss in humans.

Jim Brandenburg/Planet Earth Pictures

▲ By capturing females with cubs in their winter dens, researchers are making discoveries about the growth rates of young bears in their earliest stages of life. The metabolic pathways being used by female bears to turn their fat into milk is of great interest to medical research.

THE BEHAVIOR OF BEARS

IAN STIRLING AND ANDREW E. DEROCHER

Bears today tend to live most of their lives as solitary individuals, and there is no indication from the fossil record that their ancestors were any more gregarious. For the most part, social groups are limited to females with cubs and male–female pairs during the breeding season. As with other groups of mammals, the evolution of social organization in bears was influenced by the availability of resources, the risk of being killed by other animals, and competition for resources with other members of the same species.

Food distribution has a major effect on the development of social organization in any species. In the case of most bears, food tends to be patchily distributed, variable in quantity and quality, and difficult to defend. Thus defense of a home range by a group of bears would probably not be worthwhile, because the defendable area would be unlikely to produce enough to support the group.

BEARS AND LIONS: A COMPARISON

In considering why bears are not found in groups, it is interesting to compare their social organization with that of lions. Like bears, the ancestors of lions were solitary carnivores, as most other cats still are today. Bears and lions both give birth to helpless offspring, so substantial parental care is required when the cubs are young. In lions, the bond

▲ An alert young Alaskan brown bear takes a break from feeding to stand up and look over tall grass to check for the presence of other bears.

Competition for patchy food resources, and the evolution of a mainly vegetarian diet necessitating a large food intake because of a non-ruminant digestive tract, probably acted against the bears forming large social groups. Groups would exhaust food patches faster than individuals, resulting in the animals having to move more frequently in search of new feeding areas. The energetic cost of additional travel would be too costly because the massive build of bears makes walking long distances inefficient. In exceptional circumstances where there is a concentration of high quality food, such as at a salmon stream or a garbage dump, many bears may feed in the same area. However, such phenomena are too localized and short-lived to encourage the development of a stable pattern of social organization.

between the mother and her cubs is the basis of group formation. Because of fidelity to the birth area, the females in each group, or pride, are often related. A major advantage of group living in lions is that some males remain with the cubs and protect them from non-resident infanticidal males, leaving the females, which are generally faster and better hunters, free to supply food for all.

Fidelity to the birth area is characteristic of bears, and infanticide occurs occasionally as well, but there are two important differences between them and lions. Firstly, female lions can come into estrus at any time of year, whereas bears are seasonal breeders. Thus, a male lion that displaces a resident male may be able to mate with a lioness if he kills her cubs, regardless of the season, which is highly unlikely with bears, unless the cubs are killed during the mating period. Infanticide is therefore a less important stimulus for group living in bears than in lions.

A second, and perhaps most important difference between lions and bears relates to the treatment of

prey. By hunting together, lions can kill large prey, often enough to feed the entire group. A black or brown bear is likely to kill a hoofed mammal so rarely that it would be more advantageous not to share it. Additionally, in temperate regions, the climate is cool for part of the year, so a carcass would not decompose quickly, making it beneficial for an animal to guard it for continued use. The warmer climate in lion habitat, plus the abundance of scavengers, may make kill-sharing advantageous.

Although brown bears occasionally kill mammals as large as elk, and may sometimes hunt in pairs, their rate of kill does not approach that of lions. If bears hunted in groups, they would have to travel widely between kills, as do packs of wolves, because of the low density of prey species, and each bear would receive limited nourishment from each kill because of the need to share. Compared with that of wolves, long-distance travel by bears is slow and much more costly in energy, so solitary hunting combined with foraging is the best overall strategy.

▼ After killing a newborn deer fawn, an adult black bear quickly carries the carcass off into the forest to consume it, away from other bears that might try to steal it.

Stan Osolinski/Oxford Scientific Films

▲ In Yellowstone National Park, this brown-phase black bear killed a mule deer, probably by ambushing it while it was drinking at a stream. The sound of the water may have obscured the sound of the stalking bear.

▶ Two young brown bears take time out to play instead of trying to catch fish in a nearby fast-flowing Alaskan river.

A MAINLY SOLITARY EXISTENCE

Even in the case of polar bears, which are completely carnivorous, the small size of their major prey, ringed seals, probably negates any potential advantage from hunting as a group or sharing a kill with other bears, except their own cubs. Like brown bears hunting hoofed mammals, the rate at which polar bears kill large prey such as bearded seals, or even the small Arctic whales, does not appear to be frequent enough to stimulate the development of group hunting. Large numbers of polar bears will scavenge together at whale carcasses or dumps, as do brown or black bears, but each animal still behaves independently.

Most bears undergo winter sleep and this may also inhibit the development of sociality. By way of comparison, there is a wide range in the sociality of ground squirrels. Apparently what characterizes the most social species of squirrels is prolonged

association between adults and subadults that can occur only if the animals do not hibernate, or hibernate for short periods only.

In contrast with the varied diet of omnivores such as black bears, more than 99 percent of the giant panda's diet consists of bamboo stems, branches, and leaves. Although there are at least 30 species of bamboo that are consumed throughout the giant panda's range, in any given habitat there are usually only about two kinds available in abundance. There is seasonal variation in the use of each species and the parts of the plants that are eaten, but since bamboo grows year-round at high density, pandas can normally obtain all the food they need within much smaller areas than other species of bears. There is therefore no need for pandas to move around from season to season, change diet, or hibernate, but even so they show little social organization.

Probably because of their solitary existence, most female bears are likely to be induced ovulators, that is, they do not ovulate until they have been stimulated by mating. There is little advantage in ovulating spontaneously, as do most seals for example, if it is unlikely that there will be a male nearby. From observations in zoos and in the wild, it appears that male and female pairs may remain together for up to about two weeks. Males try to keep females in isolated areas, where they are less likely to encounter competing males, and copulation usually occurs many times. Competition between males for mating privileges can be intense and some females may mate with more than one male. Since female bears may have multiple ovulations, it is theoretically possible for members of the same litter to have different fathers. For example, one female brown bear was observed mating 10 times with four different males in two hours. How common this sort of mating behavior is, and what effect it may have had on the evolution of the social organization of bears, is unknown.

In spite of the overall trend in bears toward being solitary, some sociality exists. For example, during the ice-free period in western Hudson Bay, the whole polar bear population comes ashore and fasts, and groups of two to fourteen or more adult males often gather together closely and show extreme tolerance of each other. In such circumstances, considerable ritualized fighting may take place in which combatants are not injured.

On one occasion, two adult female polar bears, one with cubs of the year and the other with yearling cubs, socialized with each other and even attended each other's cubs over a period of six weeks while feeding together at a garbage dump. It was not known whether they were related.

It is also possible that the apparently solitary forest-dwelling bears have social tendencies. For example, reassociation of family groups after breakup has been reported. In black bears, female offspring tend to settle in or adjacent to the home

"A SLOUTHE OF BEERYS"

ANDREW E. DEROCHER

A group of bears is called a sloth, a term first used in 1452, according to *The Oxford English Dictionary*. The actual phrase was "A slouthe of Beerys." The word sloth derives from the Middle English term for slow, but it is a mystery as to why early writers thought that a group of bears moved slowly. It is also interesting to speculate about where groups of bears might have been seen. Maybe it was at some long-since-vanished site in Europe where bears congregated at a salmon stream to fish.

Currently, one would be most likely to come across a sloth of polar bears on the coast of western Hudson Bay. Towards the end of summer, when the sea ice has melted, groups of males gather together on islands and points of land. When the sea freezes over again, they disperse to hunt seals. Sloths of grizzly bears can most easily be seen at salmon spawning streams, such as McNeil River, Pack Creek, and Brooks River in Alaska. Details of how to visit these sanctuaries are given on pages 226–7.

▼ When the ice melts in Hudson Bay, Canada, sloths of polar bears gather through the late summer and fall. No breeding or hunting takes place while the bears are ashore, and in the absence of either food or potential mates to compete for, the bears become surprisingly social.

Fred Bruemmer

Daniel J. Cox

ranges of their mothers, while male cubs disperse. It has been suggested that female black bears can recognize their independent offspring and may behave toward them in a beneficial manner because of being related.

SEXUAL DIMORPHISM

The difference in size between males and females, known as sexual dimorphism, is strongly associated with species in which males mate with more than one female in a breeding season, and is thought to result from the competition between males seeking mating privileges. It has also been suggested that if males do not help care for and feed the young as, for example, male wolves do, they have additional time to seek out and mate with a number of females. Male bears do not help raise the young.

In bears, sexual dimorphism ranges from species where the difference is small to those in which males are twice the size of females. Marked sexual dimorphism characterized most of the extinct Pleistocene bears of between 2 million and 10,000 years ago, such as the cave bear and the giant short-faced bear.

Sexual dimorphism generally increases as species become larger. Although weight data are not available for most bear species, within the three North American species—the brown bear, the black bear, and the polar bear—sexual dimorphism tends to increase with size. It is also interesting to note that the pattern of increasing sexual dimorphism in relation to increasing body size is distinct even within the different populations of North American brown bears.

In one study of skull morphology of brown bears and Asiatic black bears in Japan, sexual dimorphism was detectable in all measured parts, but was only statistically significant in the canine teeth. Since the diet of males and females of each species is similar, the significant enlargement of the canine teeth in males, beyond that which would be expected because of their larger size, is probably for intrasexual threat display and because they are used as weapons. For example, in male polar bears, the canine teeth are often badly broken in fights.

Within several species of bears, intense conflicts between adult males have been reported,

▲ An adult male brown bear must mate many times with a female over a period of a week or two in order to stimulate her to ovulate. Often the male will try to herd the female to a secluded spot where he is less likely to have to defend his access to her from competing males.

Konrad Wothe/Oxford Scientific Films

Male bears of all species sometimes kill cubs, so mother bears are constantly on the lookout for predacious males. (Above) A female polar bear stands guard over her two cubs while looking around her. (Opposite, top) Another female lowers her head and prepares to meet an attack from an adult while her frightened cub hides behind her. (Opposite, center) In another instance, a male succeeds in evading the female and mauls her cub. She eventually manages to drive him off. (Opposite, bottom) A cautious female leads her 10-month-old cub around an area where males are present.

and while there is no conclusive evidence regarding mating success, it seems likely that large body size enables a male to sire more offspring. It has also been suggested that the larger size of male bears, relative to females, may have evolved in part to favor the establishment of larger home ranges, which would overlap those of several females.

The marked sexual dimorphism in polar bears is likely to be related both to the fact that they are large bears and to intense competition between males for breeding females. Although the ratio of adult males to females is roughly equal, most females only breed about once every three years, at most, so that the functional sex ratio each spring is actually three or more males for each female. A high annual variation in ice conditions and seal numbers makes food distribution for polar bears less predictable than for terrestrial bears, so female polar bears, unlike their land counterparts, do not defend territories. Instead they have large home ranges which overlap in feeding areas. They gather together in places where seals are abundant and the males are attracted to them. Males thus have to compete with each other wherever females are most numerous, which may result in greater

competition between males than occurs in terrestrial bears. Even so, it is important to note that an apparently similar degree of sexual dimorphism is also evident in some populations of brown bears.

Within the primates, sexual dimorphism is greater in ground-dwelling species than in species that climb trees. If males of tree-climbing species were significantly larger than females they might be too heavy to feed on thin stems or at the ends of branches. This factor may also influence sexual dimorphism in bears. There is little information available on the weight of sun bears, which spend much of their time in trees, but males and females are similar in size. Male and female sloth bears also differ little in size, and the difference in size between male and female giant pandas is not marked. Both sloth bears and giant pandas are capable climbers and sometimes feed in trees, though they feed more often on the ground. The least sexually dimorphic of the three North American bears, the black bear, also makes the greatest use of trees, and shows a similar degree of sexual dimorphism to that found in the spectacled bear and the Asiatic black bear, both of which also sometimes feed in trees.

COMPETITION WITHIN AND BETWEEN SPECIES

Some of the ancestral bears might have been preyed upon considerably because they were small, but it appears that as body size, teeth, and claws increased in size through evolutionary time, bears became progressively less susceptible to being killed by other animals. Smaller species of bears might have used trees as escape habitat, while larger species could stand and fight if necessary. Bears would therefore have had little stimulus to gather together in groups for defense or vigilance. While bears of several species, especially young ones, are killed from time to time by predators, such as wolves, such losses have been insufficient to stimulate changes in social organization.

In all the North American species of bears, males are known to prey on their own species, particularly cubs, but because there is little documentation of such behavior it is difficult to assess its significance. Infanticide in bears may also vary between species. For example, polar bears live in open habitat where predation of cubs by males is less likely to be successful than in forests, where visibility is limited. Also, by the time polar bear cubs are six months old, they are able to outrun adult males. Among the subtropical species of bears, there have been no reports of bears preying on their own species.

It has been suggested that competition, including predation, is significant between North American black and brown bears. When faced with a serious threat, the female black bear sends

Dan Guravich

Brian and Cherry Alexander / NHPA

Dan Guravich

BEAR NAVIGATION

LYNN L. ROGERS

Steve McCutcheon/AUSCAPE International

Bears have a mysterious ability to determine which way is home when they roam into unfamiliar areas. It is not piloting based on familiar landmarks, nor is it the ability to move in a particular direction without using landmarks. It is a form of true navigation—the ability to orient homeward, or toward a place beyond sensory contact, from a previously unvisited area. Attempts to account for bears' mental map and compass abilities include speculation that a bear senses the Earth's magnetic field and extrapolates its position from local magnetic gradients.

Bears show incredible memory of important locations. Cubs that followed their mother 32 kilometers (20 miles) to an oak stand to eat acorns one fall returned there to feed three and five years later as adults. Black bears that had become used to human observers in northeastern Minnesota showed that they knew most or all of the waterholes, refuge trees, feeding areas, and trails in their home range. The bears moved directly to preferred locations, whether those places were upwind, downwind, or out of sight.

When berry crops failed in the home range of one male black bear, he moved a record 200 kilometers (125 miles) into unfamiliar range. Researchers wondered if this 11-year-old, radio-collared bear would retrace his rather indirect route when he returned home to hibernate. He did not. One day in October, he began moving directly homeward. His route demonstrated that he knew his location relative to home and that he possessed compass sense. By ignoring trails and roadways and by blundering through rough terrain, farmland, and residential neighborhoods, he showed that he was unaware of pathways and dangers along the way. He moved only at night, when territorial bears are sleeping and most people are indoors. He apparently did not use the night sky for navigation because he continued in the right direction regardless of whether the sky was clear, overcast, or obscured by trees. His ignorance of terrain and trails may have slowed him down because he averaged only 19 kilometers (12 miles) per 24 hours, compared with 32 kilometers (20 miles) for a bear traveling through familiar range. Nine days after beginning his homeward trek, he reached familiar ground and his behavior changed. He began walking mainly on roads and trails, and he continued moving in daylight. Later that day, he left the trail he was following, went over a hill, and entered a den for the winter.

"Nuisance" bears have been able to find their way home after being tranquilized and transported up to 270 kilometers (168 miles) away. Of 54 bears that were transported 64 to 120 kilometers (40 to 75 miles) from home, 35 moved homeward after release, and of 23 that were transported 120 to 270 kilometers (75 to 168 miles) from home, 17 did so. Homing did not depend upon familiarity with release areas, upon random movement, or upon expanding search patterns. Whatever navigation methods bears do use, they apparently have a distance limit, because bears that were transported 1,400 kilometers (870 miles) from Minnesota to Arkansas moved in random directions after release.

◄ Brown bear males in areas such as this in Mount McKinley Park in Alaska spend their lives in a home range of several hundred square kilometers. They must learn the location of every food source in the region and the times of year that the food is available.

her cubs up a nearby tree for safety, flees, and then returns for them after the threat has passed. In contrast, the larger brown bear female protects her cubs by standing her ground or attacking the aggressor directly. Although brown bear cubs are capable of climbing trees, they apparently do so much less frequently in response to danger than black bear cubs.

In areas in North America where the two species overlap, brown bears are consistently one-and-a-half times to twice the size of black bears. A likely consequence of this size difference is the retention by the black bear of the forest-dwelling niche of its ancestors, because it was not large enough to protect its young, and possibly itself, on the ground from larger carnivores, such as the brown bear. The brown bear was probably able to exploit more open habitat, as well as forests, because it was larger than the black bear and thus less vulnerable to predation.

Female polar bears, which live in open habitat, also defend their cubs by attacking the aggressor directly, even if they are threatened by an adult male twice their size or a helicopter hovering overhead. In the High Arctic, female polar bears with cubs, and sometimes lone subadults as well, will often climb a hillside above the sea ice and dig a pit to lie in where they can see around them, before going to sleep. This precaution appears to be in response to the possibility of attack by larger bears.

Giant pandas sometimes seek safety by climbing trees—females will climb trees to avoid harassment by courting males. However, pandas may use trees for escape less frequently than bears of other species because of the presence of leopards which can also climb trees and are capable of killing pandas, particularly young ones.

The sloth bear is an expert climber. When cubs are small, the female will carry them into the trees on her back, whereas larger cubs may remain on the ground when the female is in a tree. If threatened, the female will leave the trees and flee on the ground, her cubs sometimes running ahead of her. It has been suggested that sloth bears do not use trees for escape habitat because of the presence of leopards, which frequently prey on tree-dwelling animals. Despite its small size, the sloth bear will attack humans if surprised, and it is regarded as dangerous by local people. As in the case of the much larger brown bear, aggressive behavior may be a consequence of being unable to rely on trees for escape.

▶ The American black bear is an excellent tree climber. Mother bears often send their cubs to safety up a tree when danger threatens. The cubs remain in the tree and wait for their mother while she escapes on her own, returning for her cubs later when it is safe.

Joe Van Wormer/Bruce Coleman Ltd

Daniel J. Cox

▲ Bears are very curious and usually pause to investigate something unfamiliar. This black bear female has her head up so she can see and smell, and her large ears erect to listen for noises. Her cubs are copying her behavior.

Jeff Foott/AUSCAPE International

DENNING AND INDIVIDUAL BEHAVIOR

Bears in winter sleep differ from hibernating mammals in that their body temperature drops only a few degrees and they are capable of rapid arousal. This limited temperature drop is necessary because pregnant females need to maintain a metabolic rate that is sufficiently high to support normal fetal development. In addition, the number of reports of predation by wolves and other bears at winter dens suggests that denning bears must also be capable of quick arousal, if necessary, in order to protect themselves and their cubs.

People who have worked with bears have been impressed by how variable the behavior of individual bears can be. Bears in the wild appear to remember a great deal about particular areas and to be able to solve problems. Although there is little experimental evidence from the wild, the extraordinary success that circuses have had with training bears suggests they are good at learning and remembering tasks. These impressions make sense, given the fact that bears are long-lived mammals that spend most of their lives within the same home range.

Cubs learn by following and imitating their mothers during the long period before weaning. Over time, they must learn and remember a great deal about the area, including where and how to find food, shelter, denning habitat, and other necessities under a variety of circumstances.

The degree of variation in the ways that bears from the same population behave within a particular area may be influenced both by genetic factors and learning. If there is considerable variability within the habitat (for example, in food types and availability, cover, and topography), over time the feeding experiences of individual bears will differ. Thus, through learning, especially by cubs from their mothers, some bears may develop individual food preferences, and may vary in the degree to which they prey on animals, or in the way they respond to disturbances.

COMMUNICATION METHODS

Because bears are solitary animals and are usually difficult to observe, their communication methods are not well understood. The degree to which bears vocalize varies from species to species. It has been suggested that black bears are more vocal than brown bears because visibility in the forest is more restricted and necessitates more extensive use of

calls. Other forest species such as spectacled bears, sloth bears, and sun bears also seem to be quite vocal. Giant pandas in zoos vocalize during estrus, and eleven sounds have been identified from wild pandas. In contrast, polar bears, which live in the most open habitat of all, vocalize little. Females and cubs may call to each other if they become separated, or if the female is leaving a site and

▲ Brown bear cubs remain with their mother for at least two-and-a-half years, watching her constantly, learning every-thing from what to eat and where to find it, to how to locate a den for the winter. These three soggy looking cubs are watching while their mother fishes for salmon.

Mark Newman/AUSCAPE International

wants the cub to follow. Males snort and chuff when behaving antagonistically with one another, but they lack the distinctive calls that characterize other carnivores.

The use of scents, including pheromones, has not been documented in bears, but they are likely to be present. For example, an adult male polar bear on the sea ice during the breeding season in the spring may walk tens of kilometers in a straight line across the ice in search of a breeding female. During this time, his path may cross the tracks of dozens of other bears but he gives no detectable response until he crosses the path of a lone adult female. Recognition is instant and he then follows the track until he catches up with her or is distracted by another female. It is not known how a male polar bear recognizes such tracks, but it seems likely that a chemical stimulus is involved.

Several species of bears are well known for marking trees. Brown bears sometimes roll on the ground in specific areas, and use special well-worn trails along which each bear that passes steps in its predecessors' footprints. While there has been no scientific confirmation, the information is probably conveyed by scents, and is likely to include territorial marking and possibly the status of the individuals.

In general, color patterns in bears are fairly conservative, especially when compared with some other mammals. Contrasting color patterns on the body may help communicate an animal's presence, especially in a forest habitat, and color patterns and contrast is greatest in bears that live in heavy forests at lower latitudes, such as spectacled bears and giant pandas, and to a lesser degree, sloth bears. Sun bears, Asiatic black bears, spectacled bears, and American black bears in most areas, usually have a white chest patch. The muzzles of these smaller forest bears, and even part of the face of the sun bear, are much lighter in color than the rest of the head or upper body.

There is less contrast in the body color patterns of brown bears, which are more adapted for living in open country, than there is in the smaller forest bears. In the polar bear, which lives in the most open habitat of any species of bear, there is no contrast in body color at all, with the exception of the black nose and eyes. The complex body markings of the giant panda may function to send signals to other members of the species.

Tom Ulrich/Oxford Scientific Films

◄ (Top) The large white chest patch characteristic of the Asiatic black bear is visible from a distance when the bear stands on its hind legs. This white flash against the dark background of a thick forest, or in poor light, may serve to signal the presence of one bear to another.

◄ Besides marking tree trunks with their claws or teeth, bears like to scratch their backs or sides against trees or rocks. This leaves hairs and scents that indicate their presence to other bears.

Wolfshead/Ben Osborne/Ardea London Ltd

It has been speculated that the chest markings in bears could accentuate a threat posture when an animal is standing on its hind legs. Bears in general tend to approach members of their own species head-on, so that concentration of marking patterns in the chest and facial areas would enhance identification and communication. Head and neck orientation, ear position, and the orientation of the mouth and teeth are probably all important for sending behavioral signals, but little research has been done in this field.

In many carnivores, tails are used for communication and are often highly patterned. Even in species with short tails, such as the lynx, the tail is held upright and is used in maintaining social contact and communication. Bears' tails are particularly small. This may be because bears socialize little, and because their most important displays seem to involve the front of the animal, whether standing on all four feet, or only on the hind feet, when the tail would not be visible.

As fascinating as bears are, there is still relatively little known about their behavior. Additional information accumulates slowly because most species are difficult to observe in the wild and are wary of humans because of a long history of persecution. The behavior of some of the subtropical bears may never be understood in any detail because it is becoming progressively more difficult to find enough undisturbed individuals in the wild in order to conduct field studies.

▲ Although giant pandas are solitary animals, they maintain contact with other pandas through vocal and olfactory signals, and can easily recognize another member of their species through their distinctive marking.

BEARS AS PREDATORS

ANDREW E. DEROCHER AND IAN STIRLING

Most bear species, other than polar bears, have been considered predominantly herbivorous, a view that is supported by their having grinding molars that are typical of herbivores. However, bears' large canine teeth suggest carnivorous possibilities, and their short, simple digestive tracts are better adapted to dealing with meat than vegetation.

Predatory behavior within the bear family ranges from polar bears, which are almost totally carnivorous, to giant pandas, which are almost wholly herbivorous. All bears are consummate opportunists, but until quite recently, the predacious nature of brown and black bears had been dismissed as insignificant. Radiotelemetry studies, however, have recently shown that both species can be effective predators.

Because of their heavy build, bears expend a considerable amount of energy every time they move. They must therefore be highly selective about their prey and the situations in which they hunt. Running after prey is only cost-efficient if the prey can be captured quickly. Polar bears on land in western Hudson Bay rarely even try to run down flightless snow geese because they would expend more energy than the goose contains if they ran for more than 12 seconds. Brown bears usually run in short bursts when hunting: if the prey starts to get away, the hunt ends. Bears will seek larger prey when there is a shortage of small prey, and within a species, males often kill the largest prey.

Polar bears are wily stalkers, and are also capable of lying motionless for several hours at a seal breathing hole they have sniffed out beneath the snow, waiting for the seal to return. Black bears also rely strongly on their sense of smell to find moose calves and white-tailed deer fawns. Once the calves and fawns can run (about 30 days old for moose) they are difficult for bears to catch.

The size of a carnivore strongly influences the size of the prey it is capable of killing, the maximum size of prey killed being slightly larger than that of the predator. For example, a 100 kilogram (220 pound) bear can handle prey weighing up to roughly 150 kilograms (330 pounds). Polar bears prey primarily on the smallish (60 kilogram/130 pound) ringed seal and the larger (up to 360 kilogram/790 pound) bearded seal. In some instances, polar bears can remove up to 44 percent of the ringed seal pups born in a particular area. They are also known to kill walruses (500 kilograms/1,100 pounds) and white whales weighing up to 600 kilograms (1,320 pounds).

Brown bears, while primarily vegetarian, can also prey significantly on hoofed mammals. In some areas, adult males reportedly kill three or four adult moose (450 kilograms/990 pounds) per year, with females killing an average of one. Caribou (150 kilograms/330 pounds), musk ox (250 kilograms/550 pounds), elk (200 kilograms/ 440 pounds), and bison (500 kilograms/1,100 pounds) have all been taken. Brown bears also prey on ground squirrels, trout, and salmon, but usually only when they are sufficiently abundant to make hunting them energy-efficient.

The extent of the predacious nature of black bears has only recently been discovered. They have been found to prey significantly on moose calves and white-tailed deer fawns. Black bears living on the tundra of northern Labrador eat large numbers of small mammals such as lemming and voles, while black bears in Alaska feed on snowshoe hares.

For other species of bears there is only anecdotal information. For example, spectacled bears are thought to occasionally prey upon woolly tapirs. It is likely that further study of the giant panda, sun, Asiatic black, and sloth bears will show that they too are opportunistic predators.

The two most predatory species—polar and brown bears—handle their prey differently. Polar bears usually feed only once on a seal and leave the remains for scavengers, whereas brown bears hide their kill by covering it with dirt and leaves, returning to feed on it later. For a brown bear, a kill may represent a large protein source worth protecting, whereas for a polar bear, the kill will be one of many. Populations of black bears (and probably brown bears) that kill large mammals have a greater number of cubs, illustrating the importance of predation.

Cannibalism, while not common, has been recorded in several species. It has been suggested that if an adult male bear kills cubs in the spring, he may be able to breed with the mother which will then raise his offspring rather than those of another male. Less frequently, adult males kill and feed on other adult bears. Which bears do this, and why, are unclear. Sometimes the cannibals are in poor physical condition, so that preying on members of their own species may simply be acts of survival.

Bears rarely attack humans, and when they do they seldom treat humans as they do the species they prey upon. Most attacks are associated with protection of offspring and surprise encounters. The only bear to commonly prey on humans is the polar bear, probably because anything a polar bear encounters on the sea ice is usually potential food.

Originally thought to be mainly herbivorous, it is now known that brown bears have considerable predatory skills. In Arctic areas of Alaska and Canada, some brown bears have learned to prey on caribou. Although bears cannot outrun caribou over long distances, they can ambush animals at places such as river crossings. Large canine teeth and powerful jaws enable a bear to kill a caribou quickly once it makes contact. Hunting caribou in this fashion was probably only practiced by a small number of bears at first and then learned by cubs watching their mothers.

Daniel J. Cox

Johnny Johnson/Bruce Coleman Ltd

▲ Two young polar bears play together amidst the breaking ice in Manitoba, Canada.

BEARS UP

CLOSE

THE BROWN OR GRIZZLY BEAR

FRED L. BUNNELL AND ROBERT K. McCANN

The largest brown bears (*Ursus arctos*) weigh 100 kilograms (220 pounds) more than the largest tigers; their claws extend 10 centimeters (4 inches); they can sprint at almost 50 kilometers (30 miles) an hour; and can carry the carcass of a bull moose easily. Of all land-dwelling carnivores, only the polar bear is bigger and stronger but, ironically, the brown bear is one of the most vulnerable species on Earth.

WHERE BROWN BEARS ARE FOUND

The brown bear was once one of the most widely distributed land-dwelling mammals. Brown bears roamed over most of Europe (including England), and throughout northern Asia south to the Himalayas, west to the Mediterranean and east to the Pacific. After emigrating from Asia, they spread throughout the western half of North America from the Mexican highlands to the shores of the Arctic Ocean and they have even been observed on the sea ice, beyond sight of land. Today there are fewer than 150,000 brown bears left, most of them in Russia and North America. In North America, where they are usually called grizzlies, they occupy less than half their former range. Only four remnant populations, totalling fewer than 500 bears, remain in central and western Europe (the Cantabrian Mountains of Spain, the Pyrenees, the Alps, and the Abruzzo Mountains of Italy). Somewhat larger populations exist in Scandinavia and in the Carpathian and Balkan mountains. From Asia Minor east, southern populations are declining. Surprisingly, there is still a substantial population of brown bears on the Japanese island of Hokkaido, although numbers are declining as a result of overharvesting.

Undoubtedly, genetic diversity has been lost, but it is unclear how this loss is distributed; the division of brown bears into subspecies is controversial. The name grizzly is often applied to interior populations of North America, and goes back at least to Meriwether Lewis, who crossed the Dakotas in 1805. Eurasian populations and some coastal populations in North America are usually called brown bears. Most taxonomists now recognize only two subspecies. *Ursus arctos horribilis*

includes all brown bears except those on the Alaskan islands of Kodiak, Shuyak, and Afognak, which are considered a separate subspecies, *Ursus arctos middendorffi*. Other researchers recognize the European brown bear (*Ursus arctos arctos*) and the Hokkaido brown bear (*Ursus arctos yesoensis*) as additional, distinct subspecies. The fact that there are few clear distinctions within the large range of brown bears suggests that all populations were at one time joined.

APPEARANCE AND COLOR VARIATIONS

All brown bears are sturdily built, with large heads. In profile, a brown bear's face looks concave (often referred to as dish-shaped), whereas black and polar bears have a sharper, more aquiline appearance. The ears of brown bears are generally inconspicuous, although this is less true after annual molting of the guard hairs, the hairs which conceal the shorter insulating underfur. A noticeable hump is usually present above the shoulders. Their claws are long and curved, and range in color from yellowish to dark brown. Their guard hairs are up to 10 centimeters (4 inches) long, and during the late spring and summer molt these hairs are lost, leaving only the shorter underfur.

Individuals vary in color from almost white through shades of blond and brown to black, and can also vary markedly in color through the year, as a result of molting or from bleaching by the sun. Guard hairs over the head, shoulders, and behind the forelegs may have light tips, but the extent of this grizzling is highly variable.

HOW BROWN BEARS DIFFER FROM ONE ANOTHER

The biggest differences among populations are in weight or size, size varying with sex, age, and season as well as geographic location. Differences among populations usually result from diet. Comparisons of weight, however, must consider the amazing gains from spring through fall. Brown bears are lightest in spring or early summer,

▶ When a brown bear lifts its head to test the wind with its sensitive nose, its slightly dished face is apparent. The lips are slightly open to admit air into the mouth as well.

▶ (Opposite) The name "grizzly" bear came about because the tips of the hairs, and sometimes much of the overall coat, are often light in color, giving the animal a grizzled appearance.

▼ Historically, the brown bear lived in the forests of western North America and north temperate Asia and Europe, as well as in the treeless habitat of the Arctic tundra and the western American plains.

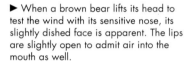
Arthus-Bertrand/AUSCAPE International/Jacana

J.M. Labat/AUSCAPE International

Franz J. Camenzind/Planet Earth Pictures

▲ In the fall, in the mountains or on the Arctic tundra, ground squirrels and marmots fatten up as they prepare to hibernate. Brown bears may dig up quantities of soil and move boulders in order to catch them.

Jeff Foott/AUSCAPE International

increasing their weight by 30 percent (adult males) to 70 percent (adult females) by denning time in fall. Peak weight gain may exceed 1.5 kilograms (3 pounds) per day. The lightest average weights of adults in spring in North America are reported for bears of the Arctic National Wildlife Reserve in Alaska (males weighed 135 kilograms/300 pounds; females, 95 kilograms/205 pounds). The heaviest average weights of adults in the spring are reported from the Alaska Peninsula (males weighed 390 kilograms/860 pounds and females 205 kilograms/455 pounds). Individuals from these coastal populations can be almost three times as heavy as those from the interior, but a large portion of the coastal animals weighed have been older animals. Other geographic trends in weight are obscure, although populations of bears from northern areas are often lighter. Few weights of Eurasian bears are available. Harvested adults in Yugoslavia averaged 185 kilograms (405 pounds) for males and 125 kilograms (275 pounds) for females, while fall weights of an adult male and female in Italy were 140 and 85 kilograms (315 and 190 pounds) respectively.

Both sexes attain their final body length fairly early in life, females completing 90 percent of their growth in body length by about five years of age, males by about seven. Adult males are usually 1.2 to 2.2 times as heavy as females, but differences in body length (tip of nose to tip of tail) are much less marked, males being 10 to 15 percent longer than females. Females complete 90 percent of their growth in weight around 8 years of age, while for males this occurs at about 12 years of age. Heavier males find it easier to obtain mates and heavier females produce more young, so obtaining substantial quantities of food is important.

MAKING A LIVING

The intelligence of brown bears and their flexible diet have enabled them to survive. One of the more striking differences between North American and Eurasian populations is in their aggressiveness. Most brown bears in North America flee from humans, but there are still enough aggressive encounters to account for the species' fearsome reputation. In Eurasia, where humans have hunted and killed aggressive bears for centuries, the surviving bears tend to be much more shy and elusive.

Large differences naturally exist in diet. Important food sources for some populations, such as spawning salmon, are never encountered by others. Geographic differences in food quality, abundance, and distribution affect adult weight, reproduction, home range size, and behavior, but it is difficult to generalize about such matters as individual bears are extremely adaptable. It is only the broadest patterns, common to all brown bear populations, that reveal why their abundance and range have declined so dramatically.

As with other animals, brown bears' lives are governed by finding food, finding mates, and avoiding being preyed upon. Their size encourages them to be wide-ranging, solitary animals. Exceptions to this solitary pattern include adult females accompanied by young, mated pairs during the breeding season, and sibling groups remaining together for a year or two after leaving their mothers. Sometimes closely related females and their young will form a short-lived foraging group, possibly as a defense against marauding adult

▲ The largest brown bears in the world are those that gain much of their nutritional intake from salmon streams in northern British Columbia, Alaska, and Kamchatka. This food source is abundant, rich in fat, and can be captured without expending much energy in traveling.

Daniel J. Cox

▲ Brown bears originally occupied treeless territory, because in such regions there were no other animals to threaten them. Instead of fleeing to escape danger, their defense was direct aggression. This was effective until humans arrived with firearms.

Steve McCutcheon/AUSCAPE International

▲ Scavenging is important to brown bears when they leave their dens in the spring, because vegetation has not yet begun to grow. To find a dead walrus, as these two immature brown bears have done, is a bonanza.

males. At rich food sites, such as garbage dumps and salmon streams, brown bears may congregate in groups of 50 or more. In such situations a male-dominated hierarchy forms, and young or small bears avoid large bears, especially males. Older females with young cubs may be prominent in the hierarchy because of their hostility towards any bear that approaches their offspring.

Out of the den, much of the brown bears' time is spent foraging or moving between foraging sites. These bears evolved from carnivore stock and have few adaptations to eating plants other than large claws for digging roots and tubers, and rather generalized teeth. As a result, their diet shifts with the seasons as they seek out the most digestible foods. Grasses, herbaceous plants, roots, corms, and berries comprise from 60 to 90 percent of their diet. They will eat almost any animal matter, but the most common items are insects, rodents, fish, and hoofed mammals. Brown bears frequently scavenge the carcasses of animals such as deer and elk, and will eat dead seals and whales that have been washed up on shore. Under some

conditions, however, they will also prey on moose, caribou, elk, and bison.

A large carcass is highly prized and brown bears will often dislodge smaller predators such as wolves and pumas from their kills or actively defend a carcass from other bears. While uncommon, brown bears will also prey on black bears and other brown bears. To meet their food requirements they may be active at any time of the day or night, although they are more likely to be active in the mornings and evenings. Where humans are in evidence, they shift their activities more towards darkness.

MEETING THEIR NEEDS

An annual home range is the area an animal needs to meet its yearly requirements. Just as diet and weight vary among populations and individuals, so do the sizes of annual home ranges. Adult males use much greater areas than adult females since they are larger and require more food. Large home ranges also increase their chances of finding mates. Brown bears on Kodiak Island, Alaska, which is rich in food, have home ranges of 133 to 219 square kilometers (51 to 84 square miles) for adult males, and 28 to 92 square kilometers (11 to 36 square miles) for adult females. Home ranges are generally larger for bears on the coastal mainland and larger still for

Jeff Foott/AUSCAPE International

inland populations, where average home range sizes vary from about 700 to 1,000 square kilometers (270 to 385 square miles) for adult males, and from 100 to 450 square kilometers (40 to 175 square miles) for adult females. Generally, as food becomes sparse or less nutritious, home range sizes increase. In Yellowstone National Park, USA, annual home ranges became three to five times larger after closure of the garbage dumps.

The availability of mates can also affect home range size. In the sparse populations of Sweden, adult females have an average annual home range of 370 square kilometers (143 square miles). The average for adult males, 2,163 square kilometers (835 square miles), is over twice that for North American males and may reflect the male's search for mates.

Newly independent subadults may explore widely before settling into a home range. Subadult males often make extensive forays 100 kilometers (60 miles) or more away from their birth area and frequently have the largest home ranges of any sex or age class. Subadult females roam less widely and are much more likely to settle into a home range

that overlaps with their mother's. Subadult males may also move extensively to avoid large males. The aggressive behavior of large males toward subadult males removes potential competitors for food and mates before they can become a serious threat.

Within their home ranges, brown bears exploit such a wide variety of habitats that few generalizations are possible, although four points seem clear. Firstly, because they rely largely on vegetation but have few adaptations for eating plants, they must seek out foods that are highly digestible. They therefore visit particular sites when the food at those places is most available or digestible, which accounts for wide-ranging shifts between alpine areas, estuaries, berry patches, and salmon spawning sites. Areas near rivers and lakes, estuaries, and avalanche chutes are often productive. Secondly, as female brown bears breed only about once every three years (they do not breed while caring for cubs), on average only one in three females will breed in any given year. Thus, for the male to successfully breed each year he must range more widely, encompassing the ranges of at least three females. Thirdly, females with young cubs may vacate the

▲ These young brown bears are just play-fighting but their behavior illustrates the way they will fight seriously as adults. When the mouth is open, the large canine teeth issue a warning to an opponent, rather like a deer's antlers, and are weapons ready for attack.

bears. When they emerge, they and their cubs often remain close to the den for several weeks, possibly to avoid other bears.

The den must provide protection and security throughout the winter. Suitable denning areas are thus an important part of the bear's habitat and they may use the same general area year after year. Usually brown bears excavate their dens, but rock caves and hollow trees are sometimes used. Occasionally, dens are hollowed out of the snow, and European brown bears have been known to den in brush, log piles, and buildings. In most cases dens are dug in areas of dry, stable soil where winter temperatures remain below freezing and the terrain is sloping. Hillside dens create better heat traps than ones dug straight down into the ground, and are easier to dig. The hillside and snow cover also provide insulation.

REPRODUCTION AND SURVIVAL

The mating strategies of brown bears vary with sex ratios, population density, and distribution. Bears congregated at localized food sources, such as garbage dumps, may be promiscuous, while in dispersed populations males may sequester females, avoiding encounters with other males. A male and a female remain together from a day or so to a few weeks to breed, with mating generally occurring from early May through to the middle of July.

Although breeding activity ends in summer, implantation of the fertilized eggs is delayed until fall, when well-fed females have gained enough weight to nurse young in the den. Females give birth to one to four cubs in their dens from about the end of January to March. Newborn cubs weigh about 400 grams (13 ounces), have little fur, and are quite helpless. They remain with their mother until they are two-and-and-half to four-and-a-half years of age and have become large enough, and sufficiently experienced, to fend for themselves. Females thus produce litters only once every three to five years.

The other major factor governing the reproductive rate is the age at which females first reproduce. This ranges from four-and-a-half years to a little over ten years in extreme cases. Litter size, the time between litters, and the age of first reproduction all appear to be related to the body weight of adult females. Populations of larger, well-nourished bears begin breeding earlier, produce larger litters, and breed more frequently.

For adult males, females in estrus can be a rare resource. One strategy males employ is to have home ranges large enough to encompass the ranges of several females. This increases the likelihood of at least one being in estrus each year and providing an opportunity to breed. It has been speculated that males may also employ a more devious approach. Since females will come into estrus again if they lose their litter prematurely, a male might be able to derive a threefold benefit by killing cubs fathered by other males. Firstly, killing the cubs reduces the

Daniel J. Cox

▲ Ovulation in female brown bears occurs only after mating many times. The male and female may remain together for a week or more, mating many times a day, before successful impregnation occurs.

▼ Most brown bears dig dens in which to spend the harsh winter months. Dens are usually located on sheltered slopes, either among tree roots or under large rocks.

best foraging areas to avoid encounters with aggressive males. Fourthly, bears must also den.

By mid to late fall, digestible food becomes scarce and brown bears enter dens to overwinter. The time they enter and leave their dens varies with food availability and possibly weather. Generally, they spend five to seven months in dens, with northern interior and barren-ground populations spending the longest time inactive. Where food and climate are most favorable, as on Kodiak Island, some adult males may not den at all. Pregnant females enter dens earlier, give birth in the dens, and emerge later than other

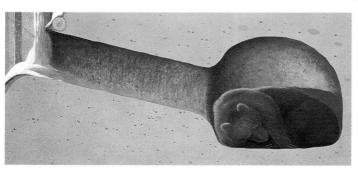

Johnny Johnson/Bruce Coleman Ltd

production of his male competitors; secondly, by consuming the cubs he derives a nutritional benefit; and thirdly, and ideally, he can then mate with the female. The success of this strategy depends upon males recognizing their own cubs.

Such male behavior may encourage females with cubs to seek out male-free habitats, and appears to affect survival rates. In many populations it is the subadult age classes, no longer in the care of their mothers, that experience the highest annual mortality rates—about 25 to 30 percent. The mortality rate of subadult males is usually larger than for females, possibly in part due to encounters with older males. Cubs also experience high mortality, ranging from about 16 to 44 percent, resulting from being preyed upon, being shot by humans, accidents, and starvation.

Natural mortality rates among adult brown bears are low, at about 5 percent per year. However, many females reproduce only a few times in their lives, because they begin reproducing late and breeding intervals are lengthy. Where the rate of kill by humans is high,

reproduction rates are lowered further. Throughout their range the greatest cause of brown bear mortality is human harvest, both legal and illegal.

Although brown bears were once widely distributed, their food requirements prevented them from forming dense populations. In the best habitats, on some Alaskan islands, densities reach one bear per 4 square kilometers (1.5 square miles), but they are generally much lower, in northern interior areas declining to one bear per 230 to 260 square kilometers (89 to 100 square miles). When humans settled in brown bear country, the bears' endless quest for food and formidable size created competition for resources and made humans fearful. In time, humans drove the bears out, and they now survive only in remote areas. Given their low reproductive rate, removing only a few females from sparse populations can place long-term population stability in jeopardy. For the decline in numbers to be halted, brown bear harvesting must be strictly controlled and management plans developed so that habitat can be shared. Brown bears have demonstrated their flexibility and intelligence. Humans must do the same.

▲ While in their dens, females and their cubs are vulnerable to predation by other bears, wolves, and humans. Dens are therefore widely spread out and are seldom reused by the same animal. If a bear enters its den while it is snowing, its scent and tracks will be covered, making it difficult to locate.

DO BEARS COMPETE?

FRED W. HOVEY AND FRED L. BUNNELL

Competition implies winners and losers. When there are individuals competing for some limited resource, the loser's survival, growth, or reproduction are reduced. Because all bear species are so similar in form and behavior, the potential for them to compete for the same resources would seem to be high. However, for competition to occur the distributions of species must overlap.

Of the eight bear species, only the spectacled bear shares no part of its range with another bear. Asiatic black bears overlap with most other bears: brown bears in China, Russia, India, Pakistan, and Afghanistan; sun bears in

Southeast Asia; sloth bears in Nepal, Bhutan, Bangladesh, and India; and giant pandas in China. While the amount of Asiatic black bear range overlap with other species is relatively small (20 percent with brown bears, 30 percent with sun bears, and

Black bear range
Brown bear range
Overlap of ranges

◀ Black bears and brown bears are widely distributed in North America, but brown bears sometimes prey upon black bears. Thus, with the exception of Northern Labrador, where brown bears are now extinct, black bears are found only in forested areas because they climb trees to escape from danger.

▼ Black and brown bears both devour enormous numbers of berries in the fall. Brown bears, being larger, have to forage for longer to meet their energy requirements.

John Shaw/NHPA

5 percent with sloth bears and giant pandas), this overlap represents a large portion of the ranges of sun bears (about 50 percent) and giant pandas (90 percent). In North America, polar bears overlap with black bears only in southern Hudson Bay, and with brown bears along the northern mainland coast. In both cases, the amount of overlap is less than 5 percent of the polar bears' range. Black bears in North America overlap nearly the entire distribution of brown bears; they are separated only in extreme areas of the Arctic tundra and western Alaska.

One theory is that competition may limit species diversity on islands. The sun bear occurs with Asiatic black bears on mainland southern Asia, but by itself on the islands of Malaysia and Indonesia. In Japan, brown bears occur only on the northern islands, whereas black bears occur only on southern ones. Although the islands of western North America contain high densities of bears, on none of them do brown and black bears occur together. Both species of bears could probably exist on any of these islands, so the fact that they do not coexist may indicate competitive exclusion.

Of the species that do occur together, American black and brown bears are most likely to compete. Firstly, most other bear species occur at such low densities that competition for resources is likely to be limited. Secondly, other species have specialized diets (such as bamboo for giant pandas, marine mammals for polar bears, and insects for sloth and sun bears), whereas black and brown bears eat the same foods. Thirdly, unlike Asian species, these bears did not coevolve. They have been together only a short time. Brown bears invaded North America from Asia only about 12,000 or 13,000 years ago, whereas black bears have been on the continent for more than 1.5 million years. Many areas that brown bears originally inhabited, such as coastlines, prairies, and other open habitats, did not contain significant populations of black bears. Human encroachment has now restricted brown bears to forested, mountainous habitats—areas to which black bears adapted

John Shaw/AUSCAPE International

▲ This black bear is eating a fish on a log, above what appears to be the entrance to a den. The den will probably not be used because the smell of food might attract predators, including other bears.

long before the arrival of brown bears. Black bears in such habitats occur in greater abundance, have higher reproductive rates, and exhibit greater adaptability to human settlement than do brown bears.

To be able to demonstrate the extent to which competition occurs between these two species, one would have to conduct experiments in which one species was removed from the range of the other so that their responses could be evaluated. That would be impractical and unethical. Available data, however, reveal potential for competition between North American black and brown bears. Brown bears, for example, are much more aggressive than black bears. This trait may have evolved from the need to defend carrion and prey from other carnivores, such as wolves, and to help females defend offspring in open, treeless habitats. Brown bears can usually usurp such resources from black bears, and they may also prey upon black bears. When food is scarce (in late fall and early spring), the two species show their greatest difference in diet, brown bears using their larger claws and shoulder muscles to dig for roots and tubers.

The most important difference between the North American black and brown bears, however, may be their size. In the regions where the species overlap, brown bears are about twice the size of black bears. Being larger, they need to eat more, but when eating important foods, like berries, brown bears are disadvantaged because black bears harvest berries at the same rate and can thus fill their stomachs in less time. Brown bears have to cover greater distances and forage for longer to meet their energy requirements. One result of this is that they are more active during darkness than black bears. Not only do black bears require less time foraging but they evade the threat of predation by avoiding times when brown bears are most active.

While it is intriguing and challenging to study competition between bear species, such competition is probably insignificant to the survival of bears when compared with the competition bears face from humans.

THE POLAR BEAR

IAN STIRLING

The polar bear (*Ursus maritimus*) is adapted to living comfortably in one of the most inhospitable, variable, and unpredictable habitats on the planet. Its apparent contentment in freezing temperatures, gale-force winds, and blowing snow has made it a symbol of the Arctic for many people around the world.

The polar bear is the largest of the carnivores. Only the coastal brown bears in a few populations that live on islands off the west coast of Alaska reach a similar size. Adult male polar bears measure 240 to 260 centimeters (95 to 105 inches) from the tip of the nose to the tip of the tail and weigh up to 600 kilograms (1,320 pounds). A few very large males reach 800 kilograms (1,760 pounds). Males do not reach their maximum size until they are around eight to ten years old. Adult females reach a maximum length of about 200 centimeters (80 inches) and are roughly half the weight of males. They reach adult size by their fifth or sixth

ADAPTATIONS TO THE ARCTIC

Of the eight species of bears in the world, only the polar bear lives on the frozen ocean. It is, as its scientific name suggests, the maritime bear. Polar bears have evolved several unique adaptations to life in the Arctic. They have heavy fur with glossy guard hairs, dense underfur, and a thick layer of fat beneath the skin to insulate them against the cold. The combined insulation of fat and fur is so effective that, as long as a bear is not exposed to wind, its body temperature and metabolic rate remain at the normal level even if the temperature drops to -37°C (-35°F)!

Norbert Rosing

▲ The polar bear evolved to exploit the sea–ice niche, and became the only maritime bear. In populations that live along the edge of the polar basin, some individuals may never walk on land.

Fred Bruemmer

year, when they weigh from 200 to 300 kilograms (440 to 660 pounds). Pregnant adult females become extremely fat and occasionally exceed 500 kilograms (1,100 pounds).

Polar bears' bodies are more elongated than those of brown bears. Their necks and skulls are also longer, but their ears are smaller. Compared with the characteristic dished profile of the face of a brown bear, polar bears have a Roman nose. Their canine teeth are quite large and the jagged grinding surfaces of their cheek teeth are adaptations to a carnivorous diet. Their claws are brownish in color, short, fairly straight, and non-retractable.

Polar bear hair is translucent and reflects solar heat down to the base of the shaft where it is absorbed by the skin, which is black. Their white color serves to camouflage them when hunting. Even the soles of their feet have small papillae and vacuoles like suction cups, to make them less likely to slip on the ice. Their eyesight and hearing are probably similar to those of humans, but their sense of smell is much better developed. A polar bear can smell a seal's breathing hole under the snow from up to a kilometer away.

One of the most remarkable adaptations of the polar bear to life in the Arctic is its ability to store immense amounts of fat during periods when food is available, and then metabolize it, as necessary, to survive periods when there is nothing to eat. For example, one thin adult female that weighed 97 kilograms (214 pounds) when caught in western Hudson Bay in late November, weighed 505 kilograms (1,112 pounds) when captured again the following August, just after the principal period of feeding on seal pups from April to July. The nursing and recently weaned young ringed

seals available during that period can be up to 50 percent fat and are more naive about predators than adults, which makes them easier to catch. Polar bears are also scavengers and will readily feed on the fat of a dead whale or walrus.

Polar bears, like other species of bears during winter, are capable of surviving on stored fat alone for long periods. This phenomenon is referred to as winter sleep, because most bears only enter this physiological condition in their dens during winter. While in winter sleep, bears do not urinate and do not need to drink because they are capable of creating water and recycling their body wastes biochemically, without using their kidneys. Furthermore, when they are living on their fat, they do not metabolize any of their lean body mass, the way a starving human would. Unlike other bears, if polar bears do not feed for 10 to 14 days, their metabolism switches over to that characteristic of winter sleep, regardless of the time of year. For example, in Hudson Bay, all the ice melts in summer so the bears come ashore towards the end of July and live on their stored fat as they would in

▼ Only pregnant female polar bears enter dens for the winter; all other polar bears continue to hunt seals on the sea ice. In particularly cold or windy weather, or if seals are difficult to find, they may dig temporary dens and occupy them for a few days to a few weeks at a time.

Dan Guravich

► This odd posture is used by a polar bear for scratching itself and cleaning its fur after feeding. This is also the way a polar bear sometimes propels itself toward a seal on the ice once it has stalked to close range but is not near enough to sprint and try to catch it.

▼ Young male polar bears have long, fairly thin faces, like this three- or four-year-old. By about six years of age, the skull has begun to broaden and in some a Roman nose has begun to form.

Dan Guravich

a winter den, until they are able to hunt seals again after the sea freezes once more, about four months later.

Food is available to polar bears, unlike other North American bears, throughout the winter so there is no need for them to enter a den, except during short periods of particularly cold or inclement weather. However, pregnant females cannot return to the ice because they must go into a maternity den in order to have their cubs, and they do not return to the ice until early March to mid-April, depending on the latitude. Thus, pregnant females in the Hudson Bay region survive entirely on their stored fat for about eight months, while at the same time giving birth to cubs and nursing them from less than a kilogram to about 10 kilograms (22 pounds). In other parts of the Arctic, females fast for five to six months.

HABITAT PREFERENCES AND SEASONAL MOVEMENTS

The preferred habitat of the polar bear is the annual ice that forms next to the shorelines of the continents and archipelagos throughout the circumpolar Arctic. The coastal marine region over the continental shelf receives nutrients from the rivers, light from the sun, and upwellings of nutrients from the deep basins, creating a zone of

high biological productivity and an abundance of seals. There are also shore leads (cracks in the ice that form parallel to the coast), usually several kilometers offshore, and polynyas (areas of open water surrounded by ice that do not freeze during winter) in which marine mammals often spend the winter, or through which they migrate.

Although polar bears have been seen near the North Pole, they generally avoid the high latitudes of the Arctic Ocean. The water below the thick multiyear pack ice that covers the central polar basin is biologically unproductive, so there are few seals there for the bears to eat.

During the winter, when the pack ice extends furthest south, polar bears may be found in the Labrador Sea, southern Barents Sea, and the Bering Sea. Occasionally, they are carried on ice floes as far as Kamchatka, and a few have shown up on the northern coastlines of Newfoundland, Iceland, and even Hokkaido, in Japan.

The major ecological factor that determines the extent of polar bears' seasonal movements is the availability of sea ice, since they need it as a platform for hunting seals. However, the further a bear travels, the more seals it must kill to provide the energy it needs just to move, before it can attend to its other basic needs such as growth, reproduction, or nursing cubs. Thus, polar bears move only as far as they have to in order to spend the maximum amount of time on the ice. In recent years, through the use of radio-collars that transmit the location of an animal to a satellite every few days, it has become possible for scientists to study the annual movements of polar bears and to understand the extent to which they are determined by ecological factors, especially sea ice.

The area within which an animal lives throughout the year is called its home range. In some areas, such as the inter-island channels of the Canadian High Arctic Archipelago, sea ice is present for most or all of the year, so bears do not need to travel great distances to remain on it. Some of these bears have a home range of only a few thousand square kilometers. In contrast, the southern edge of the pack ice in the Chukchi and Bering Seas, where seals are most abundant, moves enormous distances north and south between summer and winter every year. Some female polar bears in that region need home ranges in excess of 300,000 square kilometers (116,000 square miles) in order to be able to find enough suitable sea-ice habitat for hunting throughout the year.

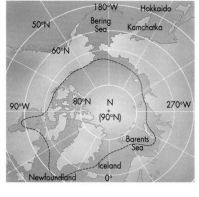

▲ The polar bear inhabits coastal regions, islands, and seas in the Arctic.

◄ The feet of a polar bear are much larger in proportion to its body than those of any of the terrestrial bears. Their feet function like paddles when swimming and like snowshoes when walking on thin ice. If the ice is too thin to walk on, the polar bear lies on its chest and spreads its legs in order to distribute its weight over a larger area to prevent it falling through.

Bryan and Cherry Alexander/NHPA

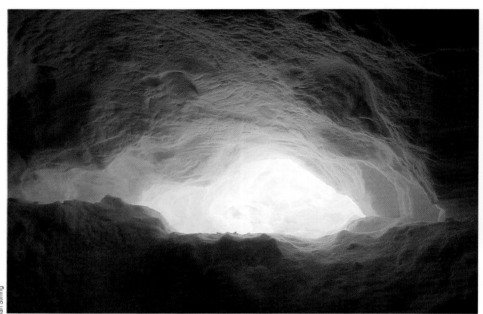

BREEDING AND MATERNITY DENNING

The three largest known maternity denning areas in the world for polar bears are Wrangel Island off the northeastern coast of Siberia, Kong Karl's Land in Svalbard, and south of Churchill, Manitoba, on the western coast of Hudson Bay in Canada. Denning also occurs in many other areas of the circumpolar Arctic, but at low densities. About 60 percent of the female polar bears that live along the north coast of Alaska have their maternity dens on the multiyear pack ice of the Beaufort Sea, while the remainder den in snowdrifts on land near the coast. It is not known whether females from other populations den on drifting sea ice as well.

Polar bears mate from about late March through late May. Since cubs remain with their mothers for about two-and-a-half years, females can wean litters only once every three years. This means that normally only about a third of the females are available for breeding in any particular year. The intense competition between adult males for access to a limited number of available females is probably part of the reason why male polar bears are so much larger than females.

Fred Bruemmer

Female polar bears apparently have induced ovulation, which means that they must mate many times over a period of a week or more before an egg is released to be fertilized. During this period, a dominant male will try to herd a receptive female away from where other males might be. Once the egg is fertilized, implantation of the blastocyst in the uterus is delayed until about late September.

Around late October or early November, pregnant female polar bears dig maternity dens in snowdrifts, usually on land within a few kilometers of the coast, in which to give birth later in the winter. The dens are often dug on south-facing slopes where the prevailing northerly winds form deep snowdrifts and where radiation from the sun is greatest in late winter and early spring, when the female and cubs first come out. When occupied, the inside temperature of a den can be 20°C (68°F) warmer than it is outside.

Gestation lasts only three months and the young are born between late November and early January. Twins are most common, sometimes there is only one cub and, fairly infrequently, triplets are born. Quadruplets are rare. At birth,

the cubs are about 25 centimeters (10 inches) long and weigh less than 1 kilogram (2 pounds). Initially their eyes are closed, and they are covered with hair so fine that in some early descriptions the cubs were reported to be hairless.

Most polar bear families break out of their maternity dens between late February and the end of April, depending on the latitude. Those further north do not leave their dens until later in the spring when the weather has warmed slightly. Even so, the ambient temperature may be -20° to -30°C (-4° to -22°F) when the female first takes her cubs outside. The family usually remains at the den site for a week or ten days so that the cubs can become used to the cold and have a chance to exercise before they take to the sea ice. They play in the snow near the den during the day, returning to its shelter with the mother at night or during stormy weather.

Because females can breed only once every three years at most, polar bear populations have a slow growth rate, which partially explains why over-harvested populations take so long to recover. (An illustration of the seasonal cycle of polar bears is given on pages 64 and 65).

▲ Intense competition between male polar bears during the breeding season can result in scarring and sometimes severely broken canine teeth.

◄ (Top, far left) Female polar bears normally have only four functional nipples, while terrestrial bears have six. This may be an adaptation to raising smaller litters of cubs in a harsh and unpredictable environment.

◄ (Top, left) Some polar bears wander like nomads over home ranges that encompass thousands of square kilometers in search of seals, while in other areas the home ranges of some females may be no more than a few hundred square kilometers.

◄ (Center) During winter, pregnant females dig maternity dens in wind-drifted snow banks in order to protect their tiny newborn cubs from the cold. The entrance tunnel rises up to the main chamber so as to trap the warmest air at the top.

◄ (Bottom) A polar bear cub weighs about 10 to 12 kilograms (25 pounds) when it leaves the den with its mother on its way to the sea ice to learn how to hunt seals. Cubs are nervous at first and rarely stray more than a few meters from their mothers.

HUNTING BEHAVIOR

Polar bears prey primarily on ringed seals and, to a lesser degree, on bearded seals. In some areas, they have also learned to kill walruses, white whales, and narwhals, but this is less common.

During winter and spring, when the sea ice is frozen, ringed seals keep breathing holes open by scraping the ice with the heavy claws of their foreflippers. In the spring, pregnant female seals dig small birth lairs beneath the snowdrifts that build up over the breathing holes and hide them. The pups, known as whitecoats, are born inside these lairs and are nursed by the females for about six weeks, until they are weaned.

▼ Lying down "still hunting" is the polar bear's preferred method of hunting seals because it requires the minimum expenditure of energy. Even when hunting conditions are good, an experienced adult only catches a seal every four or five days.

▼ (Bottom) Polar bears are powerful swimmers and have been known to swim long distances. The forelimbs and large forepaws provide the propulsion while the hind legs trail behind and act as a rudder.

Art Wolfe

Stephen Krasemann/NHPA

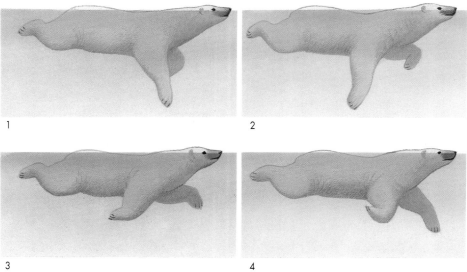

1

2

3

4

Polar bears locate birth lairs and breathing holes under the snow by smell, then they move toward them very slowly so as to minimize the sound of their approach. Sometimes they break into a lair immediately, while at others they will stand motion-less on the snowdrift over a lair for up to several hours at a time, waiting until they hear or smell a seal surfacing to breathe before attacking. In summer, after the snow melts and cracks form in the ice, the bears continue to hunt seals by stalking them when they haul out on the ice to bask, or by waiting at places where they might surface to breathe and then seizing them with their powerful jaws.

Polar bears sometimes swim underwater to stalk distant seals lying at the edge of an ice floe. When

they hunt in this manner, they appear to memorize the route to the seal before slipping quietly into the water. As the bear nears the seal, it stealthily pokes the tip of its nose out to breathe, silently slips backward until it is submerged, and then swims rapidly underwater until it needs to breathe again. When swimming, it uses only its large forepaws to paddle itself through the water, trailing its hind feet like rudders. One bear remained underwater for 72 seconds while stalking a basking seal. When the bear is finally close enough to attack, the water beside the seal explodes, with the bear leaping and clawing after its prey. Such a stalk is breathtakingly exciting to watch, but even after so much work, far more seals escape than are caught.

Polar bears must spend at least half their time hunting as usually less than 2 percent of their attempts at catching prey are successful. Even during the spring and early summer, when seals are most abundant and accessible, a bear catches only one every four or five days.

Polar bears sometimes dive and swim underwater to try to catch a sea bird at the surface by seizing it from below. One bear was seen spending several hours diving for kelp. It would put its head underwater, leaving its hind legs sticking in the air, and paddle hard with its forepaws until it disappeared below the surface. On resurfacing, with an armful of kelp, it would lie on its back in the water and carefully pick out the bits it wanted.

▲ Polar bears have occasionally been recorded swimming far from land. They sometimes swim underwater between holes in the ice to stalk unsuspecting seals lying on the surface. During cold weather, however, bears avoid going into the water unless it is absolutely necessary.

▶ In most parts of the Arctic, cubs are weaned when they are two-and-a-half years old. In Hudson Bay, some females wean their cubs at only one-and-a-half years of age when conditions are favorable. Conversely, where feeding conditions are poor some females keep their cubs until they are three-and-a-half years old.

▶ (Opposite) Polar bear cubs love to play. These cubs on a small lake enjoyed pounding the ice with their forefeet to make holes big enough in which to swim. Such play is extremely important as it helps cubs develop some of the motor skills they will need in order to survive as adults.

Leonard Lee Rue/Bruce Coleman Ltd

▼ During the late fall, levels of the male hormone testosterone are lower than at any other time of year, so males fasting along the coast of Hudson Bay, waiting for freeze-up, show little aggression toward each other. Nevertheless, males of similar size still like to undertake extended ritualized fights to hone their motor skills for when they will need them.

FAMILY LIFE

Polar bear cubs remain with their mothers for two-and-a-half years, partly because they need protection from other bears, but also because they need to be taught how to hunt. The cubs follow their mothers on the sea ice throughout the year and watch her hunt in all kinds of conditions, and then they practice hunting themselves. This learning is critical to their eventual survival. The hardest period of a polar bear's life is certainly its first year of independence when it can no longer rely on sharing the seals that have been killed by its mother.

Polar bears sometimes like to play. Except during periods of very cold weather, bears of all ages enjoy swimming, especially cubs and subadults. Young bears in particular, as they walk across the ice, will sometimes run towards the water and "belly flop" into it with a huge splash. After disappearing under the water for a few seconds their head appears and they look around. The bear will float lazily about for a few seconds up to a few minutes, then climb back onto the ice, and may repeat the sequence for an hour or more at a time.

While with their mother, and trying repeatedly to copy her behavior, cubs become bored from time to time and begin playing, but play itself can be instructive. On one occasion a female bear was seen hunting seals while her single cub, two-and-a-half years old, trailed along behind her. A well-trained cub lies still to avoid frightening a seal while its mother hunts. However, this cub soon tired of waiting. At first it just walked about where it had been lying. Soon it was running, diving, and swimming about. After about 15 minutes of cavorting, the cub ran up to a crack in the ice and took a running dive. As it flew through the air, a young seal popped up to take a breath and its head went straight into the bear's mouth! After killing the seal pup, the cub repeatedly threw it back into the water, and then retrieved it. When its mother saw what was happening, she ran over and ended the game by starting to eat. After that, the cub paid closer attention to patches of open water, in case another seal appeared, illustrating that it had learned from this piece of serendipity.

Daniel J. Cox

THE AMERICAN BLACK BEAR

MICHAEL R. PELTON

The American black bear (*Ursus americanus*) is the most common of all the bears and is distributed in North America from northern Alaska, across Canada to the northern mountains of Mexico, and to southern Florida. There are currently 16 recognized subspecies.

▼ Short, sturdy claws enable the black bear to grip a tree trunk firmly and climb quickly, and to tear rotten logs apart. Its long tongue can then, with great precision, pick out eggs and larvae.

Historically, black bears occupied the entire North American continent, with the exception of the southwestern deserts. The population is now likely to exceed half a million, and over 40,000 bears are harvested annually. States and provinces that have

sizeable populations regard the species as a game animal and conduct fall or spring hunting seasons. In some areas of the Northwest and Canada black bears are so abundant that they are regarded as pests, but in the Midwest and in the eastern parts

Judd Cooney/Oxford Scientific Films

Daniel J. Cox

of the United States the species has disappeared as a result of habitat loss. In the southeastern coastal plain, where large-scale agricultural operations have eliminated the once-extensive hardwood forests, leaving small, sometimes isolated areas of forest, only a number of small populations remain. The cumulative effects of road construction, increasingly efficient hunting methods, and the growing commercial value of bear parts, such as gallbladders, threaten the viability of these fragmented populations. Because of habitat loss and dwindling numbers of bears, the Louisiana subspecies was recently listed as threatened under the federal Endangered Species Act.

AN ADAPTABLE CARNIVORE

Average weights of American black bears range from 40 to 70 kilograms (90 to 155 pounds) for adult females and 60 to 140 kilograms (130 to 310 pounds) for adult males. An occasional male will exceed 300 kilograms (660 pounds). Bear sizes vary according to the quantity and quality of food available. The bears respond dramatically to sources of high-energy food—be it garbage, corn, or wheat—becoming larger where food is abundant and nutritious. They are generally fully grown at four years of age.

Their fur is normally uniform in color, except for a brown muzzle and an occasional white blaze on the chest. The black color phase is most prevalent in the

▼ Black bears tend to sleep during the day and feed early morning and late evening. In regions where there are many people, they may seek bedding areas in swamps or other places where it would be difficult for an intruder to approach undetected.

TREE MARKINGS BY BLACK BEARS

MICHAEL R. PELTON

Why do black bears bite or claw trees? This question has long puzzled naturalists and biologists, and has prompted a variety of theories. Early naturalists felt that such markings functioned in the same way as the urinary signposts of dogs.

The marks were originally thought to occur only on conifers, and scientists believed that their function was somehow associated with the strong resinous odors of the sap of this group of trees. However, later research revealed that marks occur just as commonly on hardwoods, the sap of which does not have a strong odor.

Marks do not occur randomly but are located along defined game trails, particularly ridge lines, with the marked portions of the tree facing the trail. Marks are usually 1.5 to 2 meters (5 to 7 feet) high on the tree and are quite conspicuous. Some trees are marked only once, while others receive repeated markings year after year, sometimes with such frequency that the scarring eventually kills the tree. Often bear hair can be collected from the crevices in the bark below the mark. Marked trees are usually right beside the trail and on the downhill side, if it is on a slope. The occasional marked trees located away from the trail (usually less than 5 meters/ 16 feet) have paths leading to them, worn into the forest soil from many years of repeated visits by bears.

Only a relatively small number of bears have been seen biting or clawing trees. Most observations have been of males making such markings before and during the breeding season, which is in summer, but females have been seen marking trees towards the end of summer and in the fall.

Daniel J. Cox

▲ Black bears pick specific trees along game trails and make deep scratches in them with their claws. The same trees may be clawed over many years and have hairs embedded in the scratches from bears rubbing against them. Although such tree markings by bears are well known, their function is not clear.

The four prevailing theories to explain marking are so far untested. The earliest idea was that markings are related to the dominance hierarchy system among the males in the population, particularly during the summer when males may compete for females in estrus, and subadult males begin to establish home ranges. A second hypothesis relates to breeding and preparation for breeding, it being suggested that marks may serve as a means of communication to ensure that males and females are synchronized properly for successful mating. The third idea is associated with territorial defense among adult females. Since it is known that some adult females are territorial, marking may serve as a means of communicating with other adult females in the area, telling them to stay away. Finally, given that marking increases when a bear enters a new area, it has been suggested that marking may be used for orientation by animals when they are visiting unknown or rarely visited areas.

Marking is a highly visual activity and obviously serves an important social function within a bear population. It seems likely that rather than there being one single explanation for why bears mark trees, there may be several.

east and the brown, cinnamon, and blond or honey phases are more common in the west. Two unique pale phases occur on the Pacific coast of Canada: Kermode bears, with white coats, and glacier bears, with blue-gray coats. Color vision; moveable lips; a long prehensile-like tongue; strong, thick, and highly curved claws; and finger-like toes allow the species to accomplish meticulous tasks, such as picking berries from bushes while avoiding the leaves. These attributes, combined with their omnivorous food habits, strength, speed, and agility, make them perhaps the world's most adaptable large carnivore.

PATTERNS OF REPRODUCTION

Female black bears generally reach sexual maturity at three to four years of age. In food-rich habitats some females may breed for the first time at two years of age, while in less productive areas they may not breed until they are five to seven years old. They normally have two cubs, but litters ranging in size from one to five have been reported. Young are born in alternate years, providing nutrition is adequate. Nutrition plays a major role in the age of reproductive maturity and subsequent production of young.

The breeding season is from mid-June until mid-August, and egg implantation is delayed for five months. After only a two-month gestation period, the young are born in late January or early February, during the winter denning period. The newborn young are rat-sized, naked, and helpless, but they develop rapidly. Mother and cubs emerge from the den in April or early May, at which time the cubs weigh 2 to 4 kilograms (4 to 8 pounds). The young stay with their mother for the next twelve to fourteen months, through the next winter, before the family unit breaks up. At this time the female comes back into estrus and breeds again. Within his home range one male may breed with a number of females, but must compete with other males to do so.

Females occasionally skip a year between their two-year reproductive cycle. Because black bears have such a low reproductive rate, population stability can easily be disrupted by such factors as a scarcity of acorns or heavy hunting pressure.

ESTIMATING POPULATIONS

Black bears are normally shy and are therefore difficult to count, so making population estimates is not easy. Using a variety of counting methods, density estimates have varied from one bear per 1.2 square kilometers (0.5 square mile) for an island population, to one per 15 square kilometers (6 square miles) for an interior mountain population. Habitat quantity and quality determine the relative density, stability, and resilience of black bear populations. Populations in less extensive habitat are thus more vulnerable to human activities. Most wildlife agencies rely on trends in harvest data for assessing populations, rather than trying to estimate numbers in other ways. In certain areas bait stations are being monitored to help determine population trends.

Daniel J. Cox

HOME RANGE AND MOVEMENTS

Male black bears move much greater distances than females, normally covering two to four times the area of a female. Whereas females may have an average annual home range of 3 to 40 square kilometers (1 to 15 square miles), males may range from 20 to 100 square kilometers (8 to 40 square miles). Home ranges vary in size from year to year, and from season to season, depending on food availability, the sex, age, and reproductive status of the bear, and population density. Normally, late summer and fall is the period of most extensive

▲ (Top) From bottom right: Black bears mate in summer, the fertilized egg implanting in the fall. Meanwhile the female feeds intensively to deposit fat. In late fall she dens, and the cubs are born in winter. The family emerges in spring to begin feeding and the cubs den with their mother the next winter. They will be weaned the following spring and the female will then mate again.

▲ Black bear cubs stay close to their mother while she searches for food. This provides them with protection and the opportunity to learn how to find food for themselves through watching everything she does.

THE COLORING OF BLACK BEARS

ANDREW E. DEROCHER

All black bears have a distinctive brown muzzle and commonly a small white or light brown V-shaped patch on the chest or throat. Most of them are indeed black, but they are also found in certain other colors. The generally recognized colors, known as phases, are black, brown, cinnamon, honey, glacier or blue, and Kermode or white, in order of rarity.

The black phase predominates east of the Mississippi River. In western North America the brown and cinnamon phases are common and, in some areas, may even comprise the majority. Brown colored black bears range from light cinnamon to a dark chestnut or chocolate, the latter often being confused with the brown bear. The honey phase appears light yellow-brown.

The uncommon glacier or blue phase is found in Alaska, northwestern British Columbia, and the Yukon Territory, Canada. Originally described as a subspecies of the black bear, it was given the name *Ursus americanus emmonsi*. This designation is no longer accepted.

The glacier bear's coat is silver-tipped, with long white or light yellow guard hairs and a rich blue-black undercoat.

The rare Kermode or white phase is found along the north-central coast of British Columbia, Canada, with a range of only a few hundred square kilometers. Some consider only the pure white bears to be true Kermodes, but they can be light red, pale orange, or light yellow. First described as a subspecies (*Ursus americanus kermodei*) of the black bear, they are now classed as a color phase. Kermode mothers can give birth to black, brown, and Kermode colored cubs and, conversely, a black female can give birth to Kermode cubs. In fact cubs of a variety of colors can occur in any black bear litter.

Little is known about the genetics of coat color in black bears. In one population, brown phase females had larger litters than black females, suggesting a genetic link between color and reproduction. Color is not closely linked to sex, but may be affected by age. Brown or cinnamon cubs sometimes turn black or dark brown within two

years, after their post-juvenile molt. Some adults also change color over time. In addition, the fur can bleach through the year, with the tip of the hair becoming lighter than the base. Susceptibility to bleaching varies, and may be inherited.

White chest patches occur in about 80 percent of black bear cubs, but often disappear with age. If the mother has a white patch, the cub is more likely to retain it for life than if the mother is entirely black. Cubs are born with blue-gray eyes but they turn brown in most bears within two years.

The causes of geographic variation in color and the possible benefits of one color over another are unclear. The glacier and Kermode phases may have resulted from a founder effect (a population being derived from few immigrants). Genetic drift (random fluctuations in the genetic composition of a population that change gene frequencies) is common in small populations and could also have produced these colors. These processes may have occurred during the last ice age when black bear populations were isolated in ice-free refuges along the coast.

If no one color phase has an advantage over another, then uncommon colors could occur just by chance. However, some color variants may have selective value. For example, in one study, fewer black than brown phase bears were seen feeding at midday in an open meadow. This may indicate that the brown phase is less susceptible to heat stress in open habitats. It is thought that fur rich in melanin, the dark pigment responsible for the black color, may be more resistant to abrasion and could therefore be advantageous in thick vegetation. It has also been suggested that the brown and glacier phases, more common where black bears overlap with grizzlies, might mimic the color patterns of the more aggressive and dominant grizzly, thereby conferring some benefit. In contrast, however, the highly visible Kermodes are also found in heavily forested grizzly habitat.

In some habitats, coloring may confer camouflage from other bears. The occurrence of black individuals in dense forests, where they are less visible in the shadows, and lighter colored bears in open, brighter prairie and subalpine regions suggests that selective pressures in different habitats might well affect color.

◀ (Left) A rare and particularly beautiful color phase of the black bear is the glacier bear, which is found only in southeastern Alaska, northwestern British Columbia, and the southwest Yukon.

◀ (Right) Cinnamon-colored black bears are common in western North America, where a dark chocolate color also occurs. Brown colored black bears are rarely seen in the eastern United States or in eastern Canada.

▼ The most paradoxical color for a black bear to be is white! The Kermode bear was once thought to be a separate subspecies, but is now known to be a color phase that occurs only in a restricted area on the coast of British Columbia.

Myron Kozak

movements, for this is when young bears disperse and the entire population searches for high-energy foods that will enable them to build fat stores for winter. The great mobility of black bears, particularly males, puts them at considerable risk. Their movements often take them beyond the confines of familiar areas and into contact with people, making them vulnerable to being run over, or shot.

HABITAT REQUIREMENTS

Prime black bear habitat is character- ized by relatively inaccessible terrain, thick understorey vegetation, and abundant sources of food in the form of shrub- or tree-borne fruits and nuts. Normally black bears depend on forest cover, although this can be sparse at times. The species' wide distribution in North America results from its ability to live in habitats that range from the chaparral shrub of the Southwest, to the dense forests of Canada and the Pacific Northwest, to the swamps of Louisiana and Florida. All these habitats are typified by thick understorey cover, in which bears can take refuge. Loss of cover and extensive human intrusion diminish the carrying capacity of habitat and cause the species to retreat into less accessible areas. Although black bears are capable of surviving in some remarkably small areas, long- term viability of even remnant populations requires areas of low human density covering a minimum of 200 to 450 square kilometers (77 to 174 square miles).

WINTER DENNING

Black bears become dormant for varying periods during winter, depending on the latitude at which they are living, their sex and reproductive status, and their nutritional condition. For some individuals, winter inactivity may consist of nothing more than settling in for a few days or weeks in a relatively

Tom Walker/AUSCAPE International

exposed nest, and being content to move to new bed- sites throughout the winter. This behavior is typical of male bears in more southern latitudes. On the other hand, pregnant females may be inactive for over five months, not leaving their dens until spring, and staying in places as long as they feel secure. Females favor large, hollow trees, if they can be found, as they offer dry, well-insulated cover. Standing trees are preferred, but fallen trees with thickets surrounding them are also used extensively. Where large trees are not available, females choose thickets and brush piles or shallow rock crevices, selecting more inaccessible and secure sites than males. Permanent snow cover in more northern latitudes offers additional insulation, and conceals the den's entrance. Males are much less selective in their choice of dens, preferring to crawl into brushpiles or thickets.

FOOD HABITS

Although black bears are classified as carnivores, and their teeth are those of an omnivore, their diet consists primarily of grasses and herbaceous plants in spring, shrub and tree-borne fruit in summer, and a

Daniel J. Cox

▲ The black bear is extremely versatile in the habitats it learns to use. Along the high- tide line at the coast, black bears search through seaweed for invertebrates, and may eat some parts of the algae as well.

▼ Although beavers are difficult for bears to capture, the black bear is one of their major predators. Beavers carry a good deal of fat so are quite a treat. Trappers use beaver carcasses to attract the bears during the hunting season.

Geri Wright/Bruce Coleman Ltd

mixture of fruits and nuts in the fall. Very little animal material is consumed, normally consisting of insects such as ants in spring and wasps in summer, but in certain areas some bears learn to be quite effective predators, usually taking advantage of specific circumstances, such as the availability of deer fawns and moose calves. Young probably learn predatory habits from their mothers. Generally, they only feed on vertebrates if an easy opportunity exists, and are more apt to eat them as carrion.

Fall is the critical feeding period for black bears, when they build up their fat reserves for winter. Their feeding at this time of year is often referred to as the fall shuffle, because of their extensive movements foraging for high-energy foods such as acorns. Bears may gain 0.5 to 1.5 kilograms (1 to 3 pounds) per day, increasing their weight from 30 to 40 percent over a period of two months.

FORMS OF BEHAVIOR

Black bears are generally active in early morning and late evening in spring and summer, but in areas where there is a risk of being disturbed by humans they may be active only at night. During the fall they may be almost frenzied, foraging both night and day for high-energy foods. Adult males are normally solitary and aggressive toward all other bears, whereas adult females tend to be territorial only toward non-related adult females. Individual bears may visit a prime feeding area at different times. This pattern of feeding is probably maintained through a hierarchical system, the larger males being dominant.

Black bears are very intelligent, have long memories, and can be extremely curious. Some individuals adapt quickly to the presence of humans, particularly when food or garbage is easily accessible, such as in national parks. Nuisance bears may need to be captured and transported a considerable distance to prevent them from returning. Unfortunately, such a procedure usually results in a short life for the bear, since few of them remain at their release sites. Most attempt to return to their home ranges, or wander aimlessly. Unable to find food in strange territory, they often wander into areas of human settlement and are then either run over by cars or shot because they habitually forage for garbage.

▲ Black bears are strong swimmers and can easily cross even major rivers. In some places on the west coast of British Columbia and Alaska they fish for salmon.

A UNIQUE POPULATION OF BLACK BEARS ON THE TUNDRA

ALASDAIR M. VEITCH

Throughout most of its range in North America, the black bear inhabits temperate hardwood and boreal coniferous forests, and in behavioral studies it has been found to be reluctant to leave the protection of these forests. However, this avoidance of open areas is certainly not found in a unique population of black bears that lives on the Ungava Peninsula of northern Quebec and Labrador, in north-eastern Canada. In this vast, uninhabited low-Arctic region black bears live all the year round on the coastal tundra of the mountainous fiords that cut deep into the Labrador coast, and on the bleak, windswept interior plateau.

Inuit hunters have reported that the black bear is a recent immigrant to this barren region, and that range expansion northward may still be occurring. The question of why the black bear has only recently begun exploiting the Ungava tundra may best be answered by considering its relationship with the now extinct Ungava grizzly, or barren-ground brown bear.

In the nineteenth century, post managers of the Hudson's Bay Company, Moravian missionaries, geologists, and explorers reported that the northeastern region of Ungava was home to a small population of barren-ground brown bears. These bears were larger and more aggressive towards humans than the few black bears that were seen north of the treeline at that time. Records show that bear skins, classified as those of grizzlies by the men who had handled such skins at trading posts in western North America, were occasionally brought in to trading posts and mission stations until 1927. Since that time, however, no further skins have been recorded.

Despite the appearance of these skins from time to time, there had always been considerable scientific scepticism regarding the existence of an Ungava brown bear population. Some biologists suggested that brown bears could not occur in Ungava because of its remoteness from the brown bear population in western Hudson Bay. These scientists believed that the so-called brown bears of Ungava were mistaken identifications of brown- or cinnamon-phase, black bears. However, recent archaeological investigations in Labrador and elsewhere have shown that the brown bear's prehistoric range in North America

Judd Cooney/Oxford Scientific Films

Alasdair Veitch

was much wider than at present, and skeletal parts of brown bears have since been found in Ontario, Kentucky, Ohio, and Labrador.

The barren grounds of North America west of Hudson Bay are presently occupied solely by the brown bear—the black bear occurs up to, but not beyond, the treeline. It has been suggested that, as the brown bear is adapted to life on the tundra, and the black bear adapted to the forest, the black bear cannot compete against the brown bear above the treeline. This scenario may also have been in effect in Ungava until early this century, when the disappearance of the brown bear allowed the black bear to venture further north.

To colonize the tundra, the black bear has had to modify its forest-dwelling lifestyle. In 1989, a study was initiated in northern Labrador to investigate these adaptations. The study involves a combination of extensive field observations and collections, and satellite and conventional radio-tracking for monitoring the bears' movements. In the first three years of study, barren-ground black bears have been found to be small- to medium-sized for the species, with annual average weights for males and females of approximately 100 kilograms (220 pounds) and 60 kilograms (132 pounds) respectively.

The diet of these bears is particularly interesting, since many of their traditional forest foods are unavailable. Over 20 percent of a barren-ground black bear's diet comes from predation and scavenging. Animal foods eaten include caribou (calves and adults), ringed seals, small rodents (lemmings and voles), birds' eggs, shrimp, and insects. Berries and grasses are the most important plant foods eaten.

As a result of the patchy distribution of plant foods, and possibly because of the need to hunt and scavenge animal foods, black bears on the tundra have much larger annual home ranges than those reported for black bears in southern forest habitats. Adult males commonly range over 500 to 1,000 square kilometers (195 to 385 square miles) and females from 50 to 200 square kilometers (20 to 80 square miles). These home range sizes are several times the reported averages for the species elsewhere.

Arctic winters are long and harsh, and black bears have responded to these conditions by increasing the length of their denning period. Typically, adult female black bears on the tundra enter their dens in early to mid-October, and males within the first two weeks of November. Males emerge in the first two weeks of May, whereas some females do not emerge until early June, giving a total of around 220 days per year spent in their den. Dens are usually excavated high on steep scree slopes to avoid detection by other bears and possible predators, such as wolves.

These black bears are at the northern extreme for the species' range in North America where food is less abundant, and one of the results of this is a generally low reproductive output by adult females due to the lack of surplus energy available for reproduction. It is therefore vital that as much as possible is learned about the ecology of these bears so that when the almost inevitable human intrusion into this Arctic region occurs, steps can be taken to ensure that the impact of development on this unique population can be minimized.

◄ (Top) Black bears use their keen sense of smell to detect insect larvae and lemmings underground, and eat grasses and berries when they are available.

◄ (Bottom) Plant productivity is limited in the harsh climate of northern Labrador. Black bears in this area must therefore rely to a considerable degree on scavenging and preying on mammals, from lemmings to caribou, in order to survive.

▼ Black bears generally avoid the open tundra. In northern Labrador, however, in an area where grizzlies are absent, black bears are demonstrating the remarkable adaptability of the species by invading atypical habitat.

▼ Inset map: Current range of black bears on tundra of northeastern Ungava Peninsula.

THE ASIATIC BLACK BEAR

DONALD G. REID

For thousands of years successive human civilizations have spread, flourished, and receded on the fertile floodplains and coastal margins of Southeast Asia. In the great mountain ranges which catch the driving summer monsoons and feed this fertility with rain-washed silt, Asiatic black bears (*Ursus thibetanus*) have lived much longer. Today both humans and the bears are here, from the foothills of the Hindu Kush in Pakistan and the headwaters of the Indus, east along the Himalayan range in northern India, Nepal, Sikkim, Bhutan, and across the Brahmaputra River into Burma. The bears range across the "land of the great corrugations" at the headwaters of the Salween, Mekong, Yangtse, and Huang (Yellow) rivers, even into the rolling mountains of northeastern China and the Pacific rim of southeastern Russia, and on Taiwan and the Japanese islands of Honshu and Shikoku.

▶ Asiatic black bears inhabit moist deciduous forests and brushy areas, mainly in hilly or mountainous country.

▼ Because of the white patch on its chest, the Asiatic black bear is sometimes also known as the moon bear. The long hairs on its neck and shoulders can give the impression of a mane.

At first glance the Asiatic black bear resembles its cousin, the American black bear (*Ursus americanus*), and the two species are similer in size. Adult male Asiatic black bears range from 100 to 200 kilograms (220 to 485 pounds), and adult females from 50 to 125 kilograms (110 to 275 pounds). Both species of black bears are black with prominent ears and muzzles, and large forelimbs. Paleontological

evidence suggests that a relatively small Eurasian bear, *Ursus minimus*, radiated from Europe through Asia and then into North America, presumably across the Beringian Platform, in the mid-Pliocene, 3 to 4 million years ago. Each of today's black bear species evolved on its own continent from this common ancestor. Viewed more closely, the Asiatic black bear is distinctly different from other black bear species. It wears a striking band of white fur across its chest, and its ears are wider at the base and less pointed.

The Asiatic black bear is primarily herbivorous, and shifts its diet seasonally to those plant parts which provide the highest concentrations of digestible energy and protein. Wherever studied so far it puts on fall fat and enters a den for at least a few months in winter. With forelimb muscles more developed than those of the hindlimbs, it is adept at climbing trees, and so can reach the plentiful fruits and nuts of the temperate broad-leaved forests. By climbing, the black bear beats its largest competitors, brown bears and wild pigs, to these rich foods.

The species has been studied for more than a few years only in southeastern Russia and in Japan. Elsewhere information on these bears has been collected in conjunction with other studies, such as those of giant pandas.

Critical information is lacking on the remaining distribution and approximate numbers of Asiatic black bears. These are large carnivores with a diverse diet of widely dispersed foods. They need large areas of land—at least 37 square kilometers (14 square miles) for an adult male in Tangjiahe, China. The forests can only support them at low densities, estimated at one bear per 7 to 8 square kilometers (2.7 to 3 square miles) in Tangjiahe, so large areas of natural habitats are needed to sustain them. Such areas are becoming increasingly rare, as the burgeoning human population of Southeast Asia spills deeper into the mountain valleys. Bears in fragmented islands of habitat risk extinction, and many small populations have disappeared this century in Pakistan, China, and Japan. The bears are hunted

Masahiro Iijima/Ardea London Ltd

▲ In common with most bears, Asiatic black bears will eat nearly anything, but they are mainly herbivorous. In the Wolong Reserve in China they eat bamboo shoots, as do the giant pandas that share the habitat with them.

extensively because their body parts, especially gallbladders, are so valuable in Asian medicine (see "Bears as Pets, Food, and Medicine," page 176). Nevertheless, where bears still exist, they leave considerable sign of passage, including footprints, droppings, claw marks, and disturbed vegetation. Scientists search this sign out, to help them picture a bear's life through the seasons.

IN THE SPRING
Spring warmth floods the valleys of the eastern Himalayas in Sichuan, China, during March. If bears have denned at low elevations in the birch, maple, and hemlock forests, they will soon rouse. However, some choose to den at higher elevations, above 2,700 meters (8,850 feet), in the evergreen fir and rhododendron forests where mature, hollow trees and rock crevices on shaded slopes provide fairly stable temperatures and are the greatest possible distance from human activity. By the second week in April all bears are active, but food may be scarce. If chestnuts, and oak and *Cycloblanopsis* acorns were numerous the previous fall, bears will search them out. The early spring growths of raspberry canes, cow parsnip, butter

bur, and hydrangea, all concentrated in the moist, sunlit forest clearings, soon become the most favored foods. These have a high water content, and are quite nutritious, with moderately high levels of protein and digestible carbohydrates.

Numerous bamboo species, growing 1 to 4 meters (3 to 13 feet) high, dominate the understorey vegetation of the temperate forests of the eastern Himalayas. In the Wolong Reserve, in China, umbrella bamboo shoots in early May, and black bears concentrate their feeding in these bamboo patches. Giant pandas feed on the same bamboo, and with their opposable sixth digit, or thumb, they can remove the fibrous, hairy sheaths from the shoots before eating. The sheaths are left in piles near the shoot stumps. Black bears ingest whole shoots, sheaths and all, and, perhaps as a result, chew them more thoroughly. The differences are evident in their droppings. At other times of year these species are not competitors, as pandas feed on other bamboo parts, while black bears diversify their diet.

In Japan's Hakusan National Park, bears end their four- to five-month winter sleep in mid- to late April, leaving their dens in hollow trees or

Joanna Van Gruisen/Ardea London Ltd

caves high in the subalpine fir, hemlock, and birch forests, from 1,900 to 2,300 meters (6,200 to 7,500 feet). Here there is little food in spring so they descend to the broadleaved oak and beech forests some 1,000 meters (3,300 feet) downslope. If the previous fall's acorns and beech nuts are scarce, the bears feed heavily on beech buds, climbing the trees and breaking branches in order to get at the food. By June, coltsfoot, butter bur, and *Sasa* bamboo shoots are pushing up through the previous year's matted dead grass and forest leaf litter.

The last snow melts in early April from the rolling Sikhote-Alin Mountains in southeastern Russia, and the bears emerge from their winter dens in hollow trees or excavated burrows. Because their digestive systems are plugged by a small amount of last fall's food remains, they need a laxative. By clawing the trunks of birch trees, they release and can lick up the flowing sap, which is believed to serve this function. Early spring growth is limited, and, as elsewhere, the bears search for nuts and acorns from the previous fall. If the squirrels, chipmunks, jays, and nutcrackers have not beaten them, the bears are in luck. Otherwise they will rob

the rodents' caches, and feed on the emerging buds of birch and Mongolian oak. By the middle of May, angelica, coltsfoot, cow parsnip, and sedges are growing well.

For female bears with young, the volume of the previous year's nut crops and the progress of spring growth are critical. If there is a shortage of nuts and acorns to forage on early in spring, the females will be unable to provide sufficient milk for their young, which need to suckle until late August. Cubs will grow slowly, and in some cases may not survive.

SUMMER ACTIVITIES

Fruits and berries ripen at different times during the summer, depending on species and elevation, and are rarely found in pure stands. Bears move frequently at this time of year, keeping track of the gradually ripening food patches.

The first fruits to ripen, by late July, in Sichuan are raspberries growing in forest clearings and slopes clearcut for their timber. Standing upright, the bears use their forepaws to guide the trailing branches to their mouths. A bear's trail through a bramble thicket is unmistakable—a mat of trampled, flattened stems punctuated here and there

▲ Asiatic black bears swim strongly. During the summer they migrate into the mountains, sometimes to an altitude of 3,500 meters (11,500 feet) or more, returning to the valleys for the winter.

121

▶ Being an excellent tree climber, the Asiatic black bear can feed on fruits and nuts before they fall to the ground, where they then become available to ground-dwelling species.

Masahiro Iijima/Ardea London Ltd

Tom McHugh/Photo Researchers Inc.

▲ Bears of different species are seldom housed together in zoos, but in this instance an Asiatic black bear mother and cub have welcomed a cinnamon-phase black bear cub.

by red- or purple-tinted droppings in which the small seeds are evident. The mature forests provide cherries of various species, *Litsea* fruit, looking like olives, and the fruits of spicebush, cotoneaster, *Eleagnus*, and *Maddenia*. Some bamboos produce shoots in July or August, and bears seek these out.

In the mountains of Japan the bears' summer diet consists of raspberries, cherries, viburnum, and dogwood. In southeastern Russia there is less variety, but the Asian bird cherries ripen by the middle of June. Bears supplement these with bilberries and cotoneaster berries, and with substantial quantities of grass. In all areas, researchers have found insects, mainly ants, most common in the summer diet. Nowhere, however,

have researchers found a large proportion of animal remains in the bears' droppings.

The breeding season begins in June, but the bears do not become any more conspicuous as a result. Sometimes fighting can be heard, perhaps males contesting for a female, but not all females breed each year. Those less than three years old are unlikely to mate, and those which gave birth the preceding winter are still suckling their cubs, and will return to a den with them for one more winter before seeking a mate again.

FALL FOODS

The bears' climbing ability is most important in fall. With the days shortening, and winter sleep only a few months away, they must eat well and put on enough fat to see them through the winter. The most suitable foods—acorns, hazelnuts, chestnuts, pine nuts, cedar nuts, beech nuts, and walnuts—are up in the trees. All these crops are rich in fat and complex carbohydrates.

At this time bears leave their most distinctive sign—ragged canopy trees that seem to have imploded their outer branches in some tangled mat by the trunk. Wary of falling from the thinner limbs, where most nuts hang, the bears pull and bend the branches in toward the trunk, and the cracking of breaking branches rings across the narrow, shaded valleys. The bears pick the nuts with their lips and shove the discarded limbs between stronger branches by the trunk, building crude leafy platforms on which they can continue feeding, or perhaps rest. In Japan this feeding sign is known as *enza*. The oak and beech leaves stay attached to the broken branches, and their brown and golden tones highlight these canopy bowers for years after a bear's visit.

Masahiro Iijima/Ardea London Ltd

The black bear's senses of smell and hearing are thought to be more acute than its sight. Such comparisons are hard to quantify, but for an animal that climbs extensively and moves in rugged terrain, good vision is no doubt also essential. Using motion-sensitive radio-collars on a couple of bears in Tangjiahe, researchers found that activity levels were consistently higher during the day than at night. Bears spent most of the night resting, except on moonlit nights, when they were a good deal more active.

In certain regions nut-bearing trees are limited, and in some years nut crops fail, so bears must look for alternative foods. In the Dachigam Sanctuary in Kashmir, bears have been found feeding early in the fall on acorns and walnuts, but by late October they switched more to the fruit of *Celtis*. In southeastern Russia bears concentrate on Korean pine nuts and oak acorns throughout the fall, but the fruit of wild grape, *Actinidia*, dogwood, and buckthorn are prominent supplements.

The critical fall foods tend to grow in the lower elevation forests, which are the first to disappear with the expansion of agriculture up the valleys. Bears have severely damaged many trees when forced to feed in shrinking stands of mature forest,

and they often turn to raiding crops such as maize. In Nepal and Japan the loss of summer habitats to slash and burn agriculture or forest plantations has created similar problems, with bears raiding crops or stripping the bark from young trees. When they come into conflict with humans the bears are considered pests in need of control, and are killed.

WINTER DENNING

Colder weather and a dearth of food drive the bears to their winter dens by early December in Sichuan, late November in Japan, and the middle to end of November in Russia. While in her winter den, the pregnant female gives birth, probably in January, to between one and three cubs, most often two. Weighing little more than 300 grams (10 ounces) at birth, the cubs are quite helpless, yet have grown to 2 or 3 kilograms (4 or 6 pounds) by the time they move with their mother from the den. The annual cycle is complete. The bears have played their part in ensuring a future for their species. Their future, overall, will depend on humans learning to accommodate bears, and becoming more compassionate and farsighted in their attitude towards the animals and their forest homes.

▲ Two young bears stand up to wrestle in the wild. Captive Asiatic black bears are sometimes trained to walk on their hind legs to entertain onlookers.

THE SUN BEAR

CHRISTOPHER SERVHEEN

The least known of the world's bears, the sun bear *Ursus (Helarctos) malayanus*, gets its name from the crescent-shaped yellowish or white mark across its chest. In Thailand it is known as the dog bear, probably because, being small and stocky, it looks somewhat like a dog. In Malaysia and Indonesia it is commonly known as the honey bear because of its attraction to wild bees' nests.

▼ The sun bear is the smallest of the world's eight species of bears. It is readily identified by the crescent-shaped mark on its chest which is white or yellowish in color.

The sun bear is the only true bear living in the lowland tropical rainforests of Southeast Asia. Its range stretches from northern Burma and Bangladesh, south and east across Laos, Cambodia, Vietnam, and Thailand, and south to the Malaysian peninsula and the islands of Sumatra and Borneo. It is likely that its range has been reduced in the northern and western portions in the last 50 years or so. In the past 20 years there have been a few reports of sightings in Bangladesh in the Chittagong Hills. The species was also certainly found at one time in Yunnan Province, in southern China, but there have been no confirmed sightings in the last few years.

The distribution of the sun bear has been adversely affected by timber harvesting, combined with the conversion and settlement of lowland tropical forest for cash-crop agriculture and subsistence farming. Many of the countries within the range of the species have lost significant amounts of forest habitat, and these losses will increase as human populations and resource demands continue to grow. The conversion of forest habitat into plantations of rubber, oil palm, coffee, and other crops is having a significant effect on the sun bear. These monoculture plantations completely eliminate forest cover and associated plant and insect species—the bears' natural foods—through the use of herbicides and continuous cutting of vegetation around the plantation species. An additional problem is that some plantation crops, such as oil palm, are attractive bear food. Sun bears, deprived of their natural foods, feed on the heart of the oil palm, thereby destroying the tree, so they are considered a pest and are killed.

Human settlement permanently converts sun bear habitat into human habitat, and brings into bear range attractive food including garbage, livestock, and domestic fruits such as bananas and papayas. Conflict with humans is an inevitable outcome for the bears and usually, again, results in their being killed.

A LITTLE-KNOWN SPECIES

Because so little is known about the sun bear, much of the natural history and biology of the species must be inferred from the animal's appearance and limited anecdotal information. It is the smallest of the bears, weighing from 27 to 65 kilograms (60 to 145 pounds), and the fur of its sleek black coat is less than 1 centimeter (½ inch) long. Large, curved claws and short, bandy legs make it well adapted for climbing trees.

The sun bear has small, round ears, strong jaws, and a short muzzle. Its long tongue is thought to be adapted to licking honey from bees' nests and for extracting insects from trees and termites' nests. The claw marks of sun bears are regularly seen on trees in the rainforest where they have been climbing. It is thought that they may also sleep in trees, but this has not been proven.

Sun bears probably also eat a wide variety of fruits. In tropical forests, many groups of trees tend to flower all at once, so that fruits may be abundant in some areas while absent in others. The movements of certain tropical forest species, such as bearded pigs, are known to be related to these fruiting cycles,

and the sun bear may behave in the same way. It may also be that the species is adapted, as most bears are, to be an opportunistic omnivore, eating whatever foods are available. If this is so, the sun bear's ability to climb trees and eat honey and insects may mean that it needs to be less nomadic than animals that depend largely on fruits.

Little is known of the reproduction of the sun bear. Captive bears have had young at various times of the year.

David C. Fritts/Animals Animals/Stock Photos

▲ The sun bear eats everything from tender palm tree shoots to insects, but is best known for its love of honey. Its long tongue is thought to be an adaptation for extracting honey and insects from deep in the cracks of trees.

◄ The smallest of the bears, the sun bear is known as the dog bear in Thailand.

Francisco Futil/Bruce Coleman Ltd

WILDLIFE HABITAT LOSS IN TROPICAL ASIA			
Country	Original wildlife habitat (1,000 hectares)	Amount remaining (1,000 hectares)	Habitat loss (percentage)
Bangladesh	14,278	857	94
Bhutan	3,450	2,277	34
Brunei	576	438	24
Burma	77,482	22,598	71
Cambodia	18,088	4,341	76
China	42,307	16,500	61
Hong Kong	107	3	97
India	301,701	61,509	80
Indonesia	144,643	74,686	49
Japan	32	14	57
Laos	23,675	6,866	71
Malaysia and Singapore	35,625	21,019	41
Nepal	11,707	5,385	54
Pakistan	16,590	3,982	76
Philippines	30,821	6,472	79
Sri Lanka	6,470	1,100	83
Taiwan	3,696	1,072	71
Thailand	50,727	13,004	74
Vietnam	33,212	6,642	80
Total	815,186	248,765	67

Source: IUCN/UNEP, 1986c.

Reproduction may be related to fruit abundance or the availability of insects, but there is less seasonality in the tropics than in the temperate environment. It is unlikely that sun bears undergo winter sleep in order to avoid limited periods when food is scarce.

Females of some bear species, such as polar bears and giant pandas, give birth to their young in dens or hollow trees. Sun bear females may behave in a similar way, but details of reproduction and cub rearing are unknown. Females have been seen with one or two cubs in the forest.

Most bear species have a reproductive pattern known as delayed implantation, in which the development of the embryo is not continuous. This is related to the need for the female to delay reproduction until she has sufficient fat deposits to successfully raise cubs. It is not known whether sun bears have this adaptation. Certainly they do not have to cope with the dramatic climatic changes that are a feature of temperate zones, as do other bears, but perhaps wet and dry seasons and seasonal changes in important foods, such as fruits, require adaptations such as delayed implantation and periods of denning.

▶ It has been suggested that the bare soles of the sun bear's feet are an adaptation to climbing. Sun bears are excellent climbers and use trees extensively for feeding and to escape from predators such as tigers. It is likely that they also sometimes sleep in trees.

Mark Newman/FLPA

AN UNCERTAIN FUTURE

Continued human destruction of the sun bear's habitat is causing population decline and fragmenting ranges. Range fragmentation increases the vulnerability of remaining populations because of the small numbers of bears remaining within any given region.

Because plantation agriculture and human settlement permanently eliminate sun bear habitat, the bear's future is likely to be tied to sustainable forestry. Sun bears may be able to live in areas that have been harvested, but until basic research has been done, the impact of forestry will remain unclear. At least by reserving large areas of forest for timber interests, where human settlement is prevented, it is presumed that habitat of some value will remain for the bears.

Forest harvest without human settlement converts primary forest to second-growth forest. Forestry methods vary from selective cutting of particular species to clear felling, which directly affects regrowth and the ability of the area to support native fauna. Detailed evaluations are necessary in order to judge the impacts of vegetation changes on the sun bear. The loss of fruiting tree species, for example, or changes in the density and distribution in second-growth forest, may affect the abundance of bees which, in turn, may have a major influence on sun bear distribution.

Another problem facing the sun bear, as well as other bear species, is the growing market in bears for the pet trade and in bear parts, such as gallbladders, for traditional medicine. Bears are becoming increasingly vulnerable to such trading through the building of roads and the spread of human settlement. The high prices paid for bear gallbladders provide an additional incentive for killing bears in plantation areas.

Resource demands throughout Southeast Asia promise continued habitat change for the sun bear. While there may be ways to manage these resources which will not adversely affect the bear, so little is known about the animal that it is difficult for scientists to propose conservation programs.

Mark Newman/FLPA

▲ Dense rainforest is the habitat of sun bears and they are largely nocturnal in their behavior.

◄ Sun bears are the most threatened of the world's bears because of the destruction of their habitat, being captured as pets, and being killed for the sale of their parts. In the not-too-distant future, sun bears may only survive in zoos.

Kenneth W. Fink/Ardea London Ltd

THE SLOTH BEAR

JOHN SEIDENSTICKER

With its shaggy coat, its bare, mobile snout, and its long, curved claws, the sloth bear seems almost other-worldly. The first Europeans to describe the animal, at the end of the eighteenth century, called it "the Ursine Bradypus or Ursiform Sloth," and gave it the name *Bradypus ursinus* because its claws were similar to those of sloths (*Bradypus*) from the New World tropics. Hence its common name.

▲ Adult sloth bears are 150 to 190 centimeters (60 to 75 inches) long. Females weigh 55 to 95 kilograms (120 to 210 pounds), while males weigh 80 to 140 kilograms (175 to 310 pounds). The reduced hair on the bear's muzzle may be an adaptation for minimizing the effects of defensive secretions from termites.

The species' true affiliation with the bears was soon recognized, however, and its scientific name was changed to *Melursus ursinus*. Recent biochemical studies have established that the sloth bear and the sun bear (*Ursus malayanus*, sometimes known as *Helarctos malayanus*) of Southeast Asia are closely related to each other as well as to the rest of the bears in the genus *Ursus*, which has resulted in the sloth bear now being named *Ursus ursinus*.

DISTRIBUTION

As recently as 50 years ago, the sloth bear was fairly abundant in the forested areas of Sri Lanka, and on the Indian subcontinent extending as far north as Assam, along the base of the Himalayas and west to the Great Indian Desert. Because sloth bear fossils have been found within this range, it is likely that the sloth bear also evolved in this region.

Early naturalists and hunters reported sightings of the sloth bear in a range of habitats including teak and sal (*Shorea robusta*) forests of the Indian subcontinent, and in the lowland, dry, evergreen forest of Sri Lanka. Sloth bears were once reported to live in the hill country of Sri Lanka and were said to be common in the grasslands and evergreen forests of southern India up to an elevation of 1,700 meters (5,500 feet). In the Brahmaputra Valley in Assam and in the Chitwan Valley in southern Nepal, sloth bears are found in the riverside forests and tall grass areas on the floodplains. In the late 1960s it was estimated that in the arid-dry lowland national parks of Sri Lanka there was one sloth bear for every 21 square kilometers (8 square miles) of land. In the mid-1970s there was estimated to be twice that density in Nepal's Royal Chitwan National Park, a density that appears to have remained about the same through the 1980s.

AN ANT AND TERMITE EATER

In the early 1970s, sloth bears were observed while scientists were engaged in studying the ecology and behavior of rhinos, tigers, and other

large mammals in Nepal's Chitwan Valley. While feeding, sloth bears seemed oblivious to humans quietly shadowing them from elephant back. One young bear was followed for more than an hour one morning. With head bowed, it walked, stopped, scraped the ground, ate a little, then moved on to repeat the process, continually sniffing and frequently changing direction. Occasionally it made loud, staccato, blowing and sucking sounds, like a jackhammer, as it alternately blew away dirt and sucked up termites or ants from a nest it had exposed with its claws.

All the sloth bear droppings that were found were examined, and analysis revealed that the bears fed on at least 17 different fruits and at least six different insects, as well as flowers, grass, and honey. From March to June about half the diet consisted of fruits and the rest was insects, while termites were a dietary mainstay throughout the rest of the year.

▼ Young, captive sloth bears in a zoo give each other the open-mouthed threat display, characteristic of bears, in which the canine teeth are prominent. The large lower lip aids in feeding on ants and termites.

The fact that termites and ants are a primary food source for the sloth bear explains much about its appearance, ecology, and behavior. The reduced hair on the bear's muzzle is probably an adaptation to cope with the defensive secretions of some termites. Its skull and facial features—such as mobile lips that can protrude, a mobile snout, nostrils that can be closed voluntarily, and the absence of the first pair of inner incisor teeth—are highly specialized adaptations for feeding on insects.

Compared with that of the carnivorous polar bear, the sloth bear has a relatively low basal metabolic rate, which may reflect the lower energy content of its diet of fruits and insects. Other adaptations in mammals that eat ants and termites, such as in the South American giant anteater (*Myrmecophaga*

tridactyla), include a low reproductive rate, little aggression between members of the same species, solitary habits, and extensive carrying of the young by the female.

Observations indicate that protected populations of sloth bears may reach higher densities than those achieved by many populations of brown or black bears, but they have a low litter size, litters averaging 1.6 cubs in Chitwan. Scientists have reported hearing sloth bears in loud vocal encounters at night, but it was unclear as to whether the sounds were related to fighting or mating. The rest of the time the bears were solitary, unlike northern bears that come together at times to feed at rich food sources such as migrating fish runs or garbage dumps.

Sloth bear mothers carry their young on their backs. The mother, in effect, becomes a movable nest, so that the cubs do not have to expend large amounts of energy traveling between feeding sites, which are often well dispersed.

AVOIDING PREDATION

Wild dogs, tigers, and leopards are potential sloth bear predators, in addition to humans. In response to a perceived threat, sloth bears sometimes flee, but they seldom climb trees on such occasions, even though they are excellent climbers. This is because leopards are tree-climbers, and occasionally prey on the bears. In abrupt, short-range encounters the sloth bear responds with a spectacular charge and then stands on its hind legs as if to attack. Usually this is a bluff, but people have been injured occasionally in encounters with sloth bears.

A SOLITARY LIFE

In Royal Chitwan National Park, sloth bear females give birth in late fall and early winter, after a gestation period of six to seven months. The young are tiny and helpless at birth. The first cubs to be observed were riding on their mothers' backs and were two to three months old. Two infant sloth bear cubs were also discovered, alone, in a hole in a riverbank. In zoos, some female sloth bears cease feeding while rearing young cubs, while others come out of the den and feed each day. Apparently females with very young cubs feed periodically, but they probably stay near the den where the cubs are hidden.

Most observations were made of females and cubs, or of solitary bears. Twice researchers saw what they thought were young bears together, animals which apparently had been recently separated from their mother. Young bears appear to gain independence at differing ages, and some remain with their mothers until their second year or even later.

Adult males and females came together only for breeding, going their own way during the rest

▼ (Top) Female sloth bears often carry their young cubs on their backs, especially when fleeing from a threatening situation. Other bear species have been seen doing this occasionally, but the sloth bear is unique in that the patch where the cubs ride has developed thicker hair, making it easier for the cubs to hang on.

▼ Sloth bears have exceptionally large, strong claws which enable them to dig into termite mounds and tear logs apart in search of ants and other insects.

Milton H. Tierney Jnr

D. Garshelis

Silvestris/FLPA

of the year. One radio-collared male in the Chitwan study area used a 8 square kilometer (3 square mile) area in the lowland tall grass and forest flood plain in April, and then from May through August it used a 4 square kilometer (1.5 square mile) area in the sal forests in the hills adjoining the grassland. The minimum area used by this male through the year was 10 square kilometers (3.7 square miles), there being some overlap of ranges from season to season.

Both males and females with young used the same areas, and researchers saw no overtly defensive or territorial behavior. They did, however, observe sloth bears marking trees. On one occasion, a large male was seen rubbing a bombax tree with his stomach. The bear then got down on all fours and rubbed it with his sides and rear end. Short, deep parallel grooves in the tree trunk had been noted earlier. With his forepaws this bear had cleaned out the grooves and probably deposited scent in the process. Grooves were noted in other large trees, with fresh marks most common from February through April, when sloth bears frequent the forest and tall grass areas near the rivers. Marks could facilitate avoidance by adult males, but serve to bring a male and a female together.

WHY SPECIALIZE IN EATING ANTS AND TERMITES?

Presumably the ancestral form of the sloth bear was a tree-climbing omnivore, similar to the sun bear, and competitive pressure and variations in food availability influenced the evolution of its feeding specialization. In the wet tropics there are seasonal fluctuations in the abundance of fruits and insects, but availability throughout the year is more stable than in a monsoon climate. The monsoonal climate of the Indian subcontinent results in a marked seasonality that restricts the fruiting of plants and the availability of many insect foods.

That sloth bear evolution was not directed towards exploiting a more predatory niche (as seen in the polar bear and some brown bear populations), or towards harvesting tubers and roots (as in the brown bear and black bear), may be explained by the presence of larger specialist animals already using these resources. The tiger, leopard, and wild dog are efficient hunters, and wild pigs

▲ Although they can climb trees, when threatened, sloth bears are likely to flee on the ground because trees do not provide safety from predators such as leopards.

▼ Termite mounds provide sloth bears with their most important source of food.

John Seidensticker

THE FIRST RADIO-TRACKING STUDY OF SLOTH BEARS

DAVID L. GARSHELIS

In 1990, Royal Chitwan National Park, Nepal, was chosen for the first intensive radio-tracking study of sloth bears because there was a relatively high number of these animals in the park, and there was easy access by elephant. Eighteen bears were captured in traps baited with honey, radio-collared, and then located by tracking their radio signals. Several of the bears eventually became so used to researchers on elephant-back that it was possible to watch them continuously for hours without disturbing them.

The goal of the study was to determine factors limiting sloth bear numbers and distribution, which included availability of suitable habitat, and the distribution of their principal food—ants and termites. There was concern that poaching, especially for gallbladders, might be significant. In two years of study, however, none of the radio-collared bears died.

No collared bears wandered outside the park, so unlike other bears that are commonly attracted to livestock and crops, sloth bears seem less vulnerable to being killed as a nuisance. Also, the home range lengths of sloth bears in Chitwan were small (8 kilometers/ 5 miles for males and 3 kilometers/2 miles for females) and seasonal shifts were limited, reducing the risk of human contact.

Radio-collared male sloth bears moved to upland areas during the onset of the monsoon (April to June) and returned to grassland and riverine forest habitats on the floodplain when the ground dried out. Presumably the floodplain offered an abundance of termites, but when the soil was saturated it was difficult for the bears to dig them out. Some radio-collared females remained in the lowlands during the monsoon, apparently feeding on insect pupae near the soil surface.

▲ Recent research on sloth bears in Royal Chitwan National Park in Nepal has relied heavily on tracking bears wearing radio collars. Local park personnel are involved closely in the study.

▶ By riding on elephants to observe sloth bears, researchers were safe from predators such as tigers.

Earlier observers in Chitwan and elsewhere, basing their findings mainly on the analysis of droppings, reported that the sloth bear diet was nearly 50 percent fruit, whereas bears in this study relied mainly on insects and ate little fruit. Because insects are available year-round, sloth bears do not have to make seasonal excursions in search of food, nor do they have to withstand periods of food scarcity that force other bears to undergo winter sleep. Radio-collared females denned for a few weeks when giving birth, but none of the bears underwent winter sleep.

Females left the natal den in January with their cubs clinging to their backs, and carried them this way for several months, a behavior known to occur regularly only for this species of bear. Carrying young may encumber the mother's movements less than if her small, slow-growing cubs traveled on their own, and also may afford the cubs protection from potential predators, like tigers, leopards, and other bears, especially in treeless grassland. Females with young cubs appeared to feed more during the daytime, possibly to avoid these nocturnal predators, whereas other sloth bears fed chiefly at night.

Sloth bear cubs stayed with their mothers for two-and-a-half years. After leaving their mother, one male and one female littermate remained together for another two years, possibly to form a defensive coalition against older bears or other predators. The part of the park where the study was conducted had few young independent sloth bears, suggesting that after leaving their mother, juveniles may be forced to disperse to less favorable habitats where they may suffer high rates of mortality. By radio-collaring juveniles still with their mothers, researchers expect to document dispersal and eventual mortality, which should enable them to better define suitable sloth bear habitat.

harvest tubers and roots. At certain times of the year, in more northerly regions, carrion is an important alternative food source for bears, but the sloth bear rarely feeds on carrion. In the tropics, carrion lasts for only a short time, and in any case, a carcass usually belongs to a potentially dangerous predator.

However, the ant- and termite-feeding niche in south Asia has been little exploited, compared with South America, Africa, or even Australia. The pangolins are the only other ant- and termite-feeding mammals in the sloth bear's range. In Chitwan, ants and especially termites are available throughout the year, while most fruits are seasonal. And it is the ants and termites the sloth bear has successfully exploited, and around which its natural history now turns.

CONSERVATION NEEDS

In many areas where the sloth bear was once common, it has now disappeared. The alarm about declining numbers was sounded in southern India two decades ago, when an extensive wildlife survey reported only five sloth bear sightings. Similar findings about declining numbers have been reported by conservationists elsewere. Sloth bears are casualties of deforestation, habitat change, poaching, confrontations with people and their agricultural interests, and a host of other problems that are common to many of the region's wildlife species. No detailed range-wide survey of sloth bear numbers and distribution exists, but the bear is known to be endangered, and its chances of survival are made more precarious by the demand for bear parts and products for use in traditional Asian medicine.

Art Wolfe

Like other bears, the low reproductive rate of the sloth bear makes it particularly vulnerable to overkill. However, because sloth bears can be dangerous it is difficult to rally support for their conservation among people who must live with them on a day-to-day basis. What the sloth bear needs in order to survive is protection, sufficient space, and understanding.

▲ Born in earth dens, most sloth bear litters consist of one or two cubs, although litters of three have occasionally been reported. In Nepal, cubs leave their natal dens with their mothers in January.

▼ Sloth bears on a forest track in India. Rearing up in alarm, the bear at the right shows its distinctive U-shaped chest patch.

Mike McKavett/Bruce Coleman Ltd

THE SPECTACLED BEAR

DIANA WEINHARDT

▶ Spectacled bears build feeding platforms high in trees where they have been eating fruits growing at the ends of limbs. They often sleep in these nests.

The spectacled bear (*Tremarctos ornatus*) is the only bear living in South America, and is the continent's second largest land animal after the tapir. Also known as the Andean bear and the ucumari, it is found in Venezuela, Colombia, Ecuador, Peru, and Bolivia. Unconfirmed sightings have been reported as far north as Panama and as far south as Argentina. The size of the wild spectacled bear population is not known. The Venezuelan population is estimated to be in the hundreds, and the population in Colombia and in Peru is decreasing drastically. Bear numbers in the high-altitude forest of Ecuador appear to be remaining steady, but Bolivia has the only strong spectacled bear population in the region.

▼ The white fur on the spectacled bear's face almost encircles the eyes and gives it the appearance of wearing glasses.

During an expedition in 1825, an unknown bear was captured in the Cordilleras Mountains of Chile and shipped to England. The well-known zoologist Frederic Cuvier wrote: "I will propose to inscribe this species in the Scientific Catalogue under the name of Ornatus, because of the two circles that decorate his head." Hence the bear was named *Tremarctos ornatus*, large "decorated" bear.

Gary Milburn/Tom Stack & Associates

INDIVIDUAL MARKINGS

The spectacled bear is dark in color ranging from black to brown, and there are a few which display a rare reddish tone. A contrasting creamy white marking, generally around the eyes, throat, and chest area, is a characteristic feature, the eye markings giving some bears the appearance of wearing spectacles. Each bear has its own distinct markings, similar to a human fingerprint.

Spectacled bears are not large by bear standards, being from about 150 to 180 centimeters (60 to 72 inches) long, and 70 to 80 centimeters (28 to 32 inches) tall at the shoulders. The weights for males and females range from 100 to 155 kilograms (220 to 340 pounds) and from 64 to 82 kilograms (140 to 180 pounds), respectively. Spectacled bears have short sturdy legs, used for making their way through dense vegetation, and long sharp claws that enable them to rip vegetation apart and climb trees. They are excellent climbers and are perhaps the most arboreal of all the bears.

FROM MOUNTAINS TO SCRUB DESERT

The spectacled bear has adapted to areas ranging from forested mountains to savanna and coastal scrub desert, with altitudes ranging from 180 to 4,200 meters (600 to 13,800 feet), but is most commonly found in the cloud and elfin forest, and the paramo. The preferred habitat is the cloud forest between 1,800 and 2,700 meters (6,000 to 8,800 feet), where food is seasonally abundant. Elfin forests are regions of stunted trees blanketed in moss and surrounded by bamboo thickets, which lie between the cloud forest and the high-altitude grasslands, and the paramo is tropical alpine habitat which the bears feed in from time to time, while moving to more favored country.

A VARIED DIET

Spectacled bears have an extremely varied diet. They eat from an assortment of over 80 different food items, including rabbits, mice, calves, vicuna, deer, birds, berries, 22 species of bromeliads, 11 species of cactus, 32 species of fruits, and 10 different plant families, including grasses, mosses, and orchid bulbs.

Food sources are selected on the basis of their availability, their geographical convenience, and the security the feeding area offers from predators. While around 40 percent of the bear's diet consists of fruits, half consists of bromeliads, so the availability of bromeliads determines whether a bear can survive in areas that do not support a year-round supply of fruits.

The spectacled bear makes a major contribution to its ecosystem through seed dispersal, seeds of a variety of plants being ingested during feeding and then distributed through the bear's droppings. The spectacled bear is one of only two species known to disperse the stony seeds of laurel trees, a highly sought-after source of timber. Tight clumps of 20 or so seedlings are evidence of such dispersal.

The bears usually build feeding platforms because the fruit-laden branches they feed from are not strong enough to support their weight. The bear climbs as close as it can to the fruit and then bends the fruit-laden branches back towards itself in order to feed. The result is a disorganized pile of broken branches, around 6 by 5 meters (20 by 16 feet) in

size, wedged in the tree alongside the limb that supported the bear's weight. Several layers of leaves are then added as bedding material. Bear hair and droppings have been found in and around such nests, leading to the assumption that nests may be used for considerable periods.

In Venezuela, tree nests have been found in conjunction with bears preying on cattle. In such instances the nests serve either as guard sites for the feeding area or as places to rest.

Spectacled bears are believed to be active at night and to sleep during the day. They sleep in large tree root cavities, on ground beds or in tree nests. A ground bed is oval in shape with a depression in the center, and is usually dug out at the base of a cliff or adjacent to the cover of vegetation. After leaving the den, female bears with cubs frequent such areas to protect their offspring from predators such as jaguars and poachers.

▼ Born during the rainy season, from about November to January, cubs emerge from the den when the greatest amounts of fruits are available.

Milton H. Tierney, Jr

▲ There may be one to three cubs in a litter, but generally there are two. At the age of three months cubs are able to follow their mothers and begin to learn how to find food.

MATING AND RAISING YOUNG

Mating occurs in April, May, and June, the time when most fruits are ripe and the bears congregate for feeding. Pairs stay together for a week or two until copulation has occurred numerous times, then the bears go their separate ways. If a male encounters another female in estrus he will also mate with her.

Gestation lasts between seven and eight months, and the newborn cubs, born in litters of one to three, are 18 centimeters (7 inches) long and weigh between 300 and 360 grams (10 and 11½ ounces). It is believed that delayed implantation of the fertilized egg occurs in the spectacled bear, like many, if not all, of the ursids. This results in cubs being born during the rainy season that lasts from November to February, and their emerging from the den at the time when large quantities of fruits are ripening.

The cubs develop rapidly. Their eyes open at 42 days, and by the time they are three months old they are able to follow their mother. In times of danger, fatigue, or when walking through tall grass, cubs have been known to ride on their mother's back. There is considerable communication between mother and cubs. They constantly trill when they are in motion, and during nursing the cubs make a loud humming noise. Distress calls are high pitched, and meet with an immediate response from the mother.

THE HUMAN IMPACT

Spectacled bears are killed for food, for money, and for their medicinal and magical properties. A farmer who kills a bear for raiding cornfields or killing cattle, can also make a good deal from selling the animal. A healthy male will provide meat worth up to US$200, not to mention the value of its skin, fat, organs, bones, and blood. The fat is said to cure rheumatism, prevent gallbladder attacks and blindness, and alleviate muscle pain. Bears' gallbladders are an ancient Andean cure for blindness and cataracts.

Bear bones are said to provide strength and virility, and are ground up and fed to children to keep them healthy. The blood is drunk warm after the bear is killed, as a tonic. The baculum, the penis bone, is worn as an amulet for manhood, and hunters retain the paws and pelts as trophies.

The spectacled bear is deeply rooted in the myths and histories of Andean cultures. The stories about it are diverse, and strongly influence people's attitudes to the animal. The bear is treated as a god in some areas, while in others it is believed to be evil and is destroyed.

In Venezuela, spectacled bears are said to emerge from the misty Andean forests, kidnap humans and use their captives for sexual bondage or to produce offspring. Male bears kidnap only young unmarried women, and female bears kidnap only young unmarried men.

The native cultures of Argentina and Bolivia have many spectacled bear stories, suggesting that the bear was once plentiful in these countries. In Bolivia, one tale tells of bears killing cattle and then haunting mountain slopes, scaring ranchers from their herds. Belief in this myth is said to be the

Bernard Peyton

▲ Despite their limited numbers in many areas, spectacled bears are frequently killed by local people for meat and for parts to be used for medicinal purposes.

◄ The patterning of white fur on the face of each spectacled bear is unique, which makes it possible for individual animals to be identified.

Milton H. Tierney, Jr

SPECTACLED BEARS IN CAPTIVITY

DIANA WEINHARDT

The first spectacled bear to be exhibited was in 1903, at the Amsterdam Zoo. During the early twentieth century, the main objective of many zoos was to exhibit as wide a variety of bears as space would allow. As spectacled bears were difficult to obtain, they were a particularly welcome addition.

Zoos are now regulated by national and international laws and treaties designed to protect wild species, which means that it is almost impossible for them to acquire wild spectacled bears. Since the 1970s, however, breeding bears has been a principal objective for zoos, and spectacled bears feature prominently in such programs. In 1962 there were 44 spectacled bears in captivity worldwide. By 1977 the number had increased to 100, and in mid-1992 there were 175 bears (50 of them born in the wild)

Milton H. Tierney, Jr

Francois Gohier/Jacana/AUSCAPE International

in 65 zoos on five continents. This increase in numbers can be attributed to the implementation of captive management programs using the Spectacled Bear Studbook and Species Survival Program.

A studbook is an historical record of all specimens of a single species which have ever been held in captivity. Regional studbooks list information pertaining to a species for one continent, whereas international studbooks encompass the species worldwide.

The Spectacled Bear Studbook originated in Germany in 1972 and was created by Dr Peter Roben of the Zoological Institute at the University of Heidelberg. In 1982, responsibility for the studbook was transferred to Mark Rosenthal, Curator of Mammals at the Lincoln Park Zoological Gardens in Chicago, Illinois.

Until the creation of the Spectacled Bear Species Survival Plan (SSP) in 1989, the Spectacled Bear Studbook was the sole captive management resource for zoos. It has now evolved into a publication containing management articles, surveys, and the most complete bibliography on the species. It is published annually in English, Spanish, German, and Russian.

The Species Survival Plan program was established in 1980 by the American Association of Zoological Parks and Aquariums to insure the long-term survival of the gene pools of selected rare, threatened, and endangered species. Breeding strategies and long-term support systems have so far been developed for 62 species in captivity, including the spectacled bear—the only bear species currently represented.

The goal of the SSP program is to include 200 species by the end of the twentieth century. These plans address the genetic and demographic problems associated with the maintenance of small populations in captivity over a 100-year period. Each SSP team consists of a species coordinator and an elected propagation group. The zoos involved in the program work cooperatively in the best interests of the species population as a whole. The SSP coordinates scientific studies, conservation programs, and programs for the improvement of animal husbandry.

For a species to be designated to the SSP the following criteria, among others, must be met. There must be: few wild populations, sufficient of the species in captivity to maintain a minimum viable population, and sufficient zoos and trained personnel to care for the animals. Zoos worldwide cooperate in the conservation of the spectacled bear, the Siberian and Sumatran tigers, the Andean condor, the radiated tortoise, the okapi, the gorilla, and many other species. For these critically threatened species, propagation in zoos may be the only means of maintaining large enough populations to insure long-term survival.

In addition to animal births, scientific studies have produced a high volume of reproductive, genetic, behavioral, nutritional, and veterinary information. This knowledge is invaluable in the current management of animal populations in zoos and in the wild.

◄ (Top) Spectacled bears were first exhibited in a zoo in Amsterdam in 1903. There are now around 175 in captivity and captive reproduction is carefully monitored to minimize inbreeding.

◄ Like other bears, spectacled bears are strong swimmers and enjoy their swimming pools when in captivity.

M. Newman/FLPA

reason why many bears are killed on sight, and since there are now many cattle ranches in such regions, bear–rancher conflicts are common.

A PRECARIOUS FUTURE
The spectacled bear faces many problems in today's world. While hunting has been banned, enforcement of the ban is difficult because of the isolated habitat and the lack of trained personnel. Road building, deforestation from uncontrolled logging, and hunting have had a disastrous effect on bear populations: habitat has been lost, and bear populations have been fragmented and cut off from important food sources. In addition, political unrest and military activities in national parks make bear research and management difficult.

The largest threat to bear survival is the colonization of habitat by highland people, some of whom have little understanding of cloud forest ecology. While a number of these people are quite

knowledgeable about the needs of spectacled bears, others feel they cause problems for local farmers and should be killed. The result is the classic conflict between an endangered species and human settlers vying for the same limited space. However, in these situations it is generally the native animal wildlife that loses in the struggle.

If the spectacled bear is to survive to the next century, conservation practices and policies must be updated and strictly enforced. New national parks must be set up and corridors established between protected and isolated areas so that the bears can migrate safely from one area to another, for if the bears remain in isolated pockets, genetic exchange will become impossible and the species will die out. Peaceful coexistence between these spectacled bears and the highland people is possible, but public education and stringent conservation management will be crucial in making it a workable reality.

▲ The spectacled bear is an excellent climber and probably has a more arboreal existence than any of the other bears.

THE GIANT PANDA

WENSHI PAN AND ZHI LÜ

The giant panda (*Ailuropoda melanoleuca*) was introduced to the Western world in 1869 when Père David, a French missionary who obtained skins and skeletal material in Sichuan, western China, sent them to the Paris Museum of Natural History.

For over 3,000 years, however, the animal has been referred to in Chinese books. In the *Shi Jing*, the earliest collection of Chinese poetry (1000 BC), the animal is described as "like a tiger and a bear." The *Er Ya*, the earliest dictionary (200 BC), describes the animal as a bamboo-eating leopard with black and white markings.

▲ Most giant panda habitat in the valleys is now occupied by humans, so pandas are restricted to a few small areas in the mountains, such as the Wolong Reserve.

Since the time Père David introduced the giant panda to the West, there has been considerable debate about how it should be classified. Some scientists believed that the animal was similar to raccoons, the Procyonidae; others insisted that the giant panda belonged in the bear family, Ursidae; while still others thought it should be placed in a separate family altogether. The most recent scientific data, based largely on molecular genetics, makes it quite clear that the giant panda is a bear. The people who live around panda habitats call the animal *hua xiong*, banded bear, or *zhu xiong*, bamboo bear.

In 1984, the fossils of several teeth were excavated in Yunnan, southern China, which are morphologically similar to those of bears and giant pandas. This animal, *Ailuropoda lufengenesis*, which lived at least 8 million years ago, marks the transition from ancient bear to ancient panda. There is no evidence to show what then happened, although the evolution of the animal in the last 3 million years seems clear. *Ailuropoda microta*,

with a body only half the size of the present giant panda, appeared in the subtropical forests of southern China in the late Pliocene and the Pleistocene (3,000,000 to 700,000 years ago). In the middle and late Pleistocene (700,000 to 10,000 years ago), *Ailuropoda melanoleuca baconi* replaced *Ailuropoda microta*. It was about one-eighth larger than the present panda, and it ranged throughout southern and eastern China, extending to Taiwan, Burma, Vietnam, and the suburbs of Beijing. Its distribution decreased abruptly during the last ice age (beginning 18,000 years ago), and at that time the present giant panda appeared.

The dramatic increase in human populations in recent years has seen most panda habitats becoming occupied by people, and as a result panda numbers have decreased sharply. Today it is estimated that only 1,500 giant pandas remain, and they are found in six remote mountainous areas in western China, the total size of their range being only about 14,000 square kilometers (5,400 square miles). These areas are: the Qinling Mountains in Shaanzi Province, the Min Mountains along the boundary of Gansu and Sichuan provinces, Wolong in the Qionglai Mountains in western Sichuan, the Liang Mountains, and the Da Xiang and Xiao Xiang mountains in southern Sichuan.

Giant pandas live in temperate forest in subalpine areas. Their habitats are limited by natural geographic features and by human farming and settlement. Usually, the panda's range is from the upper edge of the bamboo forest, at elevations of

▼ Looking east to the Wolong area from the Yu Tung Valley. The Wolong Reserve is 2,000 square kilometers (770 square miles), and is the largest giant panda reserve in China. The mountain peaks reach an elevation of 6,250 meters (20,500 feet) and the pandas here spend more than 85 percent of their time in the forests above 2,600 meters (8,500 feet).

3,000 to 3,500 meters (10,000 to 11,500 feet), down to the boundaries of the highest farms, at elevations between 1,200 and 2,500 meters (4,000 to 8,000 feet), depending on the region. The best panda habitat, at lower levels, has been permanently taken over by humans. The regions in which the pandas have found refuge are the last remaining natural areas, which also provide refuge for many other animals such as the golden monkey, the tufted deer, the porcupine, and the yellow-throated marten.

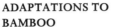

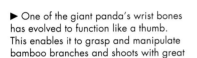
► One of the giant panda's wrist bones has evolved to function like a thumb. This enables it to grasp and manipulate bamboo branches and shoots with great dexterity when feeding.

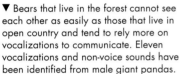
▼ Bears that live in the forest cannot see each other as easily as those that live in open country and tend to rely more on vocalizations to communicate. Eleven vocalizations and non-voice sounds have been identified from male giant pandas.

ADAPTATIONS TO BAMBOO

More than 99 percent of the giant panda's diet consists of the branches, stems, and leaves of at least 30 species of bamboo, the species eaten varying from region to region. Occasionally they eat other plants, and scavenge the meat of dead deer or takin, which illustrates that they still have the potential to be omnivorous. It is their clumsiness that prevents them from catching animals to eat, and thus renders them dependent on vegetation. The abundance of bamboo, its wide distribution, and the ease with which it can be harvested, has made it an ideal food for them.

Specialized feeding on a particular type of plant is not unusual among mammals. However, what is unusual in the case of giant pandas is that they have the simple stomach and intestines of a carnivore while leading the life of a specialized herbivore.

Both the panda's body and its behavior are adapted to its dietary habits. Its head and forepaws are specialized for handling bamboo stems. Its head is round, broad, and massive, its muzzle is short, its jaw muscles are powerful, and its large teeth are suited to crushing and grinding. Its forepaws are adapted for grasping bamboo stems through the enlargement of

the radial sesamoid, the wrist bone, which functions in the same way as a human's thumb.

When eating, giant pandas are dexterous and quick, and always choose the most nourishing parts of the bamboo. Compared with meat, bamboo is low in nutrients. It is mostly composed of cellulose, hemicellulose, and lignin which are difficult to digest. Herbivores have certain symbiotic bacteria and protozoa in their digestive tracts that degrade cellulose and hemicellulose through fermentation, but the panda has a short, simple carnivorous alimentary canal, with no adaptation for holding symbiotic bacteria. Studies in Sichuan and in the Qinling Mountains have shown that pandas are able to digest only about 21 percent of bamboo dry matter. To obtain enough nutrition for basic body maintenance, they must therefore eat a large amount of food and digest it quickly. Generally, an adult panda with an average weight of 100 kilograms (220 pounds) consumes 12 to 15 kilograms (26 to 33 pounds) of bamboo leaves and stems, or 23 to 38 kilograms (50 to 84 pounds) of bamboo shoots every day. Every day a panda spends 12 to 14 hours eating and the food it consumes stays in its digestive tract for 4 to 13 hours.

Even though a panda's maximum energy intake is from 20,500 to 25,300 kilojoules (4,900 to 6,040 calories) per day, it needs about 14,650 to 16,750 kilojoules (3,500 to 4,000 calories) per day merely for living. This suggests that its nutritional margin of safety is relatively narrow, and probably explains why pandas seldom store fat like other bears. Even without symbiotic bacteria in the gut, pandas can digest about 18 to 27 percent hemicellulose, which provides nearly one-third of their daily energy intake. It is not yet understood how pandas do this, but it is critical for their survival.

EFFECTS OF BAMBOO FLOWERING

Occasionally large areas of a particular bamboo species will flower simultaneously, resulting in all the plants dying back at the same time later in the season. This can have a disastrous effect on giant pandas. If there is only one bamboo species in an area of panda habitat, and it has a mass flowering, at the time it dies the pandas will be deprived of food until the bamboo regenerates. The most serious case recently was in the mid-1970s in the Min Mountains, where

Comstock

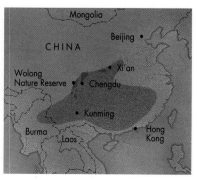

◄ The giant panda's coat is coarse and slightly oily, which helps to keep water from penetrating. The black hairs across its shoulders are 5 to 7 centimeters (2 to 3 inches) long, while those on its back and rump are half that length.

▼ A map of China showing the known prehistoric range (pink shaded area) of the giant panda, and its greatly diminished present distribution (red shaded area).

most of the bamboo bloomed at once, resulting in 13 pandas starving to death. Fortunately, almost all panda habitat supports at least two species of bamboo, and as many as 13 species grow in the Liang Mountains, at varying elevations. In some cases pandas are able to find alternative bamboo species by traveling only a kilometer or two. Moreover, studies in Wolong in the Qionglai Mountains, and in the Qinling Mountains have shown that pandas annually consume less than 2 percent of the existing bamboo.

SOCIAL BEHAVIOR

Giant pandas live alone except during the spring, when adult males and females come together, chase each other, fight, and finally mate.

Recent research in the Qinling Mountains has indicated that there is a certain amount of social organization in the panda population there. In 1987, fifteen pandas (eight females and seven males) were fitted with radio collars and have since been tracked. From September to May they live in their winter habitat at elevations between 1,200

143

▼ More than 99 percent of the giant panda's diet consists of bamboo. In the winter, they eat mainly the leaves and young stems, and in the spring they eat the shoots.

▼ (Bottom) Giant pandas walk with a steady rolling gait, holding their heads low. They can stand on their hind feet but have not been seen walking bipedally.

and 2,000 meters (4,000 and 6,500 feet), feeding on *Bashania fargesii*. From June to August they move to their summer habitat, between 2,200 and 3,000 meters (7,200 to 10,000 feet), to feed on *Fargesia spathasea*. When the two species of bamboo sprout, from May to July, the pandas follow the process of sprouting up the hillsides, which enables them to feed continuously on the shoots, the most nourishing parts of the plant. This kind of vertical movement has not been reported in other panda ranges.

In the three months of summer the giant panda's only activity is feeding. During the nine months they spend in their winter habitat they may also mate and give birth. The social organization that researchers observed in the Qinling Mountains occurred in relation to reproductive behavior in the winter habitat. Each social group consisted of a dominant male and three to five females whose home ranges were within the male's range. Females frequently appeared in exclusive core areas, even though their home ranges, with an average size of 4.2 square kilometers (1.6 square miles), overlapped. The home ranges of dominant males averaged about 11.8 square kilometers (4.5 square miles). The ranges of dominant males, which were also the ranges of groups, were largely exclusive. Fighting between males at range boundaries was observed several times outside the mating season.

The social positions of males seem to be age-related. Researchers in the Qinling Mountains noted that a male under eight years old had the lowest position and the largest range, which overlapped the ranges of at least two groups. It seems young males roam widely looking for a chance to establish a home range near some breeding females and become dominant. When males are around 15 years or older, they retreat from the best mating habitat and maintain a smaller home range on the periphery. Two males, one 9 years old and the other 14, were the strongest and were dominant in two different groups. By controlling home ranges that overlapped the home ranges of several females, these males gained the best mating opportunities. Holding dominant positions may reduce the need for males to expend energy in competition, enabling them to retain more energy for mating.

Studies in Wolong in the Qionglai Mountains, and in Tangjiahe in the Min Mountains, did not find similar social organizations.

REPRODUCTION AND CARE OF OFFSPRING
Adult male giant pandas are larger than females. They have a wider muzzle, stronger forelegs and a longer body, and weigh about 85 to 125 kilograms (190 to 275 pounds), while a female weighs 70 to 100 kilograms (155 to 220 pounds). In the field, however, it is hard to identify a panda's sex.

Males and females seldom meet other than during the mating season but they communicate by means of rubbing onto tree trunks or stones a slightly acetic-smelling substance which is secreted from the anal sacs, two glands surrounding the anogenital area. This integrates social behavior by

Keith and Liz Laidler

Jim Tuten/Animals Animals/Stock Photos

conveying messages about the reproductive state and individual identity of the sender some time after they have passed a particular site. The frequency of this scent marking increases during the mating season.

Most female giant pandas come into estrus from March to May. The period of estrus lasts for one to three weeks, but the period of peak receptivity is only about one to three days. When copulating, the male stands or squats behind the female with his forelegs propped on her back, mounting often but briefly before ejaculation. As gestation periods vary from 87 to 163 days, it is assumed that the fertilized egg develops only to the blastocyst stage and then floats free in the uterus before implanting. The delay in implantation could vary from one to four months.

Females give birth to their young in caves or hollow trees. There are usually one or two in a litter. If twins are born, females usually raise only one cub, leaving the other unattended, but several instances of a female accompanied by two young have been reported from the Min, Qionglai, and Qinling mountains. Cubs at birth weigh 85 to 140 grams (3 to 5 ounces). Blind and nearly

naked, they have a loud, high-pitched squawk that is out of all proportion to their tiny, fragile bodies. It seems that they need an emphatic signal to alert their bulky mother.

◀ Although female giant pandas often give birth to twins, most females only raise a single cub. In the wild, cubs are born in a cave, a hollow tree trunk, or some other sheltered spot away from other bears.

▼ The giant panda's distinctive black and white patterning makes it easy for them to recognize a member of their species instantly at a distance, even in heavy forest.

PANDAS AND POLITICS

DONALD G. REID

Looking like teddy bears, with marvelous coloration and an easy-going manner, giant pandas are enormously popular with the public. They are also rare and endangered, having lost most of their habitat, and being the object of frequent poaching. These characteristics make a volatile combination.

The appeal and rarity of giant pandas have made them a global symbol for endangered species and conservation, and they were once bestowed as the most significant of Chinese diplomatic gifts to zoos of selected nations. Rarity and popularity also make pandas a lucrative attraction for their owners. They are considerable money-makers for the conservation community and Western zoos, and Chinese zoos and government departments charge upwards of US$100,000 per month for the short-term loan of a giant panda overseas.

▼ Considerable efforts have been made to breed giant pandas in zoos, especially in China, and in some cases artificial insemination has been used. To date, such programs have met with limited success.

▼ (Bottom) Among the most popular animals to be seen in zoos, giant pandas are no longer given away by the Chinese authorities as diplomatic gifts, as they once were, but are rented out for relatively short periods.

Nicole Herzog-Verrey/Camera Press London

Richard Open/Camerapress

There is controversy over whether this money is being spent in the pandas' best conservation interests. Central to the discussion are differing concepts of conservation. In the Western world, conservation is generally associated with the maintenance of wild animals in natural habitats. An animal left to its own resources without human harassment is a metaphor for the pursuit of individual freedom that lies at the heart of Western cultures. China has a longer history of intervention in the landscape than many countries, and experience of wild animals in natural habitats is extremely rare for most of its citizens.

The Chinese outlook has led to emphasis being placed on saving pandas in captivity. Scientists and managers can more readily garner support for captive pandas, where they are easy to see, and where most people believe that their needs are being fully met. A condition of nearly all foreign involvement in panda conservation, including international loans, has been investment in a breeding facility or zoological garden, often with the aim of raising pandas for reintroduction to the wild. However, the inability of captive breeding to sustain zoo populations has led to these facilities being stocked with pandas taken from the wild. It is thought that if captive breeding and survival can be improved, pandas might be sustainable in captivity alone.

For Western conservationists, such a goal is unethical, quite apart from its practical difficulties. The giant panda, without its natural habitat, is gravely diminished as a subject of admiration and awe. It is relegated largely to an object of economic and academic interest. Western conservationists argue that the species' future must depend on the maintenance of wild habitats, and these are becoming increasingly less available or recoverable as time goes by. They also argue that reintroductions are risky. Panda cubs, like other bear cubs, require an extended period with their mothers to learn how to find food and shelter and avoid danger in the wild. If naive pandas are to survive release into the wild there will need to be considerable experimentation, and new introduction techniques will have to be developed. Finally, it is not only the panda that Westerners are keen to conserve. The panda's habitats include one of the most diverse assemblages of temperate fauna and flora on the globe. Their conservation is of inestimable spiritual, cultural, and economic value to the citizens of China and the world.

Ultimately, conservation actions directed at pandas will represent a compromise among the proponents of these differing ethical outlooks. The management plan ratified by the State Council of China in 1992 includes the founding of a new captive breeding center in the Qinling Mountains, and the establishment of new reserves and additions to some of the 12 existing reserves. The speed at which actions proceed will depend largely on contributions from Western conservationists and aid agencies. Contributions must come as money, expertise, and a willingness to understand the Chinese point of view and to work towards resolving the concerns of both cultures. Political will for action is built on trust, and controversies can best be avoided by communicating openly regarding planned actions and expenditures.

On 16 August, 1989, a radio-collared female gave birth to a male cub, and researchers have been able to observe the pair almost continuously since that time. In the first ten days after birth, the mother spent most of her time sitting in the den, holding her cub with a forepaw, and nursing him. Little trace of feeding and few droppings were found around the den until the cub was two weeks old. When the mother started to go outside the den to feed, the cub remained inside, sleeping. This situation lasted for four months, during which time the female carried her cub to two other dens.

The cub developed quickly. At seven days, the black of his eye patches, ears, and shoulders began to show; at 44 days, he opened his eyes and began to crawl; at 85 days, he could stand and stagger along. At 125 days, at 40 centimeters (16 inches) long and weighing 6 kilograms (13 pounds), the cub started to roam with his mother. In time, he learned to walk freely, to climb trees, and to drink from a stream. He began to eat bamboo at 13 months, and was fully weaned at 15 months. At 32 months, the time of writing, he is still living with his mother, although for some time he has been large enough to be independent. This time spent with his mother is much longer than the expected 18 or, at most, 24 months. The mother came into estrus in the spring of 1991, but did not give birth that fall. This may be the reason why the pair have been together for so long.

The first-year mortality of young had been thought to be high because the newborn are so weak and there are many carnivores, such as leopards, black bears, and yellow-throated martens that share the panda's habitat. In the Qinling Mountains, however, it was found that the cubs are well cared for by their mothers. A black bear that invaded the panda mother and cub pair's area was immediately driven out by the female.

Both male and female giant pandas reach maturity at four-and-a-half to six-and-a-half years. They live for about 20 to 22 years in the field, while the oldest one, so far, in captivity died at thirty. Males in the field are sexually active from 5 to 15 years old, the peak years of reproduction being between the ages of 8 and 14. Females may reproduce for at least 11 years. If a female gives birth during the fall and her offspring remain with her, she apparently continues to lactate through the spring mating season, and estrus is suppressed until the following year, by which time her young are fully weaned. Therefore, the maximum reproductive rate is about one litter per female every two years. In fact, the reproductive rate is lower because some females occasionally do not produce a litter, even though they come into estrus.

▶ Pandas generally remain on the ground, but they are capable climbers. They climb trees when courting and sometimes simply to sun themselves and have a rest.

John Mackinnon/Bruce Coleman Ltd

Wolfshead/Ben Osborne/Ardea London Ltd

▲ Because the giant panda's digestive system is not evolved for digesting vegetation, a panda must eat large amounts in order to survive. One panda observed in the wild fed for a little over 15 hours at a stretch, during which time it consumed about 650 bamboo shoots.

▶ Giant pandas claw trees, urinate, and rub their anal regions on trees to leave scent marks for other pandas.

John Mackinnon/Bruce Coleman Ltd.

THE CONSERVATION OF PANDAS

For millions of years the giant panda has managed to survive through climatic upheavals in which hundreds of other large mammals vanished. Today, its survival depends not on natural forces but on human goodwill. Panda habitat is constantly being invaded by people clearing land and felling timber. Present areas of habitat consist of a mere 25 forest pockets, and more than two-thirds of these support fewer than 50 pandas. Genetic research suggests that a population of at least 1,000 is needed to avoid inbreeding, because within a population less than 50 percent would be randomly breeding individuals. Inbreeding in such small populations is therefore inevitable and will result in reduced genetic variability and fitness, and subsequent extinction. Poaching is also a serious problem because panda furs can be sold illegally at extremely high prices outside China. Many poachers have been punished severely, but the practice continues.

There are currently over 100 giant pandas in zoos and breeding centers worldwide, and large amounts of money are being spent on captive breeding programs. The success rate has been low, however, and out of a total of 100 cubs born since 1963, only around 35 have lived more than six months. While the current rate of two to three cubs being born annually is better than before, further research on behavior and nutrition is needed. Funds would be spent more effectively on conserving giant panda habitat, as they breed more successfully in the wild. Certainly no more wild pandas should be captured for breeding programs.

The giant panda, now a symbol both of endangered animals and of conservation, presents us with a moral and scientific challenge. Only long-term unremitted effort will enable the animal to be preserved in what remains of its natural habitat.

▲ An American black bear sitting on a woodpile in Minnesota in the fall.

BEARS AND

HUMANS

ANTHROPOLOGY, HISTORY, AND CULTURE

BARRY SANDERS

▲ A mother bear is shown licking one of her cubs, in this early seventeenth-century French engraving. Some theological writers in the Middle Ages saw the Christian church as mimicking the bear's maternal nurturing qualities.

▼ Saint Columba is usually depicted with a palm frond and a bear on a chain. In this fourteenth-century painting from Rimini, Italy, he is shown with his bear only.

The bear can barely move through history without launching a myth or a story. Who could not be affected by a creature's miraculous ability to remain underground in a state of suspended animation through the severest part of winter, emerging precisely as the frost begins to melt? Somehow, this huge, burly animal knew the secret of turning in harmony with the great cosmic wheel. Thus, the wildest concept came to dominate primitive thinking: the hope of returning from the dead. This promise, of course, was offered by Christ to his disciples in the New Testament, which is why a number of early medieval miniatures show Christ borne aloft by a bear.

THE MATERNAL BEAR

To the Greeks and Romans the bear was the quintessence of motherly compassion, a belief they derived from observing the female bear's unique behavior. Cubs are born tiny—averaging a mere 350 grams (12 ounces)—and are hairless blobs of flesh. Ancient writers such as Pliny believed that the mother bear continually licked her little cub until it took shape. Virgil considered this activity to be the very essence of creation itself. As a consequence of its pronounced maternal devotion, both the Greeks and Romans referred to the bear only in the feminine gender.

The ancients transferred the bear's maternal concern to the world of humans. For one thing, ursa looks so familiar—our forebear in a furry coat. But more specifically, the bear's meticulous stroking and caressing resembled a human mother, who tenderly coaxes and cajoles her infant into shape, the mother's hands and voice replacing the sow's supple tongue. French mothers still call a recalcitrant child an *ours mal leche*, a badly licked bear.

According to some theological writers in the Middle Ages, the Church itself mimicked the maternal patience of the bear, licking unformed heathens into shape in the image of Christianity. Church fathers like Clemens Alexandrinus infused the concept of motherhood with the idea of spirituality. The bear's exceptional biology made it an exemplar of the loftiest Christian conception of motherhood—the Virgin Mary. While bears copulate in midsummer, the fertilized ovum does not attach to the wall of the uterus until five months later, during denning time, and the cubs are born underground. Typically, then, the bear ambles into a cave looking quite normal, only to re-emerge with a litter in tow, her cubs providing proof of the miracle of virgin birth.

AN ANCIENT LEGACY

How did such an enduring relationship with the bear begin? Walking down the trail, the Neanderthal came face-to-face with the gigantic cave bear —*Ursus spelaeus*—its long-thighed, stout body weighing as much as 400 kilograms (880 pounds). As he peered into the bear's eyes, the Neanderthal may have found a reflection of his own consciousness, but one that seemed somehow deeper.

The cave bear was a browsing animal. Instead of hunting down prey, it probably subsisted on a vegetarian diet. By observing its habits, Neanderthals may have learned what was edible, the bear teaching its first and most fundamental lesson: survival. While it is obviously impossible to know what attitude Neanderthals took to this monumental creature, we can imagine humans and bears sharing the same cave, each occupying a different niche. Excavations at various European caves provide evidence of such an association.

At Regourdou, near Lascaux in France, a Neanderthal grave site contained the upper arm bone of a bear. At other places, archaeologists exhumed bodies that were covered with patches of bear fur. Here, perhaps, the Neanderthals began putting into practice the second lesson they had learned from the bears: the hope of finding their own place in the renewal of the cosmos. The words "bury," "bier," and "burial" all derive from the same Indo-European root, *bher*, from which the word "bear" also comes.

Some 40 thousand years ago, the bear began to take on gender. She began to appear as a goddess wearing a bear mask, and seemed well on her way to becoming the Great Mother of the classical world. Clues to this transformation come from the work of archaeologists, most notably Marija Gimbutas, who has analyzed hundreds of terracotta figurines unearthed in a region that encompasses Romania to the north, Greece to the south, Austria to the west, and the Black Sea to the east—an area that produced the Vinca culture. In this period, which Gimbutas refers to as Old Europe— roughly 9,000 to 5,000 years ago— early farming people left behind bear-shaped cult vases liberally incised with chevrons, which apparently represent water, associating the bear with springs and the underworld.

Towards the end of this period the bear assumed a shape that was part human. Terracotta figurines took the form of a bear-headed woman; sometimes seated on a throne decorated with crescents (again, an indication of water), holding a bear cub Madonna-fashion, or carrying it in a sack on her back. In many of the figurines, her left hand touches her breast, once again suggesting an ursine association with water, since milk and water are often conjoined in ancient mythology. A great many of the figurines show the bear-woman actually nursing a cub.

As Old Europe became overlaid with an Indo-European culture, the old bear goddess assumed the role of a nurse who was to protect the Divine Child, the new god of vegetation, who wandered underground in winter, and arose renewed in spring. Thus, the bear goddess cradled civilization's greatest desire—the desire to be reborn.

THE LEGEND OF SALMOXIS

In an area called Thrace, just west of the Black Sea, the Egyptian historian Herodotus tells us, a group of people called the Getae sacrificed a man each year as a messenger to their god of immortality, Salmoxis. His name has been translated as "bearskin." After dispatching this human messenger, the Getae "shoot arrows at the lightning and thunder," which the classicist Rhys Carpenter interprets as an act of "weather magic," and of course the hibernating bear functions as a fairly reliable weather forecaster. The Getae clearly elevated the bear to the level of a god, and by performing their ritual sacrifice hoped to live forever, protected by the spirit of the animal.

A version of this story, without human sacrifice, was retold in other parts of Greece. The legend told of a countryman of Thrace, Salmoxis, who left his homeland for a time, and returned declaring that he held the secret of eternal life. To prove his claim, Salmoxis built a cave, shut himself in it, and fasted, vowing to return in four years. When he emerged,

◄ The shaman's bear mask of the Tlinget people of southeastern Alaska.

▲ A Roman floor mosaic dating from around the third or second century BC in Ostia, Italy, illustrates a hunter and a bear. Remarkably, a small population of brown bears still survives in northern Italy.

▼ In the famous Bara Bahau cave in the Dordogne, France, these engravings of bears were made by Paleolithic people 30,000 years ago.

the Thracians greeted him as a living miracle. He admitted to having acquired astonishing powers underground: great celestial wisdom coupled with an ability to predict the weather.

In later Thracian accounts of the legend, Salmoxis became a co-regent with the king, then a priest of immortality, and finally a god himself. He dwelt in a sacred cave and prophesied the future. In the heart of Thrace, on Mount Laphysion, ancient writers told of a cave oracle named Trophonios, whose cave opening swarmed with bees, and who had to be placated by an offering of honey cakes. Plutarch described a visitor to the cave who "remained two nights and a day underground; and when most people had given him up for dead

and his family was mourning him, at early dawn he emerged radiant." By this time, the cult of Salmoxis has clearly become an immortality ritual. All this ursine evidence surrounding Salmoxis prompted Rhys Carpenter to this conclusion: "Salmoxis can be none other than the hibernating bear, whose mysterious, foodless, mid-winter sleep has everywhere made of him a supernatural spirit to the wondering mind of primitive man."

RETURN FROM DEATH

The miracle of the bear's return from death was traditionally celebrated around 2 February. According to Balkan folklore, the bear went underground at the moment of the winter solstice and hibernated for a period of 40 days. In the Church calendar, 2 February marks the Festival of Light, Candlemas, a time to welcome the sun's return after its long winter absence. The Church calculated Candlemas by counting 40 days from

the point of the sun's deepest retreat, the winter solstice, overlaying its calendar on the bear's biological clock—basing it on the fact that somehow, deep in slumber, the bear responded to the sun's initial warming rays. The bear thus displayed a bond with the sun, as well as an empathy with the seasons.

The patron saint of Candlemas is Saint Blaise, who blessed people by conferring years of light on them. He also served as keeper of the winds, and marked the advent of spring by breaking wind, just as the bear's "fart of dehibernation"—the moment at which the bear forcefully ejects its anal plug— announced the new year on 2 February. Some scholars see in Saint Blaise the Christian culmination of a powerful and pervasive underground myth, expressed most popularly in a classical figure like Orpheus. René Gaignabet, a French cultural historian, believes that the hibernating bear presented a model for Christ's three days in the cave

and eventual resurrection. Christ the Son is symbolized by the sun, a connection that also evokes the bear's bond with the sun.

Until recently, in Arles-sur-Tech in southern France, on the Sunday following Candlemas, the townspeople would build a cave in the town square and enact an ancient ceremony that celebrated the bear. A young man would don a bearskin and go "berserk" through the streets looking for his bride. After a time of frenzy, he would grab a victim and take her inside the cave, where they were married. This ceremonial marriage occurred just as the bear had emerged from his sleep, announcing the advent of spring. Couples married on that day assured themselves a kind of immortality through childbirth.

THE CULT OF ARTEMIS
A bear cult evidently flourished off the coast of Attica, centered on the goddess Artemis, known as Artemis Brauron. Athenian girls put on brown robes

◄ According to the anthropologist Marija Gimbutas, the hundreds of bear-nurse figurines that have been discovered in eastern Europe refer to the role of the goddess as a protector of weaklings. This terracotta figure, which is about 6 centimeters (2½ inches) high, comes from southern Yugoslavia and was made in the fifth century BC.

▼ The helplessness of humans against the elements and wild animals such as the polar bear is dramatically illustrated in this nineteenth-century painting by the English artist Sir Edwin Landseer entitled "Man proposes, God disposes."

EARLY RELATIONSHIPS BETWEEN POLAR BEARS AND THE INUIT

IAN STIRLING

The relationship between the ancestors of the present-day Inuit (a term that means "the people," which has replaced the Indian word Eskimo, meaning "eaters of raw flesh") and the polar bear was complex. The polar bear was, simultaneously, a prey species, a dangerous adversary, and an animal whose spirit could be interchangeable with the hunter himself. After Sedna, the legendary human goddess of the sea who was generally held to be the supreme being, the most powerful spirit was that of the polar bear.

At the most basic level, the Inuit used polar bears for clothing, sleeping skins, and food for themselves and their dogs. There were also a number of specialized uses. For example, a hunter waiting for a seal to come up to its breathing hole might sit on a piece of polar bear skin on a snow block and rest his feet on another, to help keep the cold from penetrating. Throughout the north, the Inuit commonly used a piece of polar bear skin to brush water on sled runners in order to coat them with ice in the cold weather. The bears' canine teeth were often made into ornaments or amulets.

The early Inuit had a dual relation with most animals. As one Inuk hunter explained it to the Danish ethnologist, Knud Rasmussen,

"The greatest peril of life lies in the fact that human food consists entirely of souls. All the creatures that we have to kill and eat, all those that we have to strike down and destroy to make clothes for ourselves, have souls, like we have, souls that do not perish with the body, and which must therefore be propitiated lest they should revenge themselves on us for taking away their bodies." Unless specific rituals were adhered to, the Inuit feared the animals would be offended and withhold themselves from hunters in the future. Even worse, an animal's spirit might be angered and seek revenge. For example, at St Lawrence Island in Alaska, hunters believed a wounded bear had to be tracked down and killed in order to release its soul. If this was not done, the bear's soul would cause harm to the hunter.

Beliefs and practices varied between areas, but there were some common themes. One was the choice of the spirit of an animal to be a person's tornaq, or spiritual guardian. The shaman, the tribal medicine-man, usually had the polar bear as his tornaq because it was the most powerful of all animals.

An especially strong belief was that the spirits of men and bears were interchangeable, a belief that was reinforced by the fact that

◀ A bear walking on its hind legs resembles a human being. Wherever bears and humans coexist, this likeness has given rise to beliefs about the interchangeability of the spirit of the bear and human spirits.

▼ Miniature polar bears carved from ivory are thought to have been regarded as having special powers. Some archaeologists have suggested that the more stylized the carving, the greater its power.

▼ (Bottom) Polar bear hunting is still a vital part of the Inuit culture and economy. After being fleshed out, polar bear hides are dried and bleached in the sun.

▶ Only in Greenland has the hunter's tradition of wearing pants made from polar bear hides survived. A true hunter is immediately identified by wearing these pants, the warmest clothing that can be worn in the bitter cold of an Arctic winter.

Norbert Rosing

C.M. Dixon

Nicholas Devore/Bruce Coleman Ltd

bears have so many "human-like" traits. For example, bears are able to stand up and walk on their hind legs. Sometimes they may sit or lean against a log or a rock as if resting and thinking. Being omnivores, bears also eat many of the foods, both plant and animal, that people do. Of particular significance is the fact that the musculature of a bear's skinned carcass is uncannily similar to the body of a human. This undoubtedly explains why, in several Inuit legends, when polar bears come inside, they take off their coats and become people. When they put on their hides and go outside, they transform into bears again.

The Inuit believed that a bear would allow itself to be killed by a hunter only if it were treated properly after death. Consequently, hunters were careful to observe specific rituals after killing a bear. The most widespread practice was to observe a strict taboo against hunting polar bears after killing one, to allow its soul time to return to its family. In one legend that reinforces this concept, a woman unwittingly entered an igloo inhabited by a family of polar bears and, being frightened, hid behind some sealskins. She overheard how the youngest bear had gained respect for the Inuit, whom he had once thought were simply figures of skin and bone. This bear had been out hunting humans and had been killed by a man who later gave him a death taboo and several wonderful presents. These actions set the bear's soul free, enabling him to return to his family after four days. Later, the woman escaped and returned to her village, where she told the people what she had learned. Because of this legend, the Netsilik,

Copper, and Inland Inuit of Canada observed a strict taboo on hunting for several days after killing a bear.

Another practice that linked human beings to bears was that of providing dead bears with human implements. The Copper Inuit provided a dead male bear with a miniature bow and arrow, while a female bear was given a needle holder because, like humans, the male needed his hunting weapons and the female her domestic tools.

In rituals, usually only parts of a bear were used to represent the entire animal. The skull was most important to the Asiatic Inuit, Greenlanders, Polar Inuit, and those in the Central Canadian Arctic, while to others the skin or even the intestines held particular significance. In southern Greenland, the head of a bear was placed on the lamp platform facing southeast, which was the direction the bears came from in that district. The eyes were covered and the nostrils blocked with moss or other materials so that the bear's soul could not see or smell the hunter. Fat was smeared on the jaws to appease the bear because bears like greasy food.

At St Lawrence Island in Alaska, the head of a newly killed bear was put in a corner of the room with its mouth open and decorated in a manner that was appropriate to its sex. All hunting ceased while stories were told and songs were sung. After five days, the skull was boiled and the pieces of flesh were either thrown into the air for the spirits, or placed in the fire to appease the bear's forefathers. Afterward, the hunter put the skull on the graves of his clan's ancestors, along with other bear skulls.

▶ In this Italian earthenware dish, the bear may represent Callisto, the bear woman of early Greek mythology who mated with the all-powerful god Zeus.

in imitation of bear cubs, as part of their initiation rites. Details surrounding Artemis reveal her many bear associations. For one thing, her name translates as "bear." One of her forms, Callisto, was punished for her sexual adventures by being turned into a bear. Some classical scholars identify Artemis' mother as Demeter, whose name translates as "grain of the bear mother," as if she were born of the same seed as the ancient bear goddess. Indeed,

Demeter seemed to spend much of her time around caves. She nursed Trophonios, the oracle of the cave, who traced his own lineage back to the bear. A temple to her honor stood in the Grove of Trophonios, and her own ceremonies took place near Phigaleia, also in a cave. Long before other Olympian heroes made their descent into the underworld, Demeter had demonstrated her own immortality by making the return trip many times.

▶ The most powerful carnivore on the west coast of North America was the brown bear. This earned it enormous respect from indigenous people and a significant place in their culture and mythology.

The Bridgeman Art Library

The dance by native American people to honor the spirit of the bear is illustrated in this work by George Catlin (1794–1872).

C.M. Dixon

The story of Iphigenia, who was saved from sacrificial death by Artemis, may have spun off from episodes in which these bear-girls were ritually sacrificed. The story begins with Agamemnon, who offered his daughter Iphigenia as a sacrifice to Artemis, in order to compensate for having killed one of the goddess' sacred animals. Artemis intervened and saved her and, according to some sources, a small brown bear remained on the altar. Behind this story lurks the shadow of the prehistoric bear goddess, the outline of a ritual in which the bear is both sacred and slain.

THE FESTIVAL OF THE SLAIN BEAR

This seemingly contradictory attitude toward the bear—that it was sacred and that it had to be slain —ritually enacted an episode in one of the most persistent and widely recounted stories in the world, the Bear Mother story, which is told on page 166. In this tale, primitive people take on the bear's spirit by ingesting the animal. A continuation of that story, the Bear Son story, also told on page 166, follows the adventures of the Bear Mother's offspring who becomes a great warrior and visits the underworld. These two stories trace the historic division of the divine bear into its male and female properties.

The festival of the slain bear celebrated the most decisive moment in the story of the Bear Mother—the death of the Bear Husband. Through his own instructions, the Bear Husband transmuted his death into a moment of immortality by passing on his spirit. Just before he died, the Bear Husband taught the songs that must be sung and the prayers that must be repeated over his body to ensure humanity its measure of good fortune.

The anthropologist Irving Hallowell has studied the festival of the slain bear and has come across strikingly close parallels between the bear hunts of certain North American peoples and tribal ceremonies in Scandinavia, Siberia, and Japan. In

his article "Bear Ceremonialism in the Northern Hemisphere," published in *American Anthropologist* in 1926, Hallowell documented a circumpolar hunting tradition among sub-Arctic peoples who view the bear as a supernatural being or power. Firstly, hunters traditionally took the bear in early spring, while it was still denning. Secondly, they could refer to the bear solely in terms of deference or kinship, such as "Grandfather," "The Great One," or "Cousin," as they yelled at it to come out of hiding. Thirdly, forced out of its den, the bear had to be killed with a primitive instrument like an axe, without spilling one drop of its blood on the

▲ A bear with a salmon in its mouth is venerated on this totem pole from Bella Bella in British Columbia, Canada.

▼ A person dressed as a bear takes part in the Fiesta of the Cross in Achocalla, Bolivia.

Tony Morrison

▲ Until the 1930s the ceremony of the slain bear was carried out by the Ainu people of Hokkaido, Japan. The sacrifice of the bear was central to their religion, as they saw the bear as an intermediary between themselves and a mountain god.

ground. Fourthly, hunters were required to continue to speak to the bear after its death, imploring its soul not to be angry, and inviting it to come home with them as an honored guest. In many ceremonies, the hunters flipped a bear paw in the air in order to

determine how many days the guest would be staying. Then they severed the head from the body.

In all the ceremonies, the carcass was flayed in a carefully prescribed manner, as in Hallowell's description of the Ostyak people in Siberia:

CONJURING THE BEAR

BARRY SANDERS

For many native peoples, the bear's name, like Yahweh's, remains unutterably sacred. The bear must be addressed by different epithets. The loftiest of them suggest some sense of kinship, such as Brother, Chief's Daughter, Grandfather, and Stepmother. Others express fondness for the bear, and function more like nicknames, while still serving to address the animal without calling it by its god name. The following are some examples:

Angry One (Cree)
The Animal (Michikaman)
Apple of the Forest (Finn)
Big Feet (many native American groups)
Big Great Food (Cree)
Big Hairy One (Blackfoot)
Black Beast (many native American groups)
Black Food (Cree)
Black Place (Koyukon)
Bobtail (many native American groups)
Broadfoot (Estonian)
Dark Thing (Koyukon)
Divine One Who Rules the Mountains (Ainu)
Dweller in the Wilds (Ostyak)

▶ A bronze plaque of a bear dating from the eighth century AD, from the Perm' region of Siberia.

C.M. Dixon

Famous Lightfoot (Finn)
Fine Young Chief (Navajo)
Food of the Fire (Cree)
Forest Apple (Finn)
Four-legged Man (Ostyak)
Fur Man (Ostyak)
Golden Feet (many native American groups)
Golden Friend (Finn)
Golden King (many native American groups)

Gold Friend of Fen and Forest (Ural Altaic)
Good-tempered Beast (Cree)
Great Man (Siberian)
He Who Lives in the Den (Navajo)
Holy Animal (Lapp)
Honey Paw (Tungus)
Illustrious Pride (Finn)
Little Mother of Honey (Finn)
Lord of the Taiga (Tungus)

Master of the Forest (Lapp)
Old Man of the Mountain (Lapp)
One Who Prowls at Night (many native American groups)
Owner of the Earth (Siberian)
Pride of the Woodlands (Finn)
Reared in the Mountains (Navajo)
Sacred Man (Lapp)
Sacred Virgin (Lapp)
Snub-nose (Finn)
Step-widener (Lapp)
Sticky-Mouth (many native American groups)
The Strong One (Taglish)
That Which Went Away (Koyukon)
The Thing (Koyukon)
Unmentionable One (Blackfoot)
Venerable One (Vogul)
Wide-way (Lapp)
Winter-sleeper (Lapp)
Wise Man (Lapp)
Woodmaster (Samoyed)
Wooly One (Lapp)
Worthy Old Man (Ural Altaic)

"The stomach, lungs, and bowels are buried on the spot. The butchering of ribs, back and shoulders is done so that no bones are cut. One of the hunters gives a bit of the heart to any boy who is present, which he eats while sitting astride the still warm animal. The heart, liver, and gut are cooked in a copper kettle on a nearby fire and each hunter eats some of them all. The butchered body of the bear, along with skin and head, is then dragged home on sleds."

Finally, an elaborate festival followed—sometimes lasting several days—in which the tribe ate every bit of the bear. The hunters retold the tale of killing it, after which the bear's spirit received its send-off. Then, designated members of the tribe disposed of the bones. Wrapped in bark, they were hung from a cedar tree, along with a bark drawing of the bear. When the drawing finally dried and fell to the ground, the celebration came to an end, for the tribe knew the bear had begun its new life.

▶ This delicate ivory carving, only 8 centimeters (3 inches) high, from an Inuit midden in the northwestern Canadian Arctic, represents two bears playing. It probably also refers to the interchangeability of human and bear spirits.

▼ The similarity between bears and humans is dramatically illustrated by these male polar bears play-fighting.

BEARS IN THE SKY

BARRY SANDERS

Two bears, Ursa Major and Ursa Minor, ride through the night sky in the Northern Hemisphere. The Earth's axis points to the brightest star in Ursa Minor, Alpha Ursae Minoris, more popularly know as Polaris, or the Pole Star. One can easily get one's bearings on Earth by sighting on the first two stars in Ursa Minor, which point directly to the Pole Star. When sailors who are lost at sea count their lucky stars, they generally give thanks to the bear.

The ancient Greeks

To understand how the bears ascended into the night sky, we need to know something about Callisto, the she-bear, and her child, Arcas. Both mother and son were unruly upstarts whose punishment was to follow an orderly path in the heavens. In one story, Artemis, the guardian of chastity and childbirth, discovered that one of her attendants, Callisto, was pregnant. To punish Callisto, Artemis transformed the errant woman into her most unvirginlike nature—a bear. In another story, the goddess Hera discovered that her husband, Zeus, had impregnated Callisto, and punished Callisto by turning her into a bear.

▲ Ursa Major, the great bear, is one of the best known and most easily recognized constellations in the northern sky. The association of this constellation with a bear has been made by several quite isolated cultures in different parts of the world.

Callisto started her career as a divinity from Arcadia, in ancient Greece, where the bear cult thrived. (Arcadia takes it name from the Arkades, the bear people; Arcas is clearly a bear name as well.) Evidently, sacrifices to the bear goddess took place at a sacred place on Mount Lykaion, the highest point in Arcadia. While out hunting one day, Arcas pursued a bear which, unknown to him, was his mother in one of her many bear incarnations. He chased her into the forbidden sanctuary on Mount Lykaion and Zeus caught him. As punishment, Zeus set them in the sky: Callisto as Ursa Major, Arcas as Ursa Minor, where they can chase each other perpetually.

The Inuit

The Inuit have an elaborate explanation for the constellation of the Great Bear, which sounds like a variation of the Bear Mother story (see page 166). They tell of a woman who chanced upon a house filled with bears, which by day took on human form, and at night put on bear robes to hunt. The woman lived with the bears for a time, until she yearned to see her husband once more. The bears allowed her to leave, making her swear never to tell of their existence, but she finally betrayed them. The bears, with their uncanny intelligence, were aware of what she had done. One of them broke into her house and bit her to death, and her husband's dogs in turn attacked the bear. Then, as if by magic, suddenly both bear and dogs burned with a blinding brilliance, and rose to heaven as a constellation of stars. In the sky, the dogs continually pursue the bear.

The Hindus

The Hindus' name for the constellation is *rakh*, which in Sanskrit means "bright." According to Hindu mythology, the Great Bear keeps the universe continually whirling, causing the seasons to come and go, the crops to quicken, and the rains to fall. But the Great Bear can just as easily bring drought and famine, for he is also in control of the wind and weather. Being the progenitor of all that is vital on Earth, the Great Bear also safeguards the passage of a newborn child from the womb. In imitation of *rakh* revolving in the sky, the Hindus paint red spirals on the walls of houses where childbirth is imminent, to make certain that the child turns in the proper direction as it travels down the birth canal. Bearing a child and getting one's bearing cannot be separated, etymologically, from the Great Bear itself.

The Ostyaks

Most stories explain how the bear rose to the heavens, but never bring the bear back down to Earth. For the Ostyaks of western Siberia, though, the bear traveled easily between the two. Born of a union between the Sun and the Moon, the bear began in the sky as a heavenly force. One day, when Father Bear went out hunting, Little Bear sneaked out of the house to explore and accidentally stuck his foot through the floor of heaven, catching a glimpse of the people who were living below. He convinced his father, Numi-Torum, to allow him to visit them.

Numi-Torum placed Little Bear in a golden cradle and gently lowered him by a silver chain onto a honey blossom that was growing on Earth. His father gave him precise instructions: he was to punish the bad, reward the good, and instruct everyone in the sacred bear ceremony. At the conclusion of the first grand ceremony, Little Bear filled his backpack with silver, and Numi-Torum pulled him back up into the heavens, where he still dwells.

Soul mates

Whirling around the sky, the bear imitates the flight of birds. Birds and bears are soul mates, the bear symbolizing the immortality of the soul, the bird an emblem of the flight of the soul. Both birds and bears can be counted on as weather forecasters: certain birds disappear in the winter, just like bears, to reappear with the coming of spring.

On Earth, many tribes hunt the bear and ceremonially slay the animal, to ensure their own spiritual regeneration. A similar hunt takes place in the night sky, ensuring that the world will forever turn on its axis. Ursa Major, Ursa Minor, and the constellation Boötes, play the roles of prey and pursuer, chasing each other around the North Star. As the hunt goes on, it drives the sun from its hiding place, bringing forth light and warmth. For the Iroquois and Micmac people of North America, the Great Bear was pursued by seven hunters, all of whom were birds.

Both prey and predator, the bear lives at both ends of the food chain, and dwells at both ends of the universe—in the heavens and underground. It is the bear that keeps the heavens turning, and the seasons changing. The bear is regenerated in the sky by going into hiding when the sun rises, and is regenerated on Earth in darkness when the sun leaves—heaven and Earth in perfect balance.

▲ The handle of this fighting knife, carved in the late nineteenth century, shows the profile of a bear. It was made by the Haida people on the west coast of British Columbia, Canada, who believed that the strength of the bear spirit would aid the owner of the knife.

◄ The importance of the bear as one of the spirits of the Tlinget people on the west coast of British Columbia in Canada, and of southeastern Alaska, is confirmed by its presence on this totem pole, along with a wolf and an eagle.

THE BEAR IN LITERATURE AND ART

BARRY SANDERS

The bear dominated the beginnings of Western literature, but by the sixth century BC, the Bear Mother had all but disappeared from the scene. Her son had grown up and taken over. Unlike his gentle and nurturing mother, the Bear Son fed on fierceness in this new heroic age. A warrior and an adventurer, he journeyed from place to place establishing his reputation by performing acts of superhuman strength until he finally succumbed to his toughest foe: Christianity.

The classical scholar Rhys Carpenter makes a convincing case, through linguistic and mythological evidence, for the Bear Son as model for Odysseus, the first adventurer in Western literature. Odysseus' son, Telemachus, referred to his grandfather as Arkeisios, a name derived from a word meaning "bear-like." The ancestral line sprang from Cephalus, who mated with a she-bear to produce Arkeisios, "the Bear Son." Carpenter, in his book *Folk Tales, Fiction and Saga in the Homeric Epics*, insists that the *Odyssey* constitutes a remarkable chapter in that most pervasive story, the circumpolar account of the bear–human marriage:

"The bear names cluster so close about Odysseus that it would be mere blindness or obstinacy to overlook their clue. The central theme of the sacred legend of Salmoxis with its distant homecomer with his treasure, who feasts the chief citizens in a great hall, who disappears unexpectedly and is given up for dead, who sleeps in an underground chamber, who suddenly returns to the amazement of all—does not this supply the thematic material also for the *Odyssey*?"

SCANDINAVIAN AND ICELANDIC SAGAS

Because of his roots deep in the folk soul, the Bear Son elevated the Scandinavian and Icelandic sagas of the seventh and eight centuries AD from mere stories into tales charged with cosmic significance. In Finland's oldest poem, "The Kalevala," the bear figures at the very heart of the creation story. Meilikki, mistress of the forest, received a piece of soft wool from the heavens, and placed her treasure in a maple basket which she suspended by a golden chain from a fir tree branch. The wool gradually developed into Otso the Bear, protector of the Finnish people, who in return worshipped him as their god.

Certain warriors revealed their deep affinity with Otso by changing into bears during bouts of particularly fierce fighting. They had the gift of *hamrammir*, the ability to shape-shift. Some highly charged warriors, like the hero of the saga of Hrolf Kraki, Bodvar Biarki, could call up their bear spirit and send it forth to overpower the

enemy, in what the Icelandic sagas called *hamfarir*, "a shape journey." Even if a warrior did not possess such a gift, he could still summon up bear courage by putting on a bear pelt and then fight with the "berserker's rage." *Ber* derives from the

The Bridgeman Art Library

▲ This ornate silver-gilt model of a brown bear was made by Christopher Ritter in Nuremburg, Germany, around 1580.

► The legendary ferocity of European brown bears is captured in this melodramatic work by the artist Paul de Vos, painted in the seventeenth century.

Musée des Beaux Arts/Giraudon

root word meaning bear, and *serk* means shirt. Berserkers demonstrated their ursine might in two notable Icelandic sagas: Grettir the Strong and the Ynglinga Saga.

So powerful was the bear's spirit that merely holding a bear pelt would afford protection. In a saga called the Landnamabok, a Lapp warrior named Orvar-Odd held a bearskin up in the air in the midst of battle. On seeing it, the enemy beat a rapid retreat.

BEOWULF AND THE ROMANCES

In England, the Bear Son story is retold as "Beowulf," an eighth-century poem, the first substantial work of literature in English. The hero's name translates literally as bee-wolf, or bear. Like the bear's magic paw, Beowulf possessed the strength of 30 men in his hand alone. In one episode, Beowulf swam underwater all day in order to take on a wicked monster, and was given up for dead by his friends. He then returned from the fen, shocking his fellow warriors with a miraculous return from the underworld.

Beowulf passed his remarkable powers on to the greatest king of all England, Arthur, whose name in Latin, Arcturus, means bear. Arthur proclaimed his strength to the world by flying a bear from his banner.

Even in the romances, young lovers were well aware of the benefits of bear power. The hero of one of the most popular romances, "Guy of Warwick," finally won the object of his heart's desire, Felice la Belle, by proving himself in a long series of adventures. He triumphed in large part because he had adopted the bear as his totem animal.

▲ A mosaic pavement from Kissuf in Israel, dating from AD 576 to 578, depicts a warrior raising his sword while using his shield to deflect an attacking bear.

THE BEAR MOTHER AND THE BEAR SON STORIES

THE BEAR MOTHER STORY

A group of girls venture out to the woods one day to gather huckleberries. One of the girls has the job of singing to warn the bears of their presence, but instead she talks and chatters incessantly. A bear overhears, and takes her babbling as mockery.

As the girls head home, the chatterbox, trailing at the end of the pack, steps in some bear droppings. She complains about her bad luck, and at that instant two young men approach her. Since it is getting dark, and she might lose her way, they invite her to come home with them. She follows them, complimenting them on their lush bearskin robes.

They arrive at a house high on a mountain side. Everyone in the house is wearing bearskin robes, too. A mouse runs up to the girl and warns her that she has landed in a bears' den. A young bear, the son of a chief, tells the woman: "If you marry me, we will spare your life. If not, you will die."

She lives on as the bear's wife. When her captors leave the house, they don bearskins and act like animals. In the winter, she finds herself pregnant, and in a cliff cave she gives birth to twin boys, half-human and half-bear.

One day the Bear Mother's brothers come looking for her. She notices them in the valley below and rolls a snowball down the hill to reveal her presence. The Bear Husband knows he must die. He tells her and their Bear Sons how to kill him and teaches them the songs and prayers that will ensure good luck to their tribe. He wills his skin to Bear Mother's father, a tribal chief. With instructions from the Bear Sons, the two brothers slay Bear Husband, and take Bear Mother and her two sons back to the human world. Great rejoicing follows, the humans singing songs and eating the slain bear.

Bear Sons put away their bearskin robes and become great hunters. They know instinctively where to find bear dens, how to set snares, and how to sing all the ritual songs. Later, when their mother dies, Bear Sons put on their bearskins once again and return to live with the Bear People. But the tribe has had good fortune in their hunting ever since.

THE BEAR SON STORY

In the forest, a married woman meets a bear, who convinces her to return with him to his cave, where they live together. She gives birth to a son who is much hairier and stronger than other children. Very soon, Bear Son yearns to have his mother take him to see the human world. He pleads with her, but she refuses as she had given her word to remain as the bear's wife. Finally, however, she agrees to escape with her son back to her human husband, who adopts the bear-child.

Bear Son receives a marvelous weapon—either a knife or an axe—which he learns to use with great skill, and embarks on a series of wild adventures. In the main adventure, Bear Son finds a house in the woods, filled with food and soft beds. He pauses long enough to eat his fill and then falls asleep. The owner of the house returns— usually a dwarf, sometimes a giant—and accosts Bear Son. Bear Son wounds the monster, who then escapes into the underworld.

Bear Son follows the monster down a deep well and through a long passage, where he is beset by many disasters. Finally he reaches the underworld, a magnificent and wealthy place.

Bear Son kills the monster, rescues a beautiful princess who has been held hostage, and returns to Earth, taking her with him. His family greets him with great rejoicing and celebration, since they thought him dead. He marries the princess and they live with the great wealth he has carried back from the underworld.

◄ A lidded dish in the form of a bear with a woman on its back, nursing twin bear cubs. Made by the Haida people from the west coast of British Columbia, Canada, it illustrates part of the Bear Mother story.

THE MEDIEVAL VIEW

The medieval Church saw great symbolic potential in taming the bear. While the Church embraced the female bear with its nurturing care as a symbol of Christianity itself, the male bear—the Bear Son in all its unbridled vigor—came to stand for the wildness of the unrepentant pagan. If a surly bear could be domesticated, then surely a pagan could be brought to heel.

This struggle is delightfully played out in "The Masquerade of Orson and Valentine," a poem dating from 1488 about two brothers who were separated at birth. Valentine wound up at King Pippin's court, while his brother roamed the woods for years until he, too, stumbled into King Pippin's court. Valentine tamed his brother's wild nature with love, and christened him Orson, as a reminder of his bearish past. Valentine was named after two saints who embody the idea of Christian love. The story points out that each of us has a feral side and a civilized side, and that integration is possible only by exercising unconditional, forgiving love.

Sometimes, though, the tales about taming bears seem to go too far. For example, in the fables of Aesop, popular in the Middle Ages and into the Renaissance, Bruno the Bear was stupid, even downright gullible. The medieval bestiaries refined the caricature, portraying the bear as slow-witted, because of the inordinate amount of time he spent sleeping.

But even if Bruno played the fool, he always acted humanely. Unlike his rival, Reynard the Fox, who was all guile and deceit, Bruno felt compassion for others and forgave those who played pranks on him. Ultimately, he wins our sympathy. In Bruno, we can already begin to see the winsome nature of those cute and cuddly characters, Winnie-the-Pooh and Paddington Bear.

THE BEAR IN NORTH AMERICAN LITERATURE

As the real bear vanished from the woods in the nineteenth century, he grew larger and larger in fiction, hunted down by storytellers and stretched beyond all recognition. In 1841, Thomas Bangs Thorpe published a story entitled "The Big Bar of Arkansaw." Big Bar was a braggart who told how "the greatest bar was killed, that ever lived, none excepted." The hunt turned into an impossible affair, Big Bar explained, giving the story a sense of epic importance, for "the bear was an unhuntable bear, and died when his time came." To explain why he didn't kill the bear, Big Bar piled it on, amazing his audience with the bear's immensity: "I made a bed-spread of his skin and the way it used to cover my bar mattress, and leave several feet on each side to tuck up, would have delighted you. It was in fact a creation bar, and if it had lived in Samson's time, and had met him, in a fair fight, it would have licked him in the twinkling of a dice box."

Lauros-Giraudon

The bear makes one last, valiant stand to assert his ferocity. William Faulkner tells the story best in *The Bear*. Faulkner uses a monstrous bear, Old Ben, to stand for the wilderness itself. But this time the Bear Son (Ben means "son" in some languages) is not the hunter, but the hunted. By the end of the story, he is dead: not merely killed, but murdered by a crazed man, Boon Hoggenbeck, who was protecting his dog. Neither a participant in a ritual, nor a god in a celebration, this bear meets his ignominious end hacked into pieces by a hunting knife. In his final moments, he has lost all identity and simply "falls like a tree."

◀ This sixteenth-century French miniature of a lion-king holding a chained bear symbolizes the victory of François I over the Swiss.

▼ The story of The Arkansaw Bear was one of the tall tales about bears published in the nineteenth century.

Frontispiece—Arkansaw Bear.

▼ A nineteenth-century German illustration of a fairy tale in which two children, like Hansel and Gretel, find a house in the woods, but it is inhabited by a bear, not a witch.

J.L. Charmet/AUSCAPE International

▶ In one of the best-known fairy tales, Goldilocks enters the home of the three bears. Like humans, these bears are clothed, stand on their hind legs, and, in the case of Baby Bear, cry with remorse.

Somebody's been eating my porridge!

11p
Winnie-the-Pooh
The Year of the Child

▲ Winnie-the-Pooh, one of the most popular bears in literature, was the creation of British author A.A. Milne, and was drawn by Ernest H. Shepard. Pooh and his friends were celebrated on a postage stamp issued in Great Britain in 1979, "The Year of the Child."

▶ Baloo, the wise bear from Rudyard Kipling's *The Jungle Book*, was reduced to an animated cartoon, and then commemorated on a postage stamp.

BHUTAN 5CH

© MCMLXXXII Walt Disney Productions
Walt Disney's THE JUNGLE BOOK

▶ In the tale of "Beauty and the Beast," the beast was sometimes depicted as a bear, as in this rather genteel version.

THE FAIRY-TALE BEAR

In nineteenth-century fairy tales the bear was both fierce and nurturing—Bear Mother reunited with her son—but the animal once again bore little resemblance to the real thing. These bears existed to make a strong moral point, neatly done in the tales where the bears organized themselves, like no other animals, into families: mother cooking, father working, and children playing. Sometimes, as in "Goldilocks," humans intruded into this world and upset the delicate ursine balance. In the earliest version of "Goldilocks," published in 1837, the intruder was an old woman who, when caught in the bear's bed, escaped by jumping out of a window. When order returns at the end of the story, the bears feel stronger, safer, and more united.

In a genre of fairy tales known as animal-as-groom stories, a beautiful girl on her wedding night discovers that her husband has been transformed into an ugly bear. This situation is explored in stories like "East of the Sun and West of the Moon," and "Snow White and Rose Red." If the bride did not bolt from the bed in fear and disgust, but treated the monster with compassion, he would change back into a handsome prince.

By the century's end, society seemed so corrupt to many writers that they used animals to expose human foibles. Humor might make reform more possible and palatable, a strategy that Rudyard Kipling adopted in *The Jungle Book*, published in 1894. Even in the jungle, it seems, laws are necessary to promote order and harmony. For Kipling, only one animal exhibited enough stature to administer those laws fairly and humanely: Baloo the Bear. But Kipling made him a caricature. For all intents and purposes, the bear had died. His ursine spirit had drained away.

THE BEAR TODAY

Dozens of poets in the twentieth century—from Robert Frost to Gary Snyder—have tried to resuscitate the bear to a full and vigorous life. For the most part we have lost the ability to make spiritual contact. Winnie-the-Pooh and Paddington, the two most dominant bears of the twentieth century, only emphasize our spiritual distance from the real animal. Pooh lounges and fusses and has a variety of modest adventures; Paddington lives in a suburban home and could not be more middle-class. Both charming, certainly, but in the end all stuffing and fuzz. To make contact, we feebly attach radio transmitters to a few remaining grizzlies, but even then we are probably not on the same wavelength.

PICTOGRAPHS IN CAVES

According to some archaeologists, bears inspired the earliest cave scratchings. Over 35,000 years ago, prehistoric peoples "signed" cave walls, these experts argue, by observing the

▲ Dating from between 10,000 and 17,000 years ago, this engraving on a stone found at Péchialet in the Dordogne, France, is thought to depict two men dancing with a bear.

◀ Rajput horsemen of the sixteenth century are shown hunting bears from the relative safety of horseback.

way bears scratched trees. Alexander Marshack, in *The Roots of Civilization*, states flatly that "the Master Bear was the first teacher of the animal art and where he touched was a proper place for animal magic."

In scores of pictographs, dating between 30,000 to 10,000 years ago, archaeologists have discerned, in an array of scratches, representations of bears. One such important example comes from Péchialet in the Dordogne, France, which experts have interpreted as two men dancing with a bear. Marshack interprets another, from Mas d'Azil, also in France, showing a masked dancer before the paw of a bear, as "aspects of a bear rite, ceremony, or myth, with associated symbols and signs related to the bear story."

In a marvelous work entitled *Treasures of Prehistoric Art*, André Leroi-Gourhan compiled an inventory of Paleolithic cave art in Europe, toting up the number and kind of each animal depicted. The bear depictions show unusual characteristics. In the first place, most animals are shown paired, but not the bear (nor the rhino or lion). Leroi-Gourhan hypothesizes that this pairing indicates that early peoples saw most animals in a complementary way, male and female. But they presented the bear singly to indicate, perhaps, its androgyny—displaying characteristics of both maternal care and paternal fierceness.

Second, most animals appear in various locations in the caves, but the bear always appears in the rearmost part of the cave. Historians of prehistoric cultures suggest a connection between caves and the inside of the head where dreams inscribe themselves. Carl Jung sees the bear as the animal of dreams. He considers sleep to approximate hibernation, where the sleeper can be healed if they dream of a bear: "The dreamer is falling into the abyss. At the bottom there is a bear whose eyes gleam alternately in four colors: red, yellow, green and blue."

Historians also point out that tunnel and cave could be considered analogous to birth canal and womb. The connections between bears and childbirth lie deep in language: both *bar* and *gebaren* are the Germanic roots for "bear" and "to give birth." Bears deliver their young mysteriously, underground, and it is that miracle that may be etched into the rear of the cave.

The back of the cave could also be considered a place of supreme respect, a well-hidden spot, where the bear can be safely preserved for ever. The bear is ultimately taunted out of hiding, goaded out of his den—"Hey Grandfather, come out"—only to be ceremonially slain. The cave drawing offers a counter to that rude removal, an indelible impression of bear presence.

◄ (Top) A bear carving on a house partition screen, 4.5 meters (15 feet) high, made in about 1840, from the home of Chief Shakes' in Wrangell, Alaska. The oval opening at the base of the screen provided access to a sacred room. The bear is the clan crest of the Tlingit people.

◄ (Middle) A bear hunt featured in a tapestry made in the mid-fifteenth century in Tournai, Belgium.

◄ (Bottom) In this painting entitled "A Close Call," by the American William R. Leigh, a hunter is saved from death by his friends and their pack of dogs.

► From the earliest times, humans have competed with large carnivores for resources and space. The fear humans felt for bears is emphasized by the large numbers of hunters and dogs shown killing a bear in this eighteenth-century painting by the Frenchman Charles André van Loo, entitled "The Bear Chase."

The Bridgeman Art Library

Christie's, London/
The Bridgeman Art Library

MYTH AND REALITY

The bear disappeared strikingly fast as a subject for the visual arts. Certainly by the Christian era, the bear no longer inspired the visual or the plastic arts to any extent. It simply lived elsewhere—in rituals, celebrations, and stories. Until the 1930s, the Ainu, of Hokkaido, Japan, celebrated the slaying of the bear (see page 160).

Occasionally, a ferocious-looking brown bear stood erect, in an eighteenth- or nineteenth-century painting, ready to strike some prey, or to slap fish from a stream, the artist determined to

義經四天王出世鑑之内　六郎

功臣　亀井六郎

亀井重清ハ紀伊國牟婁郡産萬夫
不當の偏歴勇士ありあり陸奥の曽武術修行み
牛若君若干義經の鏡み留足の佐藤
庄司元春ゲ信夫の鏡み近づいて無二の
諸司み義經み随身して彼國へ下向有

とときを北山山の狩獵み憤みぐれ

show all the tooth-and-claw harshness of the wilderness. Painted in exhaustive detail, the bear seemed to call forth the wilderness itself. The bear cannot help standing for something other than itself—think of the symbol of Russia, or the stock market term. The artist must struggle to catch the animal and not the myth.

For the great majority of people, the bear lived in the heart of the woods, an invisible but dangerous presence. Only the hunter was in a position to know the bear's true nature. No artist ever came close enough. For the hunter, the bear

was the ultimate trophy, requiring more skill, stamina, and courage to bring down than even the rhino or the lion. Faulkner was aware of that. But even in the kill, the bear took on mythic, heroic proportions. Something other than the bear itself, some abstract ideal—wilderness, fear, adolescence—died along with the animal. And that, too, Faulkner knew. The bear could be had best as a trophy, a badge of courage or macho determination. That's why, in the end, bears became a subject, not for the artist's brush, but for the taxidermist's knife.

▲ In contrast with European paintings, in which numerous humans and dogs were pitted against bears, "Kamel Rokuro and the black bear in the snow," painted by the Japanese artist Kuniyoshi in 1849, shows the bear in mortal combat with a single warrior, while spectators stand at a respectful distance.

◄ The bear has been the inspiration for this finely crafted bronze figure, inlaid with malachite and gilded.

▶ This painting by Leonard Alexis (1813–1892), entitled "The Route to Maladetta," evokes the terror that people on a lonely road in the wilderness would have felt about the possibility of being attacked by a bear. The dark mountains and the gathering storm clouds accentuate the sense of isolation and foreboding.

BEARS AS PETS, FOOD, AND MEDICINE

JUDY A. MILLS

In October 1991, a Korean-American was murdered in his New York City apartment, apparently for the bear gallbladders that he had in his possession. At the same time, bear gallbladders in some South Korean traditional-medicine shops were selling, gram for gram, at much the same price as certain varieties of heroin. China keeps thousands of brown and Asiatic black bears on farms for the purposes of "milking" their gallbladders of bile in order to supply the lucrative traditional-medicine market. The trade in bear gallbladders as medicine has put a price on the head of every bear on Earth—from the sun bear to the polar bear—making all bears worth a good deal more dead, or at least taken from the wild, than alive.

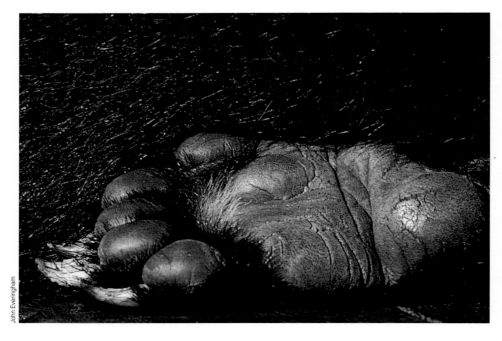

John Everingham

▲ Bear paws are in high demand in countries such as Taiwan, Korea, Hong Kong, and Singapore, for soup and other dishes. In 1990, one shipment of bear paws, representing around 1,000 dead bears, was seized in China, illustrating the extent of this illegal trade.

The bear trade is centered in Asia, where bears are popular as pets, and are used for food and medicine. Giant panda skins also have a market niche, bringing tens of thousands of dollars on the black market in a trade that continues despite the threat of the death penalty in China for killing a giant panda. Several Chinese panda traffickers have been executed and others are serving long prison terms, but the profits from one panda skin can mean instant wealth for the poor. Selling a single bear, or a bear gallbladder, can at least double a person's annual income in many Asian countries.

TAKING ONE'S BEAR FOR A WALK

Live sun bears are sought-after pets in some parts of Asia, selling for between US$100 and US$5,000 each. In Taiwan, owners walk their sun bears on leashes in downtown Taipei. In Thailand, good Buddhists buy sun bear and Asiatic black bear cubs at weekend markets not only because of the animals' cuddly likeness to puppies, but to earn merit in the afterlife. Their religious doctrine says taking in wild animals to give them food and

shelter is an act of kindness. Some pet bears in Thailand enjoy daily baths, blankets on chilly nights, taxi rides cross-country and fruit peeled for their pleasure. One beloved Asiatic black bear pet in southern Thailand received a full Buddhist funeral upon his death. But owners of pet bears usually find their bears an unwieldy burden as they grow increasingly large and strong. As a result, most bear owners are relieved to sell their adult bears when wildlife dealers come calling.

At this point, unwanted pets usually enter the food and medicine markets. In 1988, as many as 40 live bears—some of them former pets—were smuggled out of Thailand to South Korea, where their meat, blood, and gallbladders were used to fortify the Korean Olympic team.

BEAR-PAW STEW

In China and in those Asian cultures heavily influenced by the Chinese, such as South Korea, food is an economic indicator as well as a source of recreation and medicine. And among the wide range of Chinese delicacies, bear paw is said to be the most celebrated.

Bears appeared on Chinese menus during the Ming Dynasty, between 1368 and 1644. During the Ch'ing Dynasty, between 1644 and 1911, highly honored guests were served a 16-course banquet which included bear paw. China's emperors favored a menu of 100 dishes, again featuring bear paw. Imperial cookbooks include recipes for stewed bear's paw and bear-sparerib casserole. Culinary lore says the meat of the left front paw is the sweetest and most tender as it is the paw bears use to take honey from bees' nests. Eating bear paw is said to prevent colds and strengthen the body for overall good health. Bear meat generally is used to treat rheumatism, weakness, and beri-beri, and to strengthen both mind and body.

As certain Asian countries such as Taiwan, Singapore, Hong Kong, and South Korea have become more affluent, bear-paw dishes have become popular both as a status symbol and as a tonic. Prices run as high as US$700 or more per

John Everingham

serving. In 1990, braised bear paw even appeared on the menu at a restaurant in the Seoul Hilton in South Korea. South Koreans and Taiwan Chinese go on group tours to Thailand to have bears killed to order before their eyes for gourmet banquets, from which the gallbladder is taken home as a prized souvenir. High-ranking Communist Party officials in China are said, despite a legal prohibition, to dine on bear paw whenever possible.

THE TRADE IN BEAR GALLBLADDERS

Despite the immense favor of pet bears and bear-paw stew, it is the trade in bear gallbladders that drives the market for bears and threatens the survival of Asia's bear populations in equal measure with habitat destruction. The bile salts found within the gallbladder are a prized medicine, most often taken in a dried crystalline form. Anyone who tours Taipei's traditional-medicine district, Hong Kong's Kowloon shopping mecca or the widely dispersed apothecaries of Singapore will see dried bear gallbladders, which resemble large figs, displayed by the score. Black-

market vendors in the open-air markets of China peddle bear gallbladders by the kilo. Wholesalers of traditional medicines in South Korea travel to North America to buy their bear gallbladders fresh from bears killed before their eyes.

In the early 1990s, prices for bear gallbladders in Asia ranged from US$1 per gram to US$210 per gram—the latter at par with China White heroin. Prices tend to be lower in poorer countries that supply the gallbladder trade, such as Malaysia and Thailand, and much higher in wealthy consumer countries such as South Korea, Taiwan, and Japan. Perhaps because they have only about a dozen of their own bears remaining in the wild, South Koreans seem willing to pay the most and will go to the greatest lengths to obtain authentic bear gallbladders. They are known to shop for them as far afield as the remote forests of Canada and Russia, leaving in their wake whole bears dead, with nothing but their gallbladders missing.

The wide variation in prices for bear gallbladders and the extreme measures some Asians are willing to take in order to ensure the

▲ A Buddhist monk in Thailand feeds a sun bear kept on a chain as a pet. Buddhism teaches that people can earn merit by bringing bears and other wildlife in from the wild and looking after them.

John Everingham

▲ Bears are esteemed as pets throughout Southeast Asia, and are occasionally doted upon, even to the extent of women handfeeding them special treats.

▶ Sun bear cubs can be bought on the black market in Thailand and elsewhere in Asia. People tend to keep them as pets until they are approaching adult size, and then sell them for their parts when they become difficult to manage.

C. Servheen

authenticity of the product stem from the preponderance of fakes on the market. It is, in fact, impossible to distinguish the gallbladder of a bear from that of a cow or pig without laboratory analysis, although some specialists in Asian medicine say they can do so by sight, smell, or taste. As a result, fake gallbladders have flooded the market. Of course, this makes sense, considering there are fewer than one million bears on Earth and more than one billion potential consumers of bear parts as medicine.

MEDICINAL PROPERTIES

In Mandarin Chinese, bear gallbladder is *xiong dan*. It is known in Cantonese-speaking Hong Kong as *hang tan*, as *ungdam* in Korea, and as *yutan* or *kuma-no-i* in Japan. While the uses of bear gall-bladders as medicine vary slightly from country to country throughout Asia, most prescriptions grew from the ancient tenets of Chinese medicine. Bear gallbladders may have been added to the Chinese pharmacopeia as much as 3,000 years ago, and prescriptions for bear bile first appeared in writing in the seventh century. Traditional Chinese medical texts also prescribe the meat, brain, blood, bone, and spinal cord of bears for their curative powers. The gallbladder is the most prized part of the bear, however, ranking with rhino horn and wild ginseng as one of the most powerful medicines in the Asian pharmacopeia.

According to Chinese teachings, bear gallbladder is a "cold" medicine, and it is prescribed to cool the "heat" of certain illnesses and extinguish the "fire" of toxins in the body. Symptoms of "heat" include dry throat, red face, dry stools, rapid pulse, fever, headache, thirst, and profuse perspiration. "Fire" can manifest itself in such things as burns or liver disease. "Cold" medicines such as bear gallbladder lower body temperature, reduce inflammation, and detoxify.

A common misunderstanding among non-Asians is that bear gallbladders are used as an aphrodisiac. In actuality, they are prescribed for far more serious concerns such as cirrhosis of the liver, jaundice, high blood pressure, diabetes, severe burns, and heart disease. They are also used to treat hemorrhoids, eye infections, swellings from sprains, and tooth decay.

Another common assumption among Westerners is that any health benefits derived from using bear gallbladders are simply a function of mind over matter—"the placebo effect." Unfortunately for bears, the medicinal properties of their bile have been clinically proven. The active ingredient in bear bile is ursodeoxycholic acid (UDCA). While UDCA is found in the gallbladders of many mammals, including humans, it occurs in significant quantities only in the gallbladders of bears. Japanese scientists isolated UDCA from bear bile in 1927 and found a way to synthesize it from cow bile in 1955. Today, synthesized

J.A. Mills

UDCA is used by Western physicians as a means of dissolving gallstones without surgery. Clinical trials still underway are documenting UDCA's efficacy in treating cirrhosis of the liver, hepatitis, blood cholesterol, and various other life-threatening disorders.

It would seem that synthesized bear bile could be the answer to saving bears in the wild. Synthesized UDCA is pure, cheap, and reliable. According to traditional medicinal teachings, however, these attributes are not necessarily desirable. The tenets of Chinese medicine say that the advantage of obtaining medicines from nature is that they are diluted and buffered to the proper

strength, and are in the most suitable medium for assimilation by the body. In terms of expense, it is human nature to value objects of greater price and scarcity, such as gallbladders from a vanishing species.

A good example of this phenomenon comes from South Korea, where synthesized UDCA is a best-selling biomedicine and costs only a few cents per tablet. In the 1980s, one of South Korea's few remaining wild Asiatic black bears, which are strictly protected under national law, was killed by a poacher. After the culprit had been arrested, the government sold the bear's gallbladder at a public auction for US$64,000!

▲ In Thailand, sun bear cubs sometimes live as pampered pets in peoples' homes, using all the amenities, such as the drinking fountain.

MEDICINAL AND DECORATIVE USES OF BEAR PARTS

Spinal cord: Said to treat deafness and giddiness and, when rubbed on the scalp, is believed to promote hair growth and remove dandruff.

Fat: Grease from the back of the bear is said, with prolonged use, to strengthen the mind, prevent hunger, lighten the body and promote longevity. It is also prescribed to remove numbness, to treat feverish colds, to blacken hair and encourage its growth, to cure baldness and ringworm, and to remove pimples and blackheads. If bear fat is used as lamp oil, however, it may weaken the eyes and cause them to lose luster.

Hide: Popular as rug or wall hanging. Small pieces used as good luck charms in Nepal.

Head: Popular as a decorative item.

Blood: Used to treat nervousness in children.

Bones: For rheumatism and nervousness in children.

Claws: Used in countries like Nepal and Indonesia as good luck charms.

Meat: Bear paw is one of Asia's most popular, expensive and exotic dishes. Good for rheumatism, weakness and beri-beri accompanied by paralysis. Chinese texts say it should not be eaten by anyone with a chronic disease. Both canned and fresh bear meat are popular novelty foods in modern Japan.

Gallbladder: This is the bear's most coveted part. It is primarily the demand for bear gallbladder that has made the bear a commercially valuable commodity. The gallbladder is used to fight diseases of the liver, heart, and digestive system, as well as to treat conjunctivitis, blindness in newborns, infant colic, hemorrhoids, and tooth decay.

Paw: Wards off colds and generally strengthens and revitalizes the body.

▼ The killing of bears for their parts, gallbladders in particular, is a major threat to their survival.

C. Servheen

FARMING BEARS

China is now farming bears for their bile to meet the demands of its traditional-medicine industry and, Chinese officials say, taking pressure off wild bear populations. Bile is "milked" from live bears through a catheter surgically implanted in their gallbladders. As many as 8,000 or more bears currently live on such farms in China—probably more than remain in China's forests. Though the milking process is not particularly painful, it is stressful for the bears, most of which live their entire lives in small, cramped cages. Farming bears for their bile is also practiced in North and South Korea, and some Japanese have expressed interest in starting up bear-bile farms in Japan.

While bile-milking is an interesting development, as an aid to conservation it is fatally flawed. Chinese scientists are turning their research efforts away from the needs of wild bears in favor of helping bear farms increase birthrates and maximize bile production. More importantly, by supplying the demand for bear bile with farmed bile, the Chinese are further institutionalizing the perception of bears as a commodity, rather than as wild species with value in and of

THE POWER TO HEAL

BARRY SANDERS

The native people of North America and the people of India alike look to the bear as the great physician of the woods. In the United States, Pomo doctors wear bear pelts in their healing ceremonies; in Tewa, the word for "doctor" is synonymous with "bear." The Cheyenne treat diarrhea with a plant called "bear's food"; the Crow use something called "bear root" to help cure sore throats. The Potawatami call the root of any healing plant "bear potatoes." The Ojibwa call their cure-all simply "bear medicine."

Indians concoct a healing mixture called

karadi panchamritham—meaning "bear delicacy made of five ingredients" in Sanskrit—which they discovered from watching the plant-gathering habits of bears. They sometimes allow the mixture to ferment to increase its potency. This, too, might come from watching bears, for they passionately devour fermented grain. An etymological connection is certainly suggested between "barley," "beer," and "bear."

The long list of plant names in English that refer to the bear attest to the animal's wide herbal knowledge:

bearbane • bearberry • bearbine • bear's breeches
bear brush • bear claw • bear clover • bear corn
bear's ear • bearfoot • bear's garlic • bear grape
bear grass • bear's head • bear huckleberry
bear moss • bear oak • bear's paw
bear's tail • bear's tongue • bear's weed
bearwood • bear's wort

Bear's ear (*Arctotis*)   Bearberry (*Arctostaphylos alpina*)

Bear's breeches (*Acanthus spinosus*)

themselves. Finally—and of the greatest significance—farmed bile has not stopped the demand for gall-bladders from wild bears, as many devotees of traditional medicine feel farmed bile is inferior to that found in nature. It is said that the diet of wild bears, combined with the exercise they take, result in better bile salts.

The bears of the world cannot sustain the commercial pressures placed upon them for much longer. The only hope of curbing demand lies in better laws, more effective law enforcement, and in education. Of these options, education holds the most promise, since no law can be enforced without the support of those that are asked to abide by it. In other words, bears will remain a commodity as long as Asian consumers view them as a commodity.

Education programs aimed at altering Asian perceptions of bears will have to take into account the traditions of each separate bear-consuming culture. If such cultures do not alter their attitudes towards bears and the consumption of bear byproducts, entire populations of Asian bears will disappear before anyone has had a chance to document their habits and habitats. The world's other bear populations could easily follow in their wake—marking a decline similar to that of the commercially valuable rhino.

For now—as evidenced by the 360 kilogram (800 pound), trophy-class black bear found dead in a Canadian national park with nothing but its gall-bladder missing in the fall of 1991—bears living wild and free are worth far less than the sum of their commercial parts.

C. Servheen

▶ There are farms in North Korea in which bears spend their entire lives in small cages, being periodically milked for their bile, from permanently implanted catheters. This type of farming is extensive in China.

BEARS AND PEOPLE IN NORTH AMERICA

STEPHEN HERRERO

Thousands of years of coexistence have led bears and people to mutual respect and avoidance, except when a person has a gun and goes bear hunting. Bears seldom attack people, probably because those which tended to do so have been killed. When interactions between bears and people do occur, they are usually peaceful, but the few that are not keep people alert. Species identification can be important if you spot a bear in the distance. If it is a black bear you may choose to move closer to better watch the animal, still keeping a respectable distance. If it is a brown bear (a grizzly), you should keep at a considerable distance—a minimum of several hundred meters—and you should have a clear idea of what you are going to do if the bear comes your way.

Viewing bears cannot necessarily be thought of as an interaction, in that ideally the bear will be unaware that it is being watched, but watching bears from a distance is a wonderful way to get to know them. A typical sighting of a North American black bear or a grizzly bear might begin with a person spotting a dark or light-colored dot on a hillside several hundred meters away. Under such circumstances, only by using binoculars can one be sure that the blob actually is a bear.

FEEDING HABITS

Generally, the bear will be feeding or resting. If it is springtime, the animal is likely to be grazing on grass shoots and broadleaved plants. If it is a grizzly bear, it may be digging for the sweet roots of *Hedysarum* or other species. This can be quite a show of power and reveals some of the unique characteristics of this species. Root digging is not a mechanical act, but rather the careful application of force in a particular manner. The grizzly digs on a slope and peels back the turf—rather like lifting a carpet—to look underneath. Once a root is unearthed the bear uses its individual digits to manipulate and clean it before eating it.

In spring, bears do not eat only vegetation. Black and grizzly bears will often hunt newborn elk, deer, or moose, locating them either by sight or by smell. Grizzly bears will thrust their large black noses into the air, inhale deeply, and then continue on, frequently stopping and sniffing until they either scent or see their prey. If it is newborn, the bear might walk over and kill the calf without it even rising, but if it is old enough to run, a wild chase might erupt. Bears can run for a kilometer or two, attaining speeds of around 50 kilometers (30 miles) per hour. Once an elk calf is a week old, or even less, it is faster, but not smarter than a bear. Running on rough terrain usually gives the bear an edge, and within seconds it may have a high-protein meal. Anyone who has watched such a chase will be aware of the speed, power, and maneuverability of bears.

Mark Newman/Tom Stack & Associates

AT PLAY

Perhaps a bear's essence is best revealed when it is playing, and such behavior can also be watched with reasonable safety, from a respectful distance. Cubs often play for many minutes at a time, and trees are frequently part of the playground of the more arboreal black bear. On one occasion, two black bear cubs were seen playing with a small pine tree. One cub would climb it and bend it slightly groundward, then the second cub would climb the tree, causing the top to bend nearly to the ground. One of them would then jump off and the other would swing back and forth, clinging to the tree until the second one climbed the tree again. They repeated the process over and over. Even old, male grizzly bears enjoy playing. An older male was once seen crossing a snowslope in spring. He paused briefly to look down the slope, and then launched himself onto it, rolling and sliding down. At the bottom he shook himself, looked back up the slope, the top of which was hundreds of meters above him, and then climbed up and slid down again.

BLACK BEARS

The most abundant species in North America is the black bear, but do not be fooled by its name—black bears can range from near white or bluish to their common color phases of black, brown, blond, or cinnamon. Elsewhere in the book their identifying characteristics are given in detail.

Black bears are characterized by their great tolerance of people. This means that a hiker seldom has to worry about a black bear charging out of the bush, intent on attack. When attracted to campsites or

▼ In wilderness areas, and when left alone, most brown bears avoid or ignore people. However, people sometimes come far too close to take photographs. This can make a bear attack because it feels threatened.

183

roadsides by people's food or garbage, black bears will usually tolerate people nearby without incident. Nonetheless, about 95 per cent of the injuries afflicted by black bears have occurred in campsites or on roadsides where the bears have become accustomed to foraging. People sometimes hand-feed black bears and then walk away when the tidbits have been eaten. Occasionally a bite from the bear will result. Or a person sleeping in a tent might have their buttocks bulging against the side of the tent and a black bear searching for garbage might take an exploratory bite. While a few people have been injured in campsite or roadside encounters, many black bears have been killed, since they tend to become more aggressive when searching for food as their experience with people grows.

▼ Wherever the preferred habitats of grizzlies and humans overlap, such as in river valleys and around lakes, contact between the two is likely. Young grizzlies tend to investigate human property, which often results in their being shot because of their potential danger to people.

Johnny Johnson/Animals Animals/Stock Photos

Michio Hoshino/Minden Pictures

When confronted by a black bear under such circumstances, it is usually best for the people concerned to behave aggressively, shouting and walking towards it. The bear will usually move away. If it has already invited itself to your picnic and is enjoying what you hoped you would, it is best to let the bear continue. Once a black bear has begun to dine it is difficult to persuade it to leave until it has eaten everything.

What if you are hiking on a trail and you suddenly come upon a black bear? Most black bears will run as if pursued by demons, but some will direct their aggressive repertoire at you, behaving as if they will tear you to pieces if you do not back off. This is normally far from true, but impressions do count. The bear will snort, or breathe in and out loudly, and may then swat the ground, or come hurtling at you like a freight train. Stand your ground and the true nature of the drama will be revealed, with the "bluff charge" ending abruptly in front of you. The bear is telling you to leave. It does not want contact any more than you do. Accord is reached by increasing the distance between the two parties. Even females with cubs will usually flee, or they will only act aggressively, without

attacking, generally while their cubs are climbing a tree to get out of harm's way. After a while, the mother bear may climb the tree too, or she may just stand beside the trunk. In the rare instances in which campsite or roadside encounters do lead to people being injured, such injuries are almost always minor, resulting in a few stitches at worst.

Given how much black bears gesture and "shout," it is amazing how reluctant they are to attack. A search through all available records in North America since 1900 has revealed accounts of only a few incidents in which female black bears defending their young have attacked people.

There are times, however, when the black bear can be a serious threat to humans. Records show that about 35 people have been killed by black bears since 1900. In at least 90 percent of these cases it is probable that the bear was treating the person, or people, as prey. This type of incident has typically occurred during the day, the victim being a hiker. Generally no sounds or bluff charges were made by the bear—it simply attacked. A person faced with such a bear must stand and fight: if they play dead, the bear is likely to keep on chewing. Rocks, stout sticks, or knives can be used as weapons. People in

a group, if they act together, can usually deter an attacking bear. A few of these sorts of attacks have occurred at night, when the victims were sleeping. They have usually taken place in remote areas where it is likely that bears have had little experience with people. Perhaps, as these areas become settled, black bears with these tendencies will be killed.

Support for this view comes from the fact that in all of the national parks of North America—where there are many black bears and many visitors—only one person has ever been killed by a black bear. However, particularly aggressive bears are regularly eliminated from national park populations.

Bear in mind that there are over half a million black bears in North America. Once in a while a person is killed; each year, people kill tens of thousands of black bears.

BROWN BEARS

Everyone knows how dangerous brown bears are. Or are they? There is no doubt that the grizzly, the monarch of North America, goes out of its way to avoid people. Experiments in Yellowstone National Park have shown that when researchers approached as close as possible to grizzlies that were wearing

▲ At places such as the Katmai National Wildlife Reserve in Alaska, migrating salmon and anglers are abundant. Bears have access to a plentiful supply of fish so are seldom attracted to campsites for food. They have become used to humans passing by and ignore them, provided people do not approach too closely.

treated as prey, and were at least partly consumed. It is hard to imagine anything more horrifying than being pulled from one's tent by a huge animal intent cn eating you. It is ironical that our own management practices led to such incidents. Now that food and garbage are much less available to grizzlies, attacks have decreased substantially. Nonetheless, habituation of national park grizzly bears to hikers is still a problem in some places.

▲ Keeping food in a tent is dangerous because it practically invites a bear to enter and take it. If such a visit occurs during the day when no one is there, only damage to camping equipment results. If a bear enters at night while people are sleeping, either the bear or humans are likely to be harmed.

radio-collars, about 90 percent of the time the bears fled without exhibiting any aggressive behavior. In the remaining cases they fled after acting aggressively. Not one attacked. Each year hundreds of thousands of people walk in grizzly country and only a few are injured by these bears.

The circumstances associated with injuries caused by grizzly bears are quite different from black bear incidents. During the 1960s and early 1970s camping and hiking increased dramatically in North America, and garbage often accumulated around campsites. In cases where grizzly bears attacked campers, research has shown that the bear's experience was a predisposing factor. Almost always the attacking bear had a history of feeding on people's food or garbage, or had otherwise become used to humans. Most people killed in such attacks (and there have been no more than 10) were

Habituation of grizzlies to humans is not always dangerous. At McNeil River Falls in Alaska, small groups of people, led by expert guides, have come on foot to view bears for over 20 years. Sometimes one of the 30 or more brown bears that may visit the site at one time will approach to within 10 meters (30 feet) of a person. Despite this, no one has ever been injured and few bears have been shot. This outstanding safety record has been achieved because the guides make sure that people's actions are predictable, and the bears are given no opportunity to associate people with food.

The predictability that occurs at McNeil River Falls does not exist in most national parks or wilderness areas where grizzly bears are found. This sets the stage for possible surprise encounters. When a bear discovers a person within 50 meters (165 feet) or less, it will usually flee at top speed.

▼ Once brown and black bears become accustomed to feeding on garbage, it is difficult to discourage them. Because they come to associate humans with food, such bears may become angry and injure or even kill a person who does not feed them.

PEOPLE IN POLAR BEAR TERRITORY

IAN STIRLING

Being completely carnivorous, polar bears interact with humans in a way that differs from other bear–human confrontations. When polar bears attack humans, it is probably because the bears are hungry, rather than that they have been surprised at close range.

Even though humans come across polar bears much less fequently than they do other species of bears, a higher proportion of interactions results in the bear being killed because people in polar bear habitat carry firearms much more commonly than they do further south. From 1965 to 1985 in the Northwest Territories and Manitoba, Canada, humans were injured or killed on

P.L. Clarkson

Norbert Rosing

19 occasions, while in only a 10 year period ending in 1986, 230 polar bears were killed.

Most polar bear attacks occurred between midnight and 6.00 a.m., when people were asleep. This parallels the diurnal pattern of polar bears hunting seals: they tend to hunt at night and sleep during the day. The great majority of polar bears that attack humans are thin subadult males. Such animals are inexperienced and therefore less successful at hunting, and are more likely to be driven from their kills by larger bears. Faced with the choice between attacking something that smells as strange as a person and starving to death, they will opt for the former.

Typically, when a polar bear attacks a human, the final charge comes from close range and the person is usually unaware of the animal. The best protection is to have a clean, well lit camp, to keep dogs and people monitoring the approach of polar bears, and to deter bears as soon as they are discovered. They should not be given the opportunity to feed on anything. If bears associate an unpleasant experience with human contact, they are likely to avoid people in the future.

▲ During experiments to test various deterrents on polar bears near Churchill on the western coast of Hudson Bay, it was necessary to observe the bears' responses at close range. A cage was built to protect the observer which ensured that no bears became endangered through irresponsible behavior on the part of a researcher.

◄ Polar bears have no natural predators and frequently approach human settlements or campsites.

Richard P. Smith/Tom Stack & Associates

Sometimes, however, it will act aggressively rather than flee. Acts of aggression may include chomping its jaws together, making loud noises, and swatting the ground. It may even charge. There is little in people's everyday experience to prepare them for the adrenalin rush associated with a huge grizzly hurtling towards them, apparently intent on attack. Fortunately, such charges are usually bluffs.

Today, sudden encounters, especially with female grizzlies protecting their young, are the most common circumstances associated with injury. When injury is inflicted by a bear in such a situation, it usually requires a stay in hospital, although fatalities are rare. Only one person has been killed in an encounter of this sort with a grizzly bear in a North American national park.

When hiking in grizzly country it is important to be alert and knowledgeable, and to constantly assess your circumstances. By learning where bears are likely to be found at different times of year, and by taking note of field sign associated with their presence, one is in a better position to

avoid surprising them. Clearly, the fresher the sign, the greater is the chance of a bear being nearby. By making a good deal of noise when traveling through areas where you suspect bears might be hidden, you can warn them to move off before you are threateningly close. Making a noise may also make you feel more confident and in control.

If you are hiking and, despite all your precautions, a grizzly attacks, the chances are that injury will be minimized if you play dead, keeping your face and body turned towards the ground. By remaining still, on the ground, you will be seen as less threatening by the bear.

Even if you visit grizzly country a good deal, and take few precautions, your chances of injury are slim. In national parks that have grizzlies, injury rates from grizzly bears are about one person per one to two million visitors. Injury rates to persons hiking and camping in back-country areas vary from about one per 5,000 to one per 1,000,000 backcountry-user days.

▲ A bear that allows a person to come this close has probably been fed on garbage and may become annoyed if it is not fed. It will be the bear, not the person, that is punished if there is a conflict.

SAFETY IN BEAR COUNTRY

PETER CLARKSON

Although the chances of having a close encounter with a bear are extremely low, the large size, strength, and speed of bears make even the most ardent outdoor enthusiast cautious when in bear country. In the past, the perceived threat to human safety was handled by people destroying any bears that they came across, in many areas disastrously affecting bear populations. Now that we know more about bears and their ways, we know how to live with them. Peaceful coexistence is essential if bears are to survive.

Learning about bears

As bears may hibernate for five to six months of the year, they have to feed, reproduce, and find a winter den site in the remaining six to seven months. Survival depends on their storing enough energy to carry them through winter sleep and other lean times, so they are constantly on the lookout for nutritious foods. Finding food is especially important to female bears with offspring as they must feed both themselves and their cubs.

Learning about bears and their habitat will enable you to identify potential bear country, and being able to identify bear sign (tracks, droppings, diggings), and plants that are favorite bear food, will alert you to their likely presence. Knowing how bears relate to each other and to other wildlife species will help you understand how bears relate to

Michael Leach/Oxford Scientific Films

people. For instance, a female bear feels that anyone who approaches is a potential threat to her cubs, which is why females with offspring are so aggressive in close encounters.

Safety precautions

Do not travel or camp alone in bear country. Groups of three or more people are advisable, as there are more eyes to see the bears or evidence of their being in the vicinity. The more people there are, too, the more noise there is to warn a bear so that it can leave the area. The size of the group itself will often prevent a bear from approaching closely.

Be alert when traveling or camping in bear country, and look out for bears or bear sign. When hiking, choose trails with good all-round visibility as it is much easier to avoid a bear spotted at a distance than one encountered at close quarters. Likewise, camp where you can keep an eye on the surrounding area. Bears are unlikely to approach a campsite if there are few bushes nearby, and it is also easier to see them coming if they do choose to investigate.

Keep your campsite and yourself clean to reduce odors. Bears are attracted to all sorts of smells: food, garbage, latrines, fish, oil products. Garbage should be stored in airtight containers, burned, or placed in bear-proof containers. Careful planning before a trip can help reduce garbage through the elimination of unnecessary packaging and the preparation of only the amount of food needed, to avoid leftovers. Never bury garbage as bears will simply smell it and dig it up.

Store food and equipment in locations that are inaccessible to bears. In areas with large trees, a pack may be suspended between two tree trunks or branches. Some camps provide bear-proof storage

containers. The trunk of your vehicle or the inside of a motorhome are usually safe storage areas. Backpackers can use bear-proof food containers to prevent bears eating their supplies.

Never feed bears or other wildlife; animals that find food or garbage at a campsite soon come to associate camps and people with things to eat. Ask people familiar with the area about past bear activities and if there have ever been problems with bears. Never approach bears to take close-up photographs; it is not worth risking your life or the life of a bear just for a photo.

Detection methods

People are often the best detection system around. They can survey the area around the campsite or hiking trail and see if there are any bears nearby. In some situations, such as a site where a geological field party is working, a bear monitor may be used. The monitor's role is to watch out for bears and to warn the group if one is approaching.

While dogs can be effective at detecting approaching bears, only dogs trained for that purpose should be used. The inexperienced family pooch is best left at home.

Various detection systems can be used to warn of a bear approaching. A backcountry hiker may use a small portable trip-wire fence. Such fences range from simple one-strand ones that when struck will ring a bell, to more complex electrical systems that set off alarms. Systems such as light beams, infrared scanners, microwave detectors, and sonar detectors are available from security companies, and are of varying effectiveness. When choosing a system, be sure it is low maintenance and appropriate for your situation.

Once a bear has been detected, the situation can be assessed and safety precautions taken. If possible, moving everyone to a safe place should be the first priority. A decision on whether to leave the area or to deter the bear can then be made, depending on the situation.

Deterring bears

In the short term, deterrents protect people and property from immediate danger. In the long term, they give bears an unpleasant experience and prevent them from associating people and campsites with food. Deterrents reduce the number of problem bear situations.

Bears generally approach a campsite out of curiosity and most will leave quickly once they discover that there are people around. It is important, however, that they are deterred from a site the first time they are seen in the vicinity, as it is much easier to prevent a bear from becoming habituated to human foods than to break habits once they have been formed. Usually shouting, banging pots, or waving your arms about are all that are needed. In some cases a bear may not make off immediately it has seen people at a campsite or on a trail, but will circle downwind to pick up a scent to confirm what it has seen before leaving.

Not all bears will leave an area after determining that there are people around. Research on bear deterrents has shown that while noise makers such as cracker shells, boat horns, flares, or warning shots will frighten away some bears, others may become habituated to noise makers after they have heard them repeatedly, if they do not associate the noise with pain. These bears may need to be hit with a 12 gauge plastic slug or a 38 millimeter rubber baton before they will go away. If they approach within 6 meters (18 feet) capsicum spray can be used. Some deterrents may have to be used several times before the bear moves off. Whenever possible, a deterrent should be used from a safe position. In some cases a back-up firearm loaded with lead slugs may be needed.

The type of deterrent to use will depend upon the situation and what best suits the person using it. Firearms are prohibited in certain areas, such as national parks, and in any case many people feel uneasy carrying or using firearms. If a firearm is used, a 12 gauge pump-action shotgun is recommended, as it can be used to fire cracker shells or plastic slugs and also to fire lead slugs as a last resort. Anyone intending to use a firearm should take a firearms safety course.

Not all bears can be deterred. Old bears incapable of acquiring their natural foods and young bears which have not mastered foraging skills, may, in desperation, aggressively pursue food at a campsite. Unfortunately, some of these bears have to be destroyed. If it is necessary to kill a bear, it should be done as quickly and as humanely as possible, after all other options have been considered.

Bear-proofing campsites

Bears have a strong sense of smell and even the cleanest campsite may smell like a smorgasbord to a bear. To prevent bears from entering a camp or cabin, several precautions can be taken. All food, garbage, or odorous materials, such as plastic fuel containers and oil cans, should be stored in bear-proof containers. At permanent camps, attractants can be stored in bear-proof buildings or caches. A building can be bear-proofed by placing shutters on the windows and doors and ensuring that bears cannot enter the building. In some cases bear-boards (boards with nails sticking through) can be used to protect doors, windows, and building corners.

Temporary campsites can be protected by placing all bear attractants in caches raised off the ground and inaccessible to bears, or in bear-proof containers. Resealable 205 liter (45 gallon) drums can be used for storing food. Tents or buildings that cannot be bear-proofed should be emptied and left open to allow bears to enter without causing damage. If bears do not find food they are likely to leave. Electric fences, ranging from permanent multistrand structures to simple portable ones, are effective in keeping bears at a distance.

◀ In most national parks, signs and brochures advise people on how to minimize the dangers involved in a possible encounter with a bear.

▼ When in bear country, keep a constant eye open for bear sign. The large claw marks in this front paw print indicate that it was made by a brown bear.

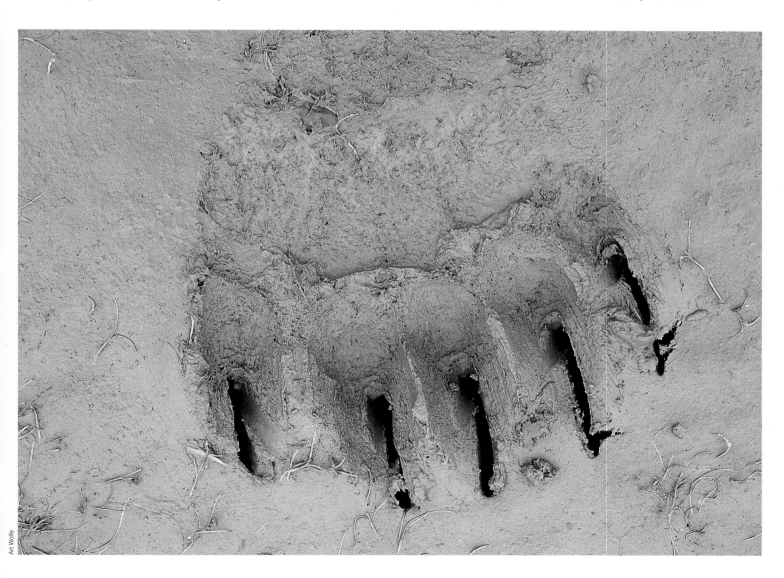

Art Wolfe

BEARS IN ZOOS

JOHN SEIDENSTICKER

As every zoo director knows, most people the world over recognize bears, and they generally come to zoos expecting to see bears. Bears were regular members of menageries long before institutions known as zoos came into existence. Today, there are about 1,100 bears living at the 400 zoos and related institutions that use the International Species Inventory System (ISIS) to track their animals. Many more bears live in smaller zoos and in other facilities that do not register their animals in ISIS.

EXHIBITING AND MANAGING BEARS

Bears are escape artists. The smallest miscalculation or mistake on the part of a keeper or exhibit designer can result in a bear getting out and about. Zoo lore and literature are rich in stories of bears escaping from their enclosures. A particularly appealing tale is the one about an American black bear and a sloth bear that made nightly forays into the grounds of a large American zoo, climbing back into their enclosures before dawn. Signs

In the traveling menageries of the nineteenth century, the wellbeing of bears was a low priority. Provoking the animals was a popular form of entertainment.

Giant pandas are rare attractions in zoos outside China, a few having been given as diplomatic gifts of great importance to zoos in Western countries.

indicated that this had been going on for some time before the exhibit was modified to prevent these nightly outings. The National Zoological Park in Washington, in the USA, has had its share of bear escapes; most have been mid-day affairs, when someone forgot to check a lock. These break-outs tell us a good deal about a bear's frame of mind. Bears are extremely curious and observant; an unlocked door is immediately spotted and investigated. If they find a weakness in an enclosure they will work at it until it gives.

Pits were once the standard zoo enclosure. The famous bear pits of Bern in Switzerland were used, off and on, from 1450 to the mid-1800s. Carl Hagenbeck, the great zoo innovator of early this century, inspired the design of the bear exhibits and holding areas that are still used in most zoos today. Hagenbeck introduced mountains of rock-

simulating concrete, concealing dens and passages, with the bears separated from the public by dry moats. In some zoos, these exhibits were first separated from the public by bars. Recently, deep dry moats have replaced bars.

Because bears can live on a generalized diet, they have been relatively easy to maintain in zoos, but their enclosures have usually been barren and empty. There are two reasons for this. Firstly, bears' curiosity and strength tends to result in their damaging objects placed within their reach. Secondly, the need to control parasites resulted in the building of concrete-floored enclosures that were easy to clean. In these sterile, hard environments some bears develop stereotypic behaviors, such as incessant pacing. Recent advances in medications to control parasites makes it possible for floors to now be mulch and grass.

▼ Following brown bears, polar bears are the second most abundant bears in zoos around the world. Their popularity stems, in part, from the fact that almost everyone recognizes them instantly.

Andi Cole

Bettmann/Hulton

Old exhibits can be modified and new exhibits designed to contain species-appropriate furnishings that promote functional behaviors in bears, and methods of feeding can be adopted that encourage natural feeding behaviors.

TRENDS IN ZOO BEAR NUMBERS

Using records from the National Zoological Park in Washington as an example, trends can be traced in zoo bear populations throughout the twentieth century. Until 1975, when the old exhibits were modified, the National Zoo maintained about 30 bears a year. Today, in about three times the area, the zoo maintains nine bears. Providing more space per bear is certainly one way to improve their quality of life.

Over the years there has also been a change in the types of bear species in the collection. Early on, the zoo exhibited mainly brown and American black bears, with a few Asiatic black bears and polar bears. By 1945, the trend towards maximizing the number of different species

▲ Brown bears were among the first bears to be held in captivity because they were widely available in western Europe at the time that zoos and menageries were developing.

◄ At the Zoological Gardens in Regent's Park, London, brown bears were a major attraction as far back as 1835.

▲ A traveling giant panda goes first class. Special cages are built and the bears are shipped by air to keep travel time and stress to a minimum.

◄ A giant panda entertains himself by investigating his reflection in a pool.

▼ Instead of bars and steep-walled holes in the ground, such as this, bear pits in modern zoos use deep, dry moats to create a less oppressive atmosphere.

exhibited was in full swing, and all the bear species, with the exception of the giant panda, were on exhibit. The zoo would have had the giant panda too, if it had been possible to arrange it. Giant pandas were eventually added to the collection, with a good deal of fanfare, through a gift from the People's Republic of China in 1972. As recently as 1975, the zoo exhibited all the species except the Asiatic black bear.

Today, zoos are turning away from the pursuit of multiple species and high numbers towards programs that focus on improving the quality of life for zoo bears. The National Zoo today maintains two giant pandas, three spectacled bears, three sloth bears, and one brown bear. Brown bears and polar bears still comprise more that half the zoo bears reported in ISIS , but increasingly

ENRICHING THE LIVES OF BEARS IN ZOOS

ALISON AMES

Bears have been held in captivity since ancient times, and sadly there have been few improvements in their living conditions over the years. They are usually kept in concrete-lined pits containing few, if any, movable objects to distract them, and without soil or sand to walk, play, or rest in. Their field of view is commonly restricted to the area within the sides of the pit and they are seldom provided with a place where they can avoid public view or the immediate company of their cage mates. Little consideration is given to their natural social behavior; for example, many zoos keep bears in male–female pairs, whereas such pairing hardly ever occurs in the wild outside the breeding season. Most captive bears are fed a limited diet of prepared food which requires little effort to eat. Under such conditions, many of them behave abnormally.

Originally designed for ease of maintenance and safety, bear pits do not cater to bears' basic physical and psychological requirements. Recently, however, many zoos have altered their day-to-day practices in caring for bears in order to create a more stimulating environment for them within existing facilities. Improved feeding routines have been established, objects have been provided for bears to investigate, and modifications have been made to existing facilities.

Changes to feeding routines include prolonging mealtimes and making feeding more interesting for the bears. For example, instead of receiving prepared meats, fruits, and vegetables, they are now being given a wide variety of whole-food items, such as meat on the bone, entire carcasses of small animals, shellfish, and whole fruits. All these require the animals to use their paws, claws, and teeth. Food delivery has also been altered so that the bears have to spend time foraging. In addition to their main meal, they are now given chopped fruit and vegetables, chopped meat, raisins, and currants. These are scattered throughout the enclosure so that the bears have to walk around in order to feed. Various types of embedded foods, such as meat frozen in blocks of ice, or food enclosed in plastic containers, stimulate the animals to use their manipulative skills. Feeding which requires activity of this sort occurs several times a day, in order to keep the animals alert and busy for longer periods. The bears' main feed occurs first thing in the morning, so as to reduce stress associated with the anticipation of food.

Bears are intelligent animals and they need opportunities for diversion within their barren enclosures. Some zoos now provide them with objects such as traffic cones, boat fenders, hosepipes, old rubber boots, and plastic containers, giving the animals an outlet for their naturally investigative behavior. Logs and leafy branches are also made available to them both for food and as play items. Once they have stripped off the bark and leaves, bears enjoy bouts of rough-and-tumble play with the remaining wood. In order to maintain interest and novelty, keepers tend to introduce certain objects and remove others on a daily basis. Bears are generally fascinated by such playthings, and are not always destructive. At times they play with the objects carefully and deliberately, and in some instances have created complex games with them.

The provision of large tree trunks, grassy areas, and pits of sand, soil, bark litter, or pebbles enables bears to behave much more naturally than they could in an empty concrete pit. All species of bears, including the polar bear, can climb, dig, build day beds, and forage with their paws and muzzles. It is these basic behaviors which need to be stimulated in captive animals. In future, bear enclosures should be designed so that their inhabitants can behave as naturally as possible.

◄▲ Innovations in the design of zoo enclosures provide bears with healthy and stimulating environments.

G.C. Kelley/Photo Researchers Inc.

◄ Bears have highly developed manipulative skills for investigating their habitat in order to find food. They will amuse themselves for hours if given novel and reasonably indestructible playthings.

▼ Rocks and concrete mounds have been added to some bear pits in an attempt to make the surroundings seem natural. However, with no trees to climb and no objects to play with, this sun bear is just plain bored.

zoos are turning their attention to the lesser-known bears of the tropics—the sloth bear, the sun bear, and the spectacled bear. An advantage for zoos with these bears is that they remain active all year, while brown and black bears go through lengthy periods of winter sleep, when they are not visible to visitors. The natural history of the northern bears is now well known through extensive field studies. Little is known, however, about tropical bears and zoo observations can make important contributions to our understanding of these animals.

BREEDING BEARS IN ZOOS

Much information on bear gestation periods, litter sizes, breeding seasons, and longevity comes from records maintained on zoo bears. With the notable exception of the giant panda, breeding bears in zoos has been relatively easy. However, improving cub survival has been a major challenge.

Wayne Lawler/AUSCAPE International

Consider the environment in which a female polar bear and most female brown bears give birth, and in which the cubs spend the first few months of life. Maternity dens are cool, dark, quiet, and undisturbed. In a zoo, however, even if the female is locked away in a den, there are the other bears coming and going with their scents and calls; there is the noise of maintenance

workers and keepers going about their rounds; the lights in the grounds are turned on and off; and often there are the noises and vibrations of the pumps and filters that clean and cool the water in the pools. In short, there is a great deal of disturbance. Unsurprisingly, the key to successful rearing of bear cubs appears to be to keep disturbances to a minimum. By adopting a strategy

of secluding females and cubs, zoos have been able to greatly improve the rate of cub survival.

Many zoos throughout the world are now joining together to foster joint bear-breeding programs. The survival of some bears, such as the tropical species, is so severely threatened that the maintenance of zoo populations may be the only way they can be preserved.

▲ Logs lying in a bear pit enable bears to lie out of sight of each other and provide surfaces for them to investigate.

◄ (Top) There is little in this cage to stimulate the sun bear held in it. In such circumstances bears often pace relentlessly.

◄ Black bears are excellent climbers and make extensive use of trees standing in their enclosures.

HYBRID BEARS

JOHN SEIDENSTICKER

The description and classification of species is important in the study of the diversity of nature. Ernst Mayr has pointed out that the number of definitions of species, reflecting different concepts of species, is virtually unlimited.

Early this century, the "big brown bears" were particularly puzzling to the taxonomists sorting through the specimens arriving at the Smithsonian Institution's Museum of Natural History from the remote corners of North America—the west, northern Canada, and Alaska. But this was not the first time that C. Hart Merriam, the scientist engaged in trying to make sense of the bears, had faced tough taxonomic problems. The big brown bears, found living throughout so much of North America, Asia, and Europe, were unquestionably closely related, but bears from different areas differed in size and in coat color. When all was said and done, Merriam concluded that there were 87 named kinds, including species and subspecies, in North America alone, and he placed them all in the subgenus *Ursus*.

▲ This hybrid from a brown–polar bear cross has the blocky head of a brown bear and the larger feet and longish hair on the lower body of a polar bear. The light color over the head and neck may hint at the first changes that occurred when polar bears evolved from brown bears.

Bears were a very popular exhibit at zoos, and all these big brown bear species created a major problem for another branch of the Smithsonian, the National Zoological Park in Washington, DC, and all the other zoos that were trying to decide which big brown bears to place together in order to breed. Early on it was learned—sometimes through deliberate efforts, and sometimes because one bear found a way to get in with another during the breeding season—that the subspecies and species that made up the big brown bear group would breed easily both with one another and with the brown bears from Asia and Europe. These matings also produced fertile hybrid offspring.

The prevailing taxonomic wisdom at the time was that mobile animals, with well-developed geographic species-isolating mechanisms (factors that result in populations in different regions not having the opportunity to interbreed) rarely hybridized in the wild. Were the successful hybridizations of the brown bears in zoos a complete breakdown of reproductive isolation among bear species, and thus an unnatural situation, or did all these big brown bears really constitute a single species? This question was part of a larger intellectual argument at the time about whether it was possible to determine the "true nature" of species by these breeding "experiments."

The situation was compounded when it was discovered that brown bears and polar bears could successfully hybridize, for taxonomists had placed these bears in different genera: *Ursus* and *Thalarctos* respectively. Bears will be bears, as a 1950 report

from the National Zoological Park shows: ". . . the male found himself in the enclosure with the female, without the planned introduction on the part of the keepers. Nevertheless, the polar bear male was seen to mate with the Kodiak bear female, a brown bear from Kodiak Island in Alaska, and produced a litter of three hybrid cubs in the winter of 1936. To determine if the second generation hybrids were viable, two female hybrids were mated with their full brother, and two litters were born." The report goes on to speculate that brown bears and polar bears might be more closely related than the taxonomy placing them in different genera would indicate.

The whole question of how many species of big brown bears existed was not really settled until the 1960s. At that time, additional evidence and more refined definitions of a species and geographic species-isolating mechanisms led taxonomists to conclude there was, in fact, only one species of brown bear, to be called *Ursus arctos*, and that while brown bears and polar bears (*Ursus maritimus*) were closely related, they were certainly different species.

Planned or inadvertent introductions and the rearing of young of different bear species together have resulted in the following hybrid offspring: polar bear x brown bear; brown bear x American black bear; brown bear x Asiatic black bear; Asiatic black bear x American black bear; and sloth bear x sun bear. The hybrids that were produced by these crosses indicate that these bear species are closely related to one another. However, with their behavioral and geographical species-isolating mechanisms, interspecific hybridization appears to occur rarely in nature.

How do these hybridizing bears relate to the other two species of bear—the giant panda (*Ailuropoda melanoleuca*) and the spectacled bear (*Tremarctos ornatus*)? By using a variety of molecular techniques, including comparative chromosome morphology, researchers have placed the bears into three subfamilies: the giant panda, with 42 chromosomes, is alone in the Ailuropodinae; the spectacled bear, with 52 chromosomes, is alone in the Tremarctinae; and the brown bear, polar bear, American black bear, Asiatic black bear, sloth bear, and sun bear, with 74 chromosomes, comprise the Ursinae.

The hybrid bears were once useful in helping to sort out relationships among the bears, but they are now no more than a relic of our past. The idea that the "true nature of species" can be determined by breeding experiments has been overrun by advances in biological technology.

◄ There are eight bear parks in Japan which house a total of approximately 1,000 bears. Bears are often over-crowded, suffer from infections, and males sometimes die from wounds incurred from fighting over females during the mating season.

George Holton

Philippe Henry/Oxford Scientific Films

◄ Zoos are now recognizing that by maximizing the natural aspects of bear holding facilities, as in this bear park in Orsa, Sweden, the bears are healthier and behave more normally, and visitors respond positively.

SELF-SUSTAINING POPULATIONS

A primary objective of zoo management today is to manage captive populations so that they are self-sustaining and retain maximum genetic diversity. Currently, however, there are a significant number of wild-born individuals of some bear species in zoos. There are a number of reasons for this. American black bears are frequently captured as orphaned cubs or as problem animals and given to zoos, and this is also the case with some brown bears. Zoo bears also tend to live for a long time. For example, 30 percent of the polar bears in the zoo population are over 20 years old. These bears were captured before policies relating to self-sustaining populations of zoo animals were developed.

BEARS IN ZOOS			
Species	**Number**	**Percentage born in captivity**	**Number of zoos**
Giant panda	7	14	4
Sloth bear	60	72	24
Sun bear	107	47	42
Spectacled bear	112	88	39
Asian black bear	117	60	34
American black bear	149	42	62
Polar bear	256	60	85
Brown bear	271	77	104

Compiled by W. Sugg from ISIS, December 1991

BEARS IN CIRCUSES

ALISON AMES

Throughout the world, over the centuries, bears have been used for human entertainment. Roman sculptures depict gladiators fighting with bears and other wild animals as a spectator sport, and dancing bears and bear-baiting in Europe date back to ancient times. Bear-baiting was a popular spectacle which involved tormenting a restrained and sometimes blinded bear with pepper, sticks, and dogs. It was not until the middle of the nineteenth century that it was outlawed in Britain by an act of Parliament.

▲ A Roman ivory bas-relief from the fourth century showing the consul Aerobindus officiating at a circus. Bears can be seen performing in the ring.

▲ (Right) A 1920s poster for the famous Ringling Bros and Barnum & Bailey combined circus, advertising their bear act in which the animals rode bicycles, walked on stilts, and even roller-skated.

In the United States, the first wild animals to be displayed were native species, including bears, caught by farmers and hunters, who then trained the animals in a rudimentary way to attract the public's attention. By the mid-eighteenth century, traveling menageries were common along the eastern seaboard.

WORKING WITH BEARS

In most modern circuses, bears are trained to exhibit their dexterity and intelligence. These qualities, combined with the size and strength of the animals, make bears fascinating to watch, and both challenging and dangerous to train.

Trainers consider polar bears to be exceptional learners, but recognize that if one of them does not immediately understand what it is being asked to do, it may lash out. This temperament, in a supreme carnivore, makes them extremely dangerous to work with, and more trainers and keepers are killed by polar bears than by any other type of bear.

The Asiatic black bear is considered as dangerous as the polar bear, but for a different reason. Although smaller and not so strong, Asiatic black bears are exceptionally clever and will try to lead their trainer into making critical errors. They are quick to spot a mistake and take advantage of it, such as a trainer turning his or her back, or approaching an animal from the incorrect direction.

By contrast, American black bears in circuses tend to be treated like domestic dogs. On the whole, these bears have extremely even temperaments, respond well to training, and appear to appreciate and benefit from human company while in captivity.

Trainers place the various sub-species of brown bear between the Asiatic and American black bears as far as danger and ability are concerned. The Kodiak brown bear receives particular attention when being trained, because of its exceptional size and strength. Little is known about the training potential of the sloth, sun, and spectacled bears. Such bears are rare, and few circuses have owned them, but trainers who have worked with sloth and sun bears say they are difficult to train.

Mike Langford/AUSCAPE International

TRAINING TECHNIQUES

Circuses have recently come under close scrutiny with regard to animal training techniques. It is often assumed that in order to get animals to perform they must be drugged, castrated, have teeth removed, bones broken, or be beaten into submission. While incompetent trainers may resort to such tactics, reputable ones believe that if someone has to "modify" an animal in such a way to get it to perform, they should not have been working with that animal in the first place.

The trainer must establish confidence, respect, and friendly relations with the bears. Terrified bears cannot focus their attention and often become rebellious and savage. Training begins at the initial meeting of human and animal, with the bear learning to accept the person in close proximity. Potential attacks are usually prevented by using a whip, but the whip is only a deterrent, and will rarely come in contact with the animal. Whips are not used to make the animals perform.

Training is achieved by positive reinforcement and the repetition of desired behaviors. Verbal and tactile praise, and food are used as rewards, and

these rewards are delayed, by degrees, until the animal manages to complete several activities, one after the other. In the final stages of training, many bears may perform together. Since bears like predictable routines, each animal will have a set repertoire of activities and know when these should take place. Often, in performances, if one bear misses its cue, or does not perform as expected, other bears in the ring will correct it for the trainer.

BEAR CARE

Caring for bears is not always easy, given the amount of traveling undertaken by the average circus. The bears have to be caged when they are traveling, before camp has been set up, and on a daily basis in between training and exercise sessions. It is undesirable to keep animals locked in small traveling wagons, but the time a bear has to spend in a cage can be made relatively comfortable and interesting. Sufficient bedding material must be provided, and food must be carefully chosen. For many years circuses have been feeding their bears on bullocks' heads, which means the bears have to work with their

▲ Performing giant pandas have become the enormously popular centerpiece of the Chinese Circus. However, critics feel that because there are so few giant pandas remaining in the wild these animals should no longer be captured for circus work.

paws, claws, and teeth to feed, as they would in the wild. If they are fed first thing in the morning, the bears will be kept occupied until their first training or exercise session.

Many circuses set up exercise pens for their animals, which are important, and some also have mobile pools for their polar bears. Starting with a complex feed early in the morning, a daily routine for circus bears may include several training and exercise sessions, and well-trained bears are often taken for walks around the grounds like domestic dogs.

It is in circus owners' interests to have contented, healthy animals. If the animals are in poor condition, they will not perform well. However, caring properly for animals is expensive and time consuming, so careful consideration should be given to animal selection. If circus owners are not prepared to spend money on large, secure exercise pens, quality food, comfortable traveling wagons, and good trainers, they should not be keeping bears. Given that captive American black bears appear to appreciate the close relationships and extensive training of the circus environment, these seem to be the most desirable bears to train.

Giraudon

▲ Bear baiting in the Campo San Angelo, in Venice, painted by Gabriele Bella in the eighteenth century. Bears were sometimes blinded before being attacked by packs of dogs, whipped, and forced to "dance" on their hind feet.

▶ European brown bears in a traveling display, dance to the beat of a tambourine in the Loire Valley in France in 1905. This photograph was used as a postcard.

Explorer/Auscape International

DANCING BEARS

ALISON AMES

Training bears to dance is an ancient practice, and there are stories of dancing bears in Indian and Turkish folklore. The sight of a large animal rearing up and shuffling from one foot to another became so popular that the practice spread throughout Europe. In Greece and Turkey it is still common to see dancing brown bears, while in India dancing sloth bears can be seen on the streets of many major cities. These animals are generally owned by gypsies who capture the animals as cubs in the wild.

In most instances a female bear will have to be killed in order for her cub to be taken away. As soon as the cub is removed from the wild, training begins. While the bear is small it is easily trained by being pulled onto its hind feet by its ears or simply by having food held above its head. When the bear becomes bigger, more forceful training methods are employed. In Greece and Turkey trainers pierce a hole

through the animal's upper lip and/or nose and insert a ring, whereas in India the hard palate of the bear is often pierced. Trainers can then easily lead the bear by pulling on a chain attached to the ring.

Accounts from literature state that the dancing bears were often trained by placing hot trays beneath their feet. Music would be played during training sessions so that bears learned to associate pain in their feet with the beat of the music. As a result, whenever music was played or a tambourine was hit they would rear up and begin lifting their feet in anticipation of pain. Today most gypsies deny having used such methods, but at Smorgony in Lithuania there was a famous school for training bears which employed this technique. One room of the school was designed so that the floor could be heated to high temperatures. The trainee bears would have their hind feet lightly wrapped in cloth so that when they were led onto the hot floor they would rear up to

▲ Woodblocks from the Middle Ages showing bears being trained to perform.

▼ A Turkish gypsy with his three-year-old European brown bear named Mercan.

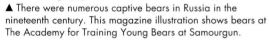

▲ There were numerous captive bears in Russia in the nineteenth century. This magazine illustration shows bears at The Academy for Training Young Bears at Samourgun.

▼ This bear in India has had the sinus bones of its nose broken to accommodate the insertion of a ring.

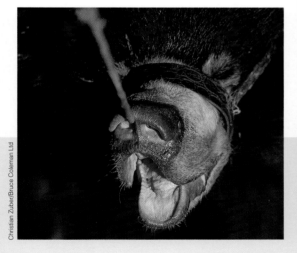

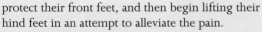

protect their front feet, and then begin lifting their hind feet in an attempt to alleviate the pain.

It is estimated that there are around 25 dancing bears in Greece, more than 100 in Turkey, and over 1,000 in India. It is now illegal to own wild-caught bears in all these countries, but the law is difficult to enforce. Often it is impossible to prove that the bears have been taken from the wild, and even if proof can be established, governments have nowhere to place confiscated animals. In Greece and Turkey there are plans to set up sanctuaries for confiscated dancing bears, but the only way the practice of training dancing bears can be eliminated is for tourists to stop paying to have their pictures taken with the animals.

STUDYING BEARS

ANDREW E. DEROCHER AND IAN STIRLING

Bears are not easy to study. To start with, they tend to be distributed at low densities over large areas in remote parts of the world. They are shy about contact with humans, and in forested areas they are difficult to see. In addition, they are large, powerful, and potentially dangerous if approached closely.

Early bear studies relied on observing animals from a distance, collecting droppings to determine their diet, and making deductions from their tracks, diggings, or animals they had killed. While a great deal of useful information was collected in this way, and such approaches are still in use, they have a number of severe limitations.

The breakthrough for studying large carnivores came with the development of immobilizing drugs and a system for delivering them that was safe for both animals and biologists. This made it possible to weigh, measure, age, tag, and put radio-collars on individual bears so that they could be studied over periods of several years.

▲ Park wardens move a drugged bear to safety, before applying ear tags and taking measurements. The bear is strapped onto a sled to ensure it is not injured while being dragged over rough terrain.

▶ When darting a bear captured in a foot snare, such as this polar bear along the western coast of Hudson Bay, Canada, it is best to do it from a safe distance.

Catching study animals is the first step in most bear research. A common method is to use a spring-loaded foot snare attached to a log or tree. A cable noose lying on the ground tightens around the bear's ankle when it steps on the trigger. The snare can be set using a bait, or it can be placed on a well-used bear trail. Traps can be made from pieces of large-diameter culvert pipe, sealed at one end and with a trapdoor at the other. The trap is baited with a favorite food: honey for sloth bears, seal for polar bears, and beaver for grizzlies. Once the bear enters the trap it closes the door on itself, as the bait is attached to a trigger release.

Small bears in snares and bears in culvert traps can be injected with drugs from a syringe attached to a short pole. Large bears are usually immobilized from a distance using a gun that fires a drug-filled dart. The dart contains a plunger that

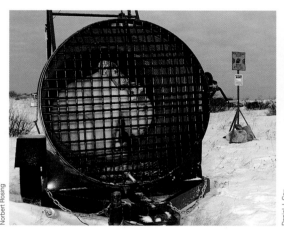

◄ (Left) Traps made with sections of culverts are used mainly for capturing problem bears around settled areas. Such traps are much safer than foot snares for both bears and people. The chance of a bear injuring itself is negligible and people who ignore warning signs and come close will not be injured.

◄ (Right) Although bear cubs are tiny at birth, they grow quickly. Female black bears are relatively docile and easy to drug in their dens, which makes it possible to study the growth rates of their cubs.

injects the drug into the bear's shoulder or rump upon impact. Such darts can be fired from a helicopter, making it possible to capture bears in open country.

It is safe to work with most bears within minutes of their being injected. After ensuring that the animal is breathing normally and lying comfortably, the following information is usually recorded: sex, length, chest girth, physical condition, head width and length, paw size, scar patterns, color, tooth wear, tooth breakage, and reproductive status (whether a female is accompanied by cubs, alone, or in breeding condition). Each bear is generally tattooed with an individual number on the inside upper lip, and a small hole is punched in the ear, through which a plastic or metal tag is attached. A small non-functional premolar tooth is extracted using dental tools. Later, in a laboratory, the tooth is examined microscopically in order to determine the bear's age.

Biological specimens can be collected to address specific questions. For example, to determine the level of toxic chemicals present in a bear, fat samples can be extracted from the rump with a small biopsy punch, or milk specimens can be obtained by injecting the hormone oxytocin to release milk. To examine blood chemistry, specimens are drawn by syringe from a vein in a back leg. Information on a female's pregnancy status can be determined from the progesterone level in the blood.

To estimate the number of bears in an area, mark and recapture studies are often used. They involve capturing a number of the population, tagging and releasing these bears, and then capturing another sample after the marked and unmarked animals have become mixed again. The ratio of marked to unmarked bears in the second sample is used to estimate population size.

Radio transmitters attached about bears' necks are also widely used and enable researchers to

DETERMINING A BEAR'S AGE

WENDY CALVERT

The age of a bear is worked out in the same way as the age of a tree—by counting annual rings. In the case of a bear, the relevant rings are found in the cementum tissue of their teeth.

Teeth are mostly dentin tissue, with enamel covering the crown and cementum covering the root. Both dentin and cementum grow throughout a mammal's life. Dentin slowly fills the pulp cavity at the tooth's center, and cementum grows outward, helping to anchor the tooth in the jaw. Such growth occurs all year, but at a seasonally uneven rate that leaves thin lines of slow growth alternating with wider lines of rapid growth.

▶ 1) A small, non-functional tooth is extracted from the bear's lower jaw and the tooth root is then softened in acid. 2) A thin section sliced from the center of the tooth is examined under a microscope. 3) Each year a thin layer of cementum is added to the outside of the root of a bear's tooth, so it is possible to determine the bear's age by counting the layers, known as annuli.

▲ Tooth cementum of a 27-year-old black bear (Ursus americanus), under magnification. Note, at the top of the figure, the diminishing spacing of annual lines from 5 to 27 years of age.

Grizzly Adams noted increments in the dentin of bear canines in the 1850s, but it was not until the 1950s, after a correlation between age and incremental layers was confirmed in other mammals, that bear teeth were first examined for age.

In bears, an annual layer consists of one thin, dark-staining line formed during the winter, and one wider, lighter line formed spring through fall. The preferred tooth is a first premolar, a small nonfunctional tooth just behind each canine. It is easily extracted from tranquilized bears or from jaws turned in by hunters. The calcium is removed by soaking the tooth in acid. It then becomes soft enough to be sectioned thinly, mounted on glass slides, stained, and examined under a microscope.

The ease of counting the layers and determining age varies among species of bears, and even among populations within a species. Because each layer of cementum tends to be thinner than the previous one, the lines in old bears are not as easy to see and are therefore more difficult to count. Despite this, an experienced reader can accurately determine the age of an old bear.

Ian Stirling

identify and locate individuals. Locations are obtained using an antenna either on the ground or in an aircraft, and recently satellites have also been used.

Radiotelemetry is commonly used to ask the most basic question: "What is the size of the home range and what habitats are occupied?" To answer this, a researcher obtains dozens of locations of several bears throughout the year, preferably over several years. Seasonal habitat-use patterns can be determined using satellite or aerial photos. Sometimes areas are examined for bear sign such as droppings, marked trees, trails, beds, and feeding areas (digging or damaged bushes). Researchers rely on analysis of feces to determine diet, but highly digestible food can go undetected and feces alone do not show the relative importance of different foods.

Bear behavior is generally studied through direct observation, the biologist watching individual bears interacting with each other and with their environment. Some researchers have studied bears that are used to having humans close by.

Ecological research on bears requires programs spanning five to 30 years, as incorrect conclusions

about habitat requirements, diet, or population dynamics can be drawn when short-term studies are used. Even in some of the longest studies conducted to date, such as those being made on grizzly bears in Yellowstone National Park in the United States and on polar bears near Churchill, Canada, researchers are only now beginning to understand their ecology. How grizzlies respond to a large forest fire, or how polar bears respond to years when there is limited food, can only be determined by following a population over many years.

Most researchers study live bears, but monitoring the sex and age of animals killed by hunters provides information on populations, and harvest records allow managers to determine the potential impact of hunting on populations.

As new research techniques evolve, scientists are quick to apply them to bears. DNA finger-printing is now being used to identify different populations and to determine cub paternity. As bear habitat shrinks and populations dwindle, scientists will need to use all their skills and every technique available to ensure that bears survive.

▲ When drugging bears near water, it is critical that the animal's nose does not go underwater, or it will drown. With experience, researchers can tell the difference between a bear that is safe to handle, and one that is resting and still capable of attack.

STUDYING HABITUATED BLACK BEARS

LYNN L. ROGERS

Black bears were once thought too dangerous to study up close, and there was concern also that close observation might cause bears to behave unnaturally. However, researchers in northeastern Minnesota have now found that wild black bears will accept and ignore human observers after a hundred or so hours of habituation.

The researchers initially fed the bears to attract them. At first the bears were wary and defensive, and even appeared aggressive, but the researchers learned to interpret aggressive behavior in terms of the bears' fear. No one was seriously hurt, and in time mutual trust developed. Some of the bears were captured and had radio-collars placed around their necks, so they could be found and observed at any time.

After a while the researchers stopped feeding the bears and began simply watching them as they went about their normal activities: foraging, napping, sleeping through the night, mating, nursing, playing, marking territories, chasing intruding bears, preying on deer fawns, and preparing dens. Remarkably, the bears learned to ignore the sounds and movements of nearby observers while remaining alert to the tiniest rustlings farther away.

Observations of the closely observed bears corresponded with the data collected on 103 radio-collared bears that had been tracked from trucks and airplanes in the same area in previous years. No differences were found in territory size, fecal contents, daily activity patterns, seasonal travel patterns, social relationships, winter sleep, and incidence of nuisance behavior. Both groups went about making a living from the forest, with the closely observed bears providing details that had been impossible to obtain from a distance.

For example, to learn what bears eat, researchers had previously relied on examining droppings, and had been concerned that they provided incomplete information. Close observation of bears confirmed this. Insect larvae, meat, and succulent plants turned out to be favorite foods, but are so digestible that they seldom show up in droppings. It was found that the bears were particularly partial to tent caterpillars, which are distasteful to most birds. Some habituated bears each ate up to 25,000 of them a day during caterpillar outbreaks.

Observations such as this are providing information, for the first time, on how much wild bears eat. One bear, aided by squirrels that had gathered nuts into piles for winter, ate over 3,000 hazelnuts in a day. Grass had previously been found in spring droppings but the species and habitat source could not be identified. Habituated bears revealed both, and showed the importance of grassy lowlands and wetlands to bears in spring. Fawn parts had been found in droppings, but it was not known whether the fawns had been killed or scavenged. Two habituated bears studied were observed to have killed 13 fawns between them in a year.

Such a killing occurred one morning when observers were accompanying a six-year-old mother and her two cubs. The bears were going from log to log in search of ant pupae when the mother began casting about on a new scent. Finding a scent trail, she loped up a wooded hill, sniffing the ground and air. The observers and the cubs ran with her. The mother found she had run too far, whirled, nudged past an observer, and leaped on a fawn that was bedded under the lower branches of a fir sapling. She killed the fawn, chased away the doe that appeared, and returned to the kill. She and the cubs

initially shared the milk that was curdled in the fawn's stomach. Within hours, they had cracked the last of the fawn's bones to feed on the marrow. At day's end, the mother led the cubs and a new set of observers a short distance across a bog to a hill where she bedded next to a gnarled old pine tree that the cubs could climb in case of danger. She nursed the cubs, snuggled down with them for the night, and fell asleep with the observers resting a few meters away. All her

Daniel J. Cox

actions, the number of bites she took of each food, and the habitats she crossed were recorded in notes or on a field computer.

Another bear is revealing the extent to which heart rate and temperature change with the seasons. For example, just before entering a den for the winter, she fell asleep with an observer's hand on her femoral artery, and her pulse dropped to only 22 beats per minute—less than one-third her summer sleeping heart rate.

Studies of habituated black bears are now being conducted in several locations across North America. They are showing how black bears react to predators, prey, biting insects, jets, unidentified sounds, rain, wind, snow, and strong sunlight. They are revealing the uncanny memories bears have of feeding locations, waterholes, refuge trees, and sources of danger. They are showing how bears' activities change with the seasons. They are documenting vocalizations, body language, scent-marking methods, social and territorial behavior, and even the killing of intruding bears. They are also documenting that mothers recognize and tolerate their offspring after the young become independent. Most importantly, the bears are providing information on habitat use and behavior that can help forest managers provide habitat for bears in the face of a growing human population.

▼ This young black bear, feeding on berries, ignores a human observer standing only a few meters away. Being able to watch black bears in this way is providing a wealth of information about their food habits.

THE FUTURE OF BEARS IN THE WILD

CHRISTOPHER SERVHEEN

O f the eight species of bears in the world, six are declining both in numbers and in range. This decline is directly attributable to increasing human populations and spiraling human resource demands.

Bears have an evolutionary history that dates back some 10 million years. During this time, many variations in the basic bear form have come and gone. Extinctions resulted mainly from competition between bear species, shifts in the availability of food, and catastrophic environmental changes. Today, the bears that remain must contend with humans in order to survive, and humans never lose in competition but to themselves.

THE PAST
The future for bears can best be understood by looking at the past. Bear range first began to be affected by humans some 3,700 years ago, when

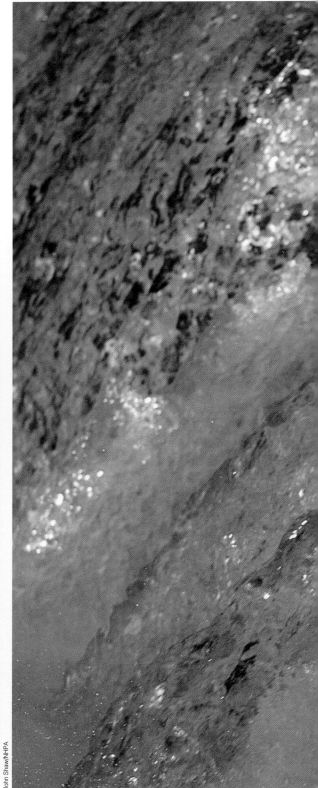

▲ Extensive hunting of brown bears in medieval Germany, as illustrated in this nineteenth-century hunting magazine, resulted in their extermination in eastern Germany by 1770 and in Bavaria by 1836.

▼ In Sweden, forests in brown bear country are being logged in relatively small blocks, leaving undisturbed areas as escape habitat for the bears.

the brown bear disappeared from what is now Denmark. The exact cause is not known, but it is likely to have been related to humans. Brown bears were also once found in the British Isles, but were considered a threat to humans and livestock: the last one was killed there around the beginning of the twelfth century. Until the late sixteenth century, the brown bears of Europe occurred as a single

population from Spain and Portugal across France, Germany, Italy, Austria, and into eastern Europe. Hunting of bears was a right usually reserved for noblemen, but despite this limitation the increasing human population led to widespread killing of bears both for sport and to control their preying on livestock. Over the years, methods of killing bears were also becoming increasingly sophisticated.

▼ A brown bear catching a salmon in the clear waters of a river in Katmai National Park in Alaska. These bears are all but extinct in continental United States south of the Canadian border.

In this postage stamp from early this century, an Arctic explorer is shooting a bear of mythic proportions. Explorers were almost always shown killing bears.

▲ Brown bears once occurred throughout western Europe, but they were eliminated because they competed with humans for space and preyed upon livestock.

▼ One of the best hopes for long-term brown bear conservation lies with protected areas in Alaska. Bears are a tourist attraction in these refuges, providing an economic motive for their protection.

▶ (Opposite, top) The brown bears of Hokkaido, Japan, are now mainly limited to national parks. Even in these parks they are insufficiently protected by existing laws.

▶ (Opposite, bottom) Dumps are attractive to scavenging bears, which run a high risk of ingesting toxic materials. In this instance, a pale cinnamon phase black bear is in amongst the garbage.

By the late seventeenth century, the brown bears of Spain were reduced to the northern Cantabrian Mountains, and this population had become separated from the nearest population to the east, in the Pyrenees Mountains, on the French border. This separation marked the beginning of

ESTIMATES OF FOREST AREAS AND DEFORESTATION RATES IN THE TROPICS

Country	Closed forest area (1,000 ha)	Percent deforested per year
Tropical America:		
Paraguay	4,070	4.7
Costa Rica	1,638	4.0
Haiti	48	3.8
El Salvador	141	3.2
Jamaica	67	3.0
Nicaragua	4,496	2.7
Ecuador	14,250	2.4
Honduras	3,797	2.4
Guatemala	4,442	2.0
Colombia	46,400	1.8
Mexico	46,250	1.3
Panama	4,165	0.9
Belize	1,354	0.7
Dominican Republic	629	0.6
Trinidad and Tobago	208	0.4
Peru	69,680	0.4
Brazil	357,480	0.4
Venezuela	31,870	0.4
Bolivia	44,010	0.2
Cuba	1,455	0.1
French Guiana	8,900	no data
Suriname	14,830	no data
Guyana	18,475	no data
TOTALS	678,655	0.6
Tropical Asia:		
Nepal	1,941	4.3
Sri Lanka	1,659	3.5
Thailand	9,235	2.7
Brunei	323	1.5
Malaysia	20,995	1.2
Laos	8,410	1.2
Philippines	9,510	1.0
Bangladesh	927	0.9
Vietnam	8,770	0.7
Indonesia	113,895	0.5
Pakistan	2,185	0.3
Burma	31,941	0.3
Cambodia	7,548	0.3
India	51,841	0.3
Bhutan	2,100	0.1
Papua New Guinea	34,230	0.1
TOTALS	305,510	0.6

Source: FAO, 1981. Tropical Forest Assessment Project (GEMS): Tropical America, Tropical Asia. FAO/UNEP, Rome, Italy

the fragmentation of the European brown bear population. The decline of exclusive hunting privileges for the nobility in the nineteenth century resulted in the accelerated elimination of the brown bear from most of western Europe. Bears were left with few areas of habitat, and were generally viewed by humans as predatory pests. Villagers who killed bears were considered heroes, and there were men who bragged of killing 50 or more bears during a lifetime.

Today, Europe's remaining brown bears live in a number of fragmented populations in a few remote mountainous areas, and even in regions such as these their survival is questionable unless intensive management plans can be established. The story of the demise of brown bears in Europe, a tragedy which has taken place largely in the last 150 years, is a story that can currently be told about most bear populations worldwide.

SHARED HABITAT PREFERENCES

Bears and humans have similar habitat preferences, such as valley floors where soils are fertile and access is easy. The regions where wild food for bears is available and at its most abundant are also likely to be where crops and livestock will be raised most successfully and, in turn, where people will want to establish farms and settlements. In addition, bears are opportunistic omnivores and will readily eat the foods that humans favor. Inevitably, all this places bears on a collision course with people.

Bears will kill livestock, destroy beehives, raid oil-palm plantations, damage fruit trees as they harvest the fruit, raid grainfields and stored crops, and dig up gardens. Most people are intolerant of these activities and remove the offending bears. As human habitations and farming activities move further into bear habitat, attractive human-related foods become increasingly available to bears. Areas of human settlement therefore tend to act as population "sinks," attracting bears from surrounding areas. The bears then come into conflict with humans and are subsequently eliminated. This population sink potential dramatically magnifies the detrimental effects of human settlements in bear habitat.

THE SPECIES MOST AT RISK

Those species of bears in most trouble are the giant panda, the sloth bear, the spectacled bear, and the Asiatic black bear. Of particular concern are the bears of Asia, where human populations are increasing most rapidly. In many parts of Asia, large areas of forest habitat are being lost as a result of human settlement and timber harvesting, and this forest is essential to bear survival. Little information is available on the distribution of the Asian bears, and even more disturbing is the lack of basic information on their biology and habitat needs. Without such information, the impact of intensive habitat alteration cannot be assessed. Asian bears face local extinctions and habitat fragmentation in large parts of their range.

The giant panda The giant panda is the most threatened of the world's bears, with only around 1,000 remaining in six island populations in the mountains of central China. Although a detailed management plan has recently been completed, implementation of the complex actions needed to guarantee the panda's survival is questionable. Poaching of giant pandas continues, despite the death penalty: a single giant panda skin can fetch tens of thousands of US dollars in Taiwan or Japan.

The giant panda has been called a "blueprint for extinction" by Dr. George Schaller, the world's foremost authority on the species. The reasons for this vulnerability are: limited and isolated range, and increasing human presence in the range; dependence on a single food source, bamboo; and a high value placed on parts, which promotes poaching. Preserving the giant panda from extinction is one of the world's most challenging conservation problems.

The sloth bear The sloth bear lives on the Indian subcontinent, a part of the world where there are high densities of people. This species competes little with humans for much of the year as it feeds largely on insects and tree fruits. Its greatest threat is increasing numbers of people in its range and the fragmentation of populations. In many areas where it was once common it has now disappeared, and it is now found mainly in reserves in India and Nepal. Sloth bear survival outside such reserves is unlikely in the long term, and if populations are solely restricted to reserves, this will result in severe fragmentation. Its range is likely to be further reduced in the future as human needs for forest products and space escalate.

The spectacled bear The spectacled bear of South America faces increasing pressures as humans convert its habitat to agricultural uses. More and more people are moving into mountainous areas, pushing the range of the spectacled bear higher and eliminating lowland habitats. Fragmentation of populations is ongoing, and in many areas nothing is known about the bear's distribution. The threats to this bear are severe.

The Asiatic black bear The distribution of the Asiatic black bear was once second only to that of the brown bear, but its range includes much of Asia where the human population is increasing rapidly. The bear directly competes with humans for food by feeding on crops, and in most areas of its range it has been reduced to small isolated populations that face local extinction. Parts of the bear are much sought-after for traditional Asian medicine, increasing its vulnerability.

The species has been virtually eliminated from the Korean peninsula, and has been driven to extinction from overhunting on the island of Kyushu in Japan. The remaining Japanese populations are

Odazima

Myron Kozak

WHY BEARS ARE SO VULNERABLE

ANDREW E. DEROCHER

There is a principle in ecology that only one species can occupy a given niche, or position, in the ecological web. If two species are present in a niche, one will eventually exclude the other. Humans and bears have a long history of competing for the same resources. While in earlier times, mutual respect and avoidance produced an equilibrium, unjustified fear, fueled by myth and sensationalist media coverage, has recently combined with firearms to upset the balance. Few people are prepared to coexist with bears, with the result that bears that come near humans are often termed "problem bears" even before they cause any disturbance.

▶ In many areas, much of the black bear's diet consists of berries. If there is a crop failure, the bears become extremely hungry and enter settled areas in search of food. People feel threatened, and bears are frequently shot.

▼ An Alaskan hunting guide's trophy room. Under the US Marine Mammal Protection Act of 1972, American sport hunters cannot kill polar bears in Alaska or import their legally taken hides from other countries.

Daniel J. Cox

Harvest and habitat loss can have a devastating effect on bears. Ironically, this vulnerability relates to the very aspects of their population dynamics that made them such a successful group. Bears are adapted to maintain a stable population in a variable environment. They tend to live at low densities and females do not reproduce until they are experienced enough to care for their cubs. They have a small number of young at a time and look after them for two to three years to give them the best chance of survival. To compensate for a low reproductive rate, bears generally live for more than 20 years, which gives them time to replace themselves. However, these traits mean that bears cannot recover quickly from population depletion. Even a population managed to allow a harvest can easily be depleted, while it may take years to recover.

Studying bears is far from easy, and they are therefore difficult to manage. If the number of bears in a population is not known, incorrect management decisions can be made, resulting in over-harvesting. Changes in a population indicating over-harvesting, such as shifts in the age or sex composition, are not always apparent and may not be noticed until the damage has been done.

Computer modeling of polar bear populations has shown that if the harvest of females exceeds about 2 percent, the population will decline. The protection of females is critical for bear conservation, but a bear's sex is often difficult for a hunter to determine before shooting. Even protection of females with offspring is difficult to enforce because cubs may not be seen. In small populations, removing even a few adult females can result in local extinction.

Behavioral traits such as a highly variable diet (except giant pandas where extreme specialization makes them vulnerable), rapid learning, high curiosity, wide dispersal of young, large home range, low population density, and ferocious defense of offspring were critical for bears to survive through evolutionary time. However, these behaviors now bring bears into conflict with humans. Their curiosity and ability to digest a varied diet allow them to substitute crops and cattle for natural foods, and they are quick to exploit any new food source. If people do not kill the bears,

Stephen J. Krasemann/Bruce Coleman Ltd

Steve McCutcheon/AUSCAPE International

▲ Guided brown bear hunting assists the economies of some of the mountainous areas of Alaska and northwestern Canada. The number of bears harvested is carefully controlled in order to protect populations from declining.

their garbage often does. Bears sometimes enter dumps and poison themselves by eating such things as engine oil, tin cans, car batteries, and antifreeze. Conflicts often require the removal of a bear and, increasingly, there is nowhere to release it.

Habitat loss is critical to bears because they require vast areas to support populations large enough to prevent inbreeding and maintain genetic variability. Most reserves are either not large enough, or the right shape, to encompass ecosystems of sufficient size to contain a viable bear population, resulting in many bears coming into contact with humans around the edges.

Protected areas of natural beauty are not necessarily suited to bears. Prime bear habitat usually includes wet areas near creeks and lakes, and the bottoms of valleys—areas that support the best timber, provide the best climate for growing crops, and are used for roads, dams, and urban development. When the areas bears require overlap with regions humans wish to exploit, the bears are killed or forced to leave. Displaced animals have nowhere to go and, inevitably, they come into conflict with humans.

Learned behavior can also influence the vulnerability of bears to humans. For example, females that feed at rubbish dumps will frequently pass on this habit to their cubs.

Sometimes bears from some distance around will concentrate in a small area if food is abundant there, such as at a salmon stream or a berry patch. Hunting at such locations can result in a large portion of the population being removed before a reduction in numbers is noted.

Careful planning of buffer zones can leave critical bear habitat intact while allowing logging and mining in remote areas. Given the chance, bears are often able to adapt to new environments. An additional problem arises, however, in that the building of roads provides increased access for hunters and poachers. Possibly the most significant threat is now posed by poaching for international trade in bear parts for traditional medicines.

The low reproductive rates of female bears mean that substances such as polychlorinated biphenyls (PCBs) in the food chain and the various impacts of global climatic change could tip the balance of many populations towards extinction.

If bears are removed from an area, they are difficult to reintroduce, a major reason being the absence of experienced females to teach their cubs how to fend for themselves. Also, once bears have been removed, the resident human population is often reluctant to see them reintroduced. Bears are a highly successful group, but they are now becoming unable to cope with the rapid rate of change.

John E. Swedberg/Ardea London Ltd

▲ The barren Arctic coast of Alaska is becoming more populated as oil exploration increases. This camp at Prudhoe Bay is only a few kilometers from an area where polar bears hunt seals.

being overharvested through pest and sport hunting, and the bear is likely to continue to decline in numbers and range unless some change is instituted in its management. The remaining populations on the densely populated islands of Taiwan and Hainan are hanging on, but little is known about them or how long they can survive.

The Asiatic black bears in eastern Siberia are in the best condition of any populations of this species, but increasing timber harvesting in this region, combined with ease of access for Asians willing to pay high prices for bear gallbladders and paws, may mean that these populations will soon also be at risk.

The sun bear The sun bear is a forest-dwelling species found in the lowland tropical rainforest of Southeast Asia, and its habitat is being eroded increasingly by human settlement and timber

harvesting. Settlement is resulting in a growing number of conflicts between humans and sun bears, with a resultant decline in bear numbers, and is causing habitat fragmentation and isolation of populations. This bear's future will depend upon the maintenance of forest areas of sufficient size to support viable populations, where human settlement is prohibited. Sun bears may be able to sustain themselves in forest areas where timber harvesting has taken place and the forest has been allowed to regenerate, but they cannot survive where the forest has been cleared and where human settlements proliferate. Given the extent of human population expansion within the range of the sun bear, the future for this species is unclear.

The brown bear The brown bear is the most widespread of the bears, but this will not guarantee its future. Humans rapidly eliminated the brown bear from much of Europe and North America, and the populations that remain are far from secure. A recent survey of Canadian brown bears estimated that more than 60 percent of the populations in Canada are presently at risk.

THE NEAR EXTINCTION OF THE GRIZZLY BEAR

CHRISTOPHER SERVHEEN

The brown bear, or grizzly, once existed in essentially an unbroken population across the western half of North America from the Arctic Ocean to central Mexico. It is estimated that there were perhaps 50,000 grizzly bears in 1800. When Lewis and Clark explored the interior of the continent in 1803 and 1804, they encountered some 17 grizzlies and tried to shoot almost every one of them.

Settlers viewed the grizzly bear as a dangerous animal—a predator on livestock and a competitor for space. Much of the literature of the old West consists of tales of bear hunts, of people being killed or mauled by bears, or of bears that were notorious, crafty livestock killers. The settlers viewed the grizzly bear in the same way that they viewed native Americans—as something to be tamed, controlled, or eliminated.

Grizzlies were shot, trapped, poisoned, and lassoed with ropes from horseback. First they were eliminated from the fertile lowland areas and the great plains, then from the mountain valleys. In time the only grizzlies that remained were those that lived in the mountains. The entire race of grizzlies that lived on the prairies was gone by the late 1800s, less than 100 years after the arrival of the first white people in this vast area.

Along with the settlers came cattle and sheep, which did best in the rich, wet areas where grasses and other plants flourished. These plants were also important foods for the grizzly, whose diet is 80 to 90 percent vegetation. As the livestock ate the natural foods of the bears, the bears began increasingly to prey on livestock, and the settlers spared no effort in eliminating the bears. At first livestock were kept on the lowlands, but by the early twentieth century sheep were being driven into mountain pastures during summer. As they invaded the mountain haunts of the grizzly, deadly predator-control poisons like strychnine came with them. At the time when sheep numbers reached their peak, in the 1920s and 1930s, grizzly bear numbers were at their lowest. Many areas that are now designated as wilderness were widely grazed by livestock during these years.

The decline of the grizzly did meet with some concern. In Montana, decreasing grizzly numbers prompted closure of bear hunting for several years in the 1940s. But the voices heard in support of the grizzly were few. It was not until the Craigheads' work on the biology of the grizzly bear in Yellowstone National Park, and the subsequent closure of the park's rubbish dumps, that the plight of the grizzly was recognized.

In 1975, 173 years after the Lewis and Clark expedition, and after 98 percent of the grizzlies and their habitat had been destroyed, the grizzly bear was declared a threatened species under the US Endangered Species Act. Today more than US$2 million is spent annually trying to ensure that the remaining bears survive.

The Bettmann Archive

The largest numbers of brown bears are in Russia, but current political changes and increasing exploitation of resources throughout eastern Siberia, the area that has the largest remaining populations, place them at risk. The need for hard currency that can be gained through the exploitation of bear habitat is likely to result in its rapid destruction in many areas.

Polar bears Polar bear populations appear to be less threatened than other bear species, but they continue to be vulnerable, especially in the face of oil and gas development. Polar bear conservation is perhaps the best example of what can be done to address the needs of a bear species, once governments cooperate through limitation of harvest and habitat maintenance (see The International Agreement on the Conservation of Polar Bears, page 230).

The North American black bear
The North American black bear is the most abundant of the world's bears. It is doing well in most areas where habitat has not been fragmented and throughout much of its range its status is secure because it is valued as a game animal and is managed as such. Where populations are small and isolated, however, they are being driven to extinction.

◀ On the open plains, grizzlies were no match for the greater speed of horses and there was nowhere to which they could escape.

▼ The US Endangered Species Act declared the grizzly bear a threatened species in 1975.

▼ The grizzly, once abundant on the western plains, is now restricted to parts of Montana and Idaho.

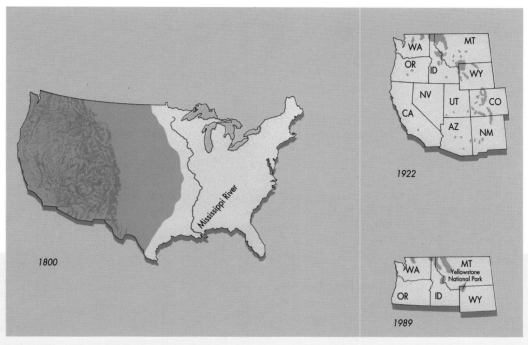

1800

1922

1989

Erwin and Peggy Bauer/Bruce Coleman Ltd

GRIZZLY ADAMS

ANDREW E. DEROCHER

James Capen Adams, who became known as Grizzly Adams, was born in 1807 in Medway, Massachusetts, in the United States. After working as a shoemaker, an animal trainer, and a cattle rancher, all with only limited success, he took to the hills in California and began fur trading and catching animals for zoos and traveling shows.

In his prime, Adams was of medium build, wiry and muscular. He had nerves of steel and was an excellent shot. On one outing, he came across a female brown bear, or grizzly, and her yearling cubs. While he was positioning himself to shoot the mother, she spotted him and stood on her hind legs to get a better look. His first shot hit her in the chest. The bear charged, so he seized his second rifle and fired a shot through her open mouth and into her brain. He lassoed her cubs, one male, one female, bound and muzzled them, and chained them to a tree.

Unlike the image portrayed in movies, Adams was a stern animal trainer. Lady Washington, the female cub, was beaten into submission, and was taught to follow by being dragged behind a mule. Despite such treatment, she became a faithful companion. To remain warm at night, Adams slept with the bear at his back and a fire at his front. Lady Washington and his other grizzly companion, Ben Franklin, were trained to carry packs and the deer he shot when out hunting.

Adams eventually moved to San Francisco and set up the Mountaineer Museum, advertising his show by wandering about town accompanied by his grizzly, Ben, and various other bears. His menagerie included black bears, cougars, jaguars, elks, monkeys, a baboon, a sea lion, snakes, and a buffalo. Adams and his museum became notorious, and he added to his fame by telling tall tales of his exploits. After four years, however, he still had made no money, so he took his animals east to travel with the great P.T. Barnum's traveling show.

His career was cut short when one of his trained bears, General Fremont, struck him a fearful blow on the head. Despite the injury, Adams continued to show his animals until close to his death in 1860.

Grizzly Adams has been romanticized as a mountainman, but he exploited bears rather than cared for them. He considered them a challenge to subdue or kill, and the bears that he killed were sold for meat, hides, and fat— all at a handsome profit. He was not a naturalist of note and, unlike some other early hunters, he never called for the conservation of bears or their habitat. He was, in fact, a major force in the extermination of brown bears from California.

Archive Photos

◀ The story of Grizzly Adams is so popular in the United States that the mountainman and his bear companions became the subject of a successful television series.

THE CONSERVATION NEEDS OF THE WORLD'S BEARS

It is possible for people to live with bears and guarantee their future, if consideration is given to the bears' needs. The bear species that are in the best condition today—the polar bear and the North American black bear—are doing well because they are managed by government programs, and the people who live with them value them. The bears are highly regarded as a game species for regulated hunting, as beautiful animals for viewing and photographing, and as members of the natural community. The people who live with these bears are willing to contribute to management programs and to consider bear needs when harvesting timber, undertaking recreational activities, and disposing of their garbage.

In general, the six remaining bear species do not have this level of support from local people, and it is unlikely that consideration of the needs of bears can be established in local communities in developing countries in time to ensure the survival of these bears and their habitat. Instead, it may be necessary to link bears' survival with more commonly held goals, such as watershed maintenance, sustainable forestry and other commodity production, and quality of life.

As an example, watershed maintenance for reliable water supplies could be linked with sustainable forestry. Sustainable forestry would result in harvest practices that would contribute to forest regeneration for future timber requirements, and would bring about the securing of large contiguous areas of forest that would be devoid of human settlement. The halting of habitat fragmentation would, in turn, ensure the continuance of bear populations of sufficient size to guarantee long-term survival.

The quality of life approach in developing countries could be related to the assurance of continued resources to provide food and jobs for future generations. An approach such as this could also be related to benefits that derive from bears either directly, as in bear parts for traditional medicine, or indirectly, as in tourist dollars from people who are interested in hunting, viewing, and photographing bears.

The future of Asiatic black bears, sun bears, Asian brown bears, and perhaps sloth bears will depend upon the innovative development of programs to promote and support initiatives such as these. Habitat preservation and species-support programs need to be integrated directly with ecosystem management and the maintenance of biodiversity. Bear conservation could, in fact, become a key factor in sustaining the critical biological systems of the areas in which they live, and would be of immense benefit to humans, for the ecosystems required for bear survival are equally necessary for human survival.

Mike McKavett/Bruce Coleman Ltd

◄ Sloth bears in India are dependent on national parks for the protection of sufficient areas of habitat to enable small populations to survive.

HABITAT FRAGMENTATION

Habitat fragmentation results in bear populations living in small units of habitat in small numbers. Fragmentation dramatically increases the risk of extinction of these small populations because they have limited resource diversity and there is no possibility of bears immigrating from other populations. Habitat fragmentation is currently causing the extinction of small populations of brown bears, North American black bears, sun bears, sloth bears, Asiatic black bears, spectacled bears, and giant pandas.

Many bear population fragments are so small that even absolute protection will not guarantee their survival, even though a few bears may persist for many years. Intensive management is necessary to ensure bear survival in population pockets, involving either the placement of additional bears in such areas on a regular basis, or developing linkages between isolated areas through habitat acquisition.

The best solution to habitat fragmentation is, of course, to avoid it in the first place through management practices, so that bears can continue to live in large, contiguous populations. Human activities that fragment populations, such as settlement, forest clearing, the establishment of plantations, and water impoundments should be carefully evaluated with regard to their likely impact on bear habitat.

Significant fragmentation has already taken place in most areas of bear habitat, except for some areas in eastern Siberia and perhaps some limited areas in Southeast Asia. Once such fragmentation has occurred—usually as a result of many small land-management decisions—it is almost irreversible. It is a sad fact that existing

Gerald Cubitt/WWF

▲ Although sun bears, like this one in Tanjung Puting National Park, are protected in Indonesia, deforestation and increasing use of land for agriculture continue to diminish bear habitat. There is also concern that parts from Indonesian bears are being marketed elsewhere in Southeast Asia.

Morten Strange/NHPA

◄ The jungles of the world once provided a haven for many of the world's large tropical carnivores, such as the sun bear. Roads, such as this one in Malaysia, are now penetrating the rainforest, as the demand for timber grows.

THE REINTRODUCTION OF BLACK BEARS IN ARKANSAS

KIMBERLY G. SMITH, JOSEPH D. CLARK, AND SCOTT D. SHULL

Arkansas' history is so closely linked to black bears that it was known as "the bear state" until early this century. Legends of big bears in Arkansas figured prominently in the mythology of the American frontier, and not so long ago a popular series of children's books told of the mythical "Arkansaw Bear."

The black bear became a valuable commodity for the early settlers, providing skins, meat, oil, and grease, and bear skins stretched out to dry in front of a house were regarded as a status symbol. "Southern fried cooking" has its roots in the use of bear oil, which gave food a distinctive flavor and crispy texture.

Unregulated hunting, and habitat loss due to forestry and agricultural activities, caused bears to be nearly eliminated from Arkansas by 1920, and by 1930 they had disappeared in the surrounding areas of Missouri and Oklahoma. The last stronghold of the native Arkansas bear was in the eastern delta region, not far from the present White River National Wildlife Refuge, where there were estimated to be only 25 bears in 1940, and 40 to 50 bears in 1950. There are currently thought to be about 160 to 175 bears in and around the refuge.

In 1958, the Arkansas Game and Fish Commission (AGFC) began reintroducing black bears in the Interior Highlands (the Ozark and Ouachita mountains) of western and northern Arkansas, where there had been no bears since the turn of the century. Forty bears captured in Minnesota were released initially, followed by more from Minnesota and a number from southern Manitoba, Canada, during the summers of 1962 through 1968. The bears were released in a somewhat clandestine manner. When the Director of the AGFC agreed to the trapping of up to 100 bears in Minnesota in 1965, he stated in his letter of authorization that the project was to receive no publicity. The project ceased because of cost and increasing public concern about bears wandering into the towns.

The bears to be relocated were captured in barrel traps, often in urban areas, but they were not habitual nuisance bears. In the last years of the project, emphasis was placed on transplanting females and young males. The animals were transported to Arkansas in pick-up trucks, each of which accommodated six bears in individual cages. Release areas were chosen for their remoteness and the availability of food and water. Feeding troughs of dog food were placed at the release sites, so that the bears would not go hungry while learning about their new home, and the food was eaten by some of the bears.

Bears in northern Minnesota and southern Manitoba, Canada, belong to the same subspecies, *Ursus americanus americanus*, as the ones originally found in the Ozark and Ouachita mountains. An estimated total of 254 bears were released at three sites, although, because detailed records were not kept, a number of bears may have been released in other areas as well. Two release sites were in the Ozark National Forest—Piney Creek Wildlife Management Area (WMA), and Black Mountain, now known as White Rock WMA—and the release site in the Ouachita National Forest was in Muddy Creek WMA. Up to 1973, the White Rock WMA release had been considered a failure, because there had been no evidence of sustained reproduction and only the occasional bear had been sighted, while both the other sites were deemed successful. However, the bears did survive in the White Rock WMA, and that area now has one of the highest densities of black bears in the state. Its history provides a valuable lesson in the time that is sometimes needed to ensure the successful reintroduction of a long-lived, slow-reproducing predator that lives at low density.

In 1988, the AGFC initiated a three-year study in the Ozarks and Ouachitas to determine bear numbers, and researchers estimate that there are now about 2,100 bears in the Interior Highlands. Not surprisingly, bears are also appearing with increasing frequency in the neighboring states of Oklahoma and Missouri, and it is thought that there may be an additional 300 bears in those states. Thus, from the initial stocking of about 250 individuals, black bear populations in and around western and northern Arkansas have increased nearly tenfold in 20 to 30 years, making it the most successful reintroduction of a large carnivore in the world.

Reasons for success

A number of factors contributed to the effectiveness of this project: the bears were released over a lengthy period; a relatively large number of bears were released each year; bears were released into high-quality habitats; and a number of remote release sites were used. With the benefit of hindsight, it may also have been significant that details of the project did not receive any publicity. Although records from the project are sketchy, it appears that bears were released in Arkansas in as many as eight separate years over an 11-year period

OZARK PLATEAU

Piney Creek WMA

White Rock WMA

ARKANSAS RIVER VALLEY

Muddy Creek WMA

DELTA

OUACHITA MOUNTAINS

White River National Wildlife Refuge

GULF COASTAL PLAIN

◄ Map of Arkansas showing the reintroduction release sites and the present distribution of black bears within the state. Bears in the White River National Wildlife Refuge represent the relict population of native Arkansas bears.

• Release sites

◼ Present bear range

► Hunters outside Pine Bluff in eastern Arkansas, at around the turn of the century. These men made their living by supplying game to the local markets.

▼ Numbers of nuisance bears captured and relocated by Arkansas Game and Fish Commission personnel from 1977 through 1991. Nuisance bear captures were particularly high during 1990, a year when natural food was in short supply.

Courtesy Arkansas Game and Fish Commission

Numbers of Bears

50

40

30

20

10

0

77 78 79 80 81 82 83 84 85 86 87 88 89 90 91

Year

(1958 through 1968). Probably between 20 and 40 bears were released most years. Again, with the benefit of hindsight, this may have been the maximum effective number of a large carniv-orous mammal to reintroduce per year in areas of that size. Releasing wild-caught animals, as opposed to ones that had been raised in captivity, probably also increased the chances of success, as wild-caught bears would have known how to fend for themselves, even though their surroundings had changed.

The decision to have a number of release sites at the core of the historical range of bears in Arkansas was important as it meant that the chances of success were not pinned to a single site. The Ozarks and Ouachitas are high-quality habitats for black bears, because of the abundance and variety of fruits and berries in summer, and acorns and nuts in fall. The region is also now relatively predator-free for black bears, because wolves and mountain lions no longer exist in the Interior Highlands. Adult bears therefore have a high survival rate in both areas.

Surprisingly, major differences exist between the bear populations in the Ozarks and Ouachitas. In the Ozarks, from 1988 to 1990, the average litter size was only 1.4 cubs, compared with 2.4 in the Ouachitas, and first-year survival of cubs was about five times greater in the Ouachitas. Equally intriguing is the fact that about 25 percent of the black bears in the Ozarks were brown in color, while only about 3 percent of the black bears in the Ouachitas were brown. As records are incomplete it is impossible to establish details about the colors of bears released at each site, but personal accounts indicate that few, if any, brown-colored black bears were released in the Ouachitas. Assuming that coat coloring is genetically controlled, such variation could represent genetic differences between pop-ulations, which may reflect a bias in the original stocking program.

The human response

Large predators compete with humans for space, so it is not surprising that as bear numbers have increased, so have the frequency of their conflicts with humans. Complaints related to black bear activity have risen steadily in Arkansas since the 1970s, and the number of bears captured following complaints by land-owners reached a record high in the late 1980s. AGFC personnel now spend more time dealing with complaints about bears than with complaints related to all other animals combined. Ironically, the increase in bear–human problems, referred to as "nuisance

activity," has now become a serious issue for wildlife managers and many of the citizens of Arkansas.

Bears engage in nuisance activity primarily when searching for food. Problems range from a bear simply being present (which some landowners perceive as dangerous) to actual property damage. Nuisance activity is particularly common in years when natural foods, such as berries and acorns, are in short supply. At such times bears are more likely to come close to human dwellings, usually to feed on garbage or pet food. Bears also occasionally damage and enter buildings in search of food. Recently, for example, a woman in the Ozarks found a bear rummaging through the cabinets in her kitchen.

At times, considerable losses are experienced by honey growers in the Ozarks, when bears destroy beehives. Bears also damage grain crops and orchards, and occasionally prey on livestock. Landowners sometimes shoot nuisance bears, although this is illegal without a state-issued depredation permit.

In Arkansas, two- to three-year-old male bears are responsible for 84 percent of the nuisance activity. Young males are not tolerated by dominant older male bears in high-quality habitats, and so are forced into marginal habitat, such as agricultural land. This increases the likelihood of conflict with humans. Currently, nuisance bears are captured in barrel traps and released several kilometers away. Preliminary results suggest that the trauma associated with being caught and transported a short distance is enough to discourage these bears from making further contact with humans.

Although the reintroduction of black bears in Arkansas has been spectacular in terms of the numbers of bears present today, the project cannot be considered completely successful until people fully accept the presence of bears in the Interior High-lands. Judging from negative public perceptions regarding bears expressed in the late 1960s, it is doubtful that the release program would at that time have met with much public support. However, in a recent

▲ A nuisance bear is released in a remote area of the Ouachita Mountains, 200 kilometers (125 miles) south of the region where it was trapped.

Kevin Lynch

survey of Arkansas landowners, the group that was thought most likely to be opposed to bears, over 80 percent wished to see the numbers of bears remain the same, or increase, in their area. Apparently, the reintroduction of bears is now viewed positively by a considerable number of Arkansas landowners, suggesting that perhaps, in the future, the state may once again be famous for its black bear populations.

Save Mountain Habitats

▲ Appropriately, the brown bear appears on a postage stamp promoting mountain habitats.

▼ Brown bears require huge tracts of wild land if they are to survive. Only remote areas of Alaska and northwestern Canada still offer this possibility in North America.

losses are likely be permanent because of the high social and economic cost involved in reversing the situation. Few governments can afford the expense of maintaining small isolated bear populations. For example, China has determined that it will cost almost US$10 million to link the six separate populations of giant pandas in order to increase their chances of survival.

Future activities in unfragmented bear habitat must be carefully evaluated in order to minimize their impact. As we lose bear habitat, we lose the option to have bears.

ANIMAL RESERVES
As the press of human population growth limits the potential for large areas of land to be set aside as animal reserves, it is essential that bear management be carefully integrated into human economic and environmental systems. In any case, reliance on

reserves for the future of bears will result in fragmented populations risking extinction, unless such reserves are designed to meet the needs of populations of at least 300 to 500 bears. Development interests may prefer wildlife to be confined to parks and reserves, thus freeing them from the expense of habitat management, but this is an abdication of environmental responsibility. Integration of bear management, not isolation of management, is the key to a future for bears.

EDUCATION PROGRAMS

People need to be better informed about bears if they are to value them and be prepared to ensure their survival. Education programs should be directed at schools, to inform those who will be making decisions about resource management in the future. Today, scientists know what needs to be done to conserve bears and bear habitat. The challenge is to gain public support so that the necessary conservation measures are implemented.

The history of humans and bears goes back to when they shared the same caves in order to survive. At that time there were more bears than humans. Today, humans have the advantage in numbers and can outcompete any species in their relentless demand for resources, but they also have the knowledge and the ability to balance their needs with those of other living creatures. The next 20 years will show whether we are prepared to use this knowledge to assure a future for the world's bears.

▲ The delicate balance between the polar bear and the Inuit on the edge of the polar ocean is illustrated by an adult female and her yearling cub investigating a sled that might be used one day to hunt them.

VIEWING BROWN BEARS IN ALASKA

JACK W. LENTFER

Alaska is well known for its coastal brown bears (*Ursus arctos*) and the hunting they provide. Less well known are the conservation measures which have protected certain areas of brown bear concentration from hunting for decades and thereby provide excellent opportunities for people to see them. Not so long ago there were people who thought of brown bears mainly as competing predators for salmon, or as animals for hunting, but it is now generally recognized that areas managed to preserve brown bears contribute to outdoor recreation and tourism, and thus benefit the Alaskan economy. Three of the best protected areas are McNeil River, Pack Creek, and Brooks River.

Probably the most famous of these three bear sanctuaries is McNeil River, about 350 kilometers (210 miles) southwest of Anchorage on the northeastern coast of the Alaska Peninsula. Its unique concentration of bears was recognized in the 1950s, when it was decided to protect the area from hunting. In 1967 the McNeil River State Game Sanctuary was established and the area was closed to hunting. Brown bears gather there from mid-June through August, to feed first on red salmon ascending Mikfik Creek to spawn and then on chum salmon that concentrate below the McNeil Falls, just upstream from the ocean. As many as 60 to 100 individual bears can be identified by physical characteristics, such as coat color, at McNeil River, and none have radio-collars or tags.

Jeff Foott/AUSCAPE International

Bear viewing here is supervised by an Alaska Department of Fish and Game representative who walks with visitors from the camping area and stays with them at the various viewing sites. The bears have learned to associate these sites with humans. Although the bears sometimes approach to within 10 meters (30 feet), they have never received food, or had access to garbage, and so ignore the people.

There are still two unresolved issues concerning the management of the McNeil River Sanctuary. A fishway constructed in 1991 at the mouth of Paint River 5 kilometers (3 miles) north of McNeil River will allow salmon to bypass falls and start new salmon runs in the Paint River drainage. This may reduce the number of bears on view at McNeil River. There are also questions relating to hunting. Although hunting is not allowed in the McNeil River Sanctuary and in the area to the south, hunting increased in the 1980s north of the sanctuary. Some McNeil bears spend time in this area and are thus at risk. There is disagreement between advocates of hunting and those who are opposed to hunting in areas where animals have become habituated to humans.

Visitor use is regulated by issuing lottery and standby permits, valid for four consecutive days. Ten visitors per day are allowed from 1 July through 26 August, which includes the period of greatest bear concentration. There is a high demand for permits, and only a small number of applicants are successful. Permit applications can be obtained from the Alaska Department of Fish and Game, 333 Raspberry Road, Anchorage, Alaska 99518, USA.

Pack Creek is in upper Seymour Canal on Admiralty Island, 45 kilometers (28 miles) south of Juneau in southeastern Alaska. Bears have been protected from hunting here since the mid-1930s. The protected area has recently been enlarged and the Pack Creek core area has become the Stan Price State Wildlife Sanctuary. As many as 30 brown bears congregate to feed on chum salmon and pink salmon at Pack Creek, and the best time to see them is usually from mid-July to mid-August. Bears can be viewed from the ground and from an observation tower reached by a 2 kilometer (1 mile) walk from the beach.

A maximum of 24 people are allowed per day, and visitors are supervised by the Alaska Department of Fish and Game and the US Forest Service. Permit applications can be obtained from the Forest Service Information Center, 101 Egan Drive, Juneau, Alaska 99801, USA. Areas adjacent to Pack Creek, including Swan Cove to the north and Windfall Harbor to the south, are also closed to brown bear hunting. These areas provide opportunities to see brown bears in a true wilderness setting with few other people around and without the need for a permit.

Brooks River is in Katmai National Park on the Alaska Peninsula 470 kilometers (290 miles) southwest of Anchorage, and bears have been protected from hunting there since the area became a national park in 1931. Bears congregate in July to feed on red salmon going up Brooks River to spawn. About 35 different bears can be identified near Brooks Camp. On arrival, visitors to Brooks River are told about bear behavior and safety measures. Permits are required for campground use only. Bears can be seen near the lodge and campground, but the most popular viewing area is at a low falls on Brooks River between Naknek Lake and Brooks Lake, an easy walk of 3 kilometers (2 miles) from the lodge.

Brooks River is 55 kilometers (33 miles) from King Salmon, and can be reached by boat or plane. Camping permits and information can be obtained from the National Park Service, PO Box 7, King Salmon, Alaska 99613, USA.

◀ At McNeil River, campsites are kept clean and no garbage is thrown away. Because of this, bears do not associate humans with food and simply ignore observers, even when they are at close range.

▼ A young brown bear surfaces at McNeil River. In the 20 years that people have been viewing bears at this sanctuary, no one has been attacked.

POLAR BEAR TOURISM AT CHURCHILL, MANITOBA

IAN STIRLING

Churchill, Manitoba, on the western coast of Hudson Bay in Canada, is probably the easiest place in the world to see polar bears. In fact, the town proudly calls itself "The Polar Bear Capital of the World" and people come from all over the globe each fall to see these spectacular carnivores up close. These tourists now provide the town with a significant proportion of its income. Like the large mammals of East Africa, the polar bears of Churchill have achieved recognition as a significant part of the world's international wildlife heritage.

The town of Churchill, on Hudson Bay in Canada, is known for the facilities it provides for viewing polar bears in the wild.

There is a simple reason why polar bears are so abundant near Churchill in the fall. For most of the year, they hunt seals on the sea ice of Hudson Bay but, in early summer, the ice breaks up. The last ice to melt lies off the coast of Manitoba and Ontario, so that is where the bears come ashore to wait for freeze-up in the late fall. Adult males tend to remain along the shoreline, while family groups and subadults go inland. For the four months they are ashore, there is little to eat, so the bears survive on their reserves of stored body fat. By mid-fall, some of the bears along the coast begin to move north along the beaches. Since Churchill is situated on the coast, this seasonal movement of the bears brings some of them close to town. In fact, polar bears have been reported in the Churchill area in the fall ever since the first Europeans wintered there at the end of 1619, and were known to the native trappers of the region well before that.

Polar bears usually avoid humans but, by fall, some of the younger bears, and females nursing cubs, are beginning to run low on their stored fat and are becoming hungry. They too move out to the coast and some move north toward Churchill. The smell of garbage attracts some bears into town in search of food. In the late 1960s and early 1970s, it was not unusual to see 20 or more polar bears in the town dump in October, often

Konrad Wothe/Oxford Scientific Films

scavenging side by side with people. Some bears ventured into town and broke into buildings. Overall, the bears were remarkably well behaved but they did cause a certain amount of property damage, frightened many people and, in 1968, a bear killed a schoolboy (after it was provoked). Not surprisingly, through this period, the bears were principally regarded as pests and were dealt with as such. Some of the problem bears around town were trapped and released elsewhere (after which many promptly returned), some were sent to zoos, and many were simply shot. Nevertheless, each fall, the media had a field day with articles and films depicting a town besieged by bears, and Churchill's fame grew.

Because of the publicity, people began coming to town to see polar bears, which, at first, usually meant renting a truck or hiring a taxi and driving to the dump. However, two events coincided in 1980 to change the future of polar bear tourism in the town. Len Smith, a local Churchill man who was fascinated by polar bears, built the first "tundra buggy." It resembled a bus but had large, wide tires to minimize damage to the tundra. With his tundra buggy, Len took people out to view polar bears in safety, for both the bears and the humans. That fall, the National Geographic Society made a documentary, *Polar Bear Alert*, about how Churchill coped with the annual influx of polar bears, and one of the features was a trip in the tundra buggy. This resulted in further publicity. In 1981, the first commercially booked polar bear tour with a tundra buggy took place, and since then the business has gone from strength to strength.

By 1981, the Manitoba Department of Natural Resources recognized that it was unacceptable simply to kill so-called problem bears. It therefore built a "jail" in which up to 16 single bears and four family groups could be housed. Thus, instead of being shot, a problem bear is simply "jailed" until freeze-up and then released onto the ice. Since the bears live on their stored fat through this period anyway, they do not have to be

◄ Some of the polar bears that come into Churchill are captured and flown in a net under a helicopter several kilometers to the north, while still drugged, and are then released.

Daniel J. Cox

fed and therefore the risk of their associating food with humans is avoided. The program has been remarkably effective, and saves the lives of several polar bears every year.

The total value of the polar bear tours is far greater than the economic return would be from hunting the animals. The success of tourism at Churchill is now inspiring the development of other sites for viewing live, undisturbed polar bears. Currently, a balance is being sought between the amount of activity the bears and the tundra can withstand before the impact of vehicles and well-meaning tourists has a negative effect. There is also concern for maintaining the quality of the visitors' wilderness experience.

◄ Polar bears appear placid when investigating a tundra buggy, but they can move with blinding speed. It is dangerous for anyone to put their head or arms outside a vehicle.

▼ One of the sights a visitor to Churchill can enjoy from a tundra buggy.

THE INTERNATIONAL AGREEMENT ON THE CONSERVATION OF POLAR BEARS

IAN STIRLING

The polar bear is not an endangered species today, but 25 years or so ago there was concern that it might become so. Through the 1960s, the growing value of polar bear hides, combined with the increasing use of oversnow machines, stimulated an unprecedented increase in the number of bears being killed. For example, in Alaska, the number of trophy kills increased from 139 in 1961 to 399 in 1966. In Canada, between 1953 and 1964, the recorded harvest fluctuated between 350 and 550, while in 1967 it jumped to 726. The unrecorded kill is unknown. In Svalbard, an Arctic archipelago which is governed by Norway, the annual postwar harvest was over 300 bears, while in Greenland it was over 100. Although hunting of polar bears ceased in the Soviet Union in 1956, it has been estimated that over 150,000 polar bears were killed or captured in Soviet Eurasia between the beginning of the eighteenth century and that time.

In 1965, the first international meeting on the conservation of polar bears was held in Fairbanks, Alaska. Subsequently, scientists from the five polar bear nations (Canada, Denmark, Norway, USA, and the USSR) met at regular intervals, and in 1973 an international agreement on the conservation of polar bears and their habitat was negotiated and signed in Oslo, Norway. This landmark agreement was the first of any kind signed by all the nations surrounding the Arctic Ocean. Under the terms of the agreement, the harvest of polar bears, which is taken mainly by native people, is controlled within scientific guidelines, and research and management of polar bears are coordinated internationally.

From an ecological point of view, Article II may be the most profound part of the agreement. It states "Each Contracting Party shall take appropriate action *to protect the ecosystems of which polar bears are a part* (author's emphasis), with special attention to habitat components such as denning and feeding sites and migration patterns and shall manage polar bear populations in accordance with sound conservation practices based on the best scientific data." Since then, an enormous amount of research has been undertaken on everything from population dynamics, movements, reproduction, maternity denning areas, behavior, and relationships to prey species, to levels of toxic chemicals. As a result, overhunting no longer threatens the survival of the polar bear.

However, given the level of uncertainty about global climate change and pollution, there is no room for complacency. Furthermore, although the Polar Bear Agreement has functioned well as an instrument of conservation, it is not legally enforceable and no infrastructure has been set up to ensure compliance.

Despite these reservations, at a time when large carnivores in particular are under great pressure throughout the world and environmental degradation continues on a global scale, the history of polar bear research, and the management strategies that have been adopted, constitute an international success story in conservation.

Steve McCutcheon/AUSCAPE International

Norbert Rosing

Norbert Rosing

▲ (Top) Hunting polar bears is important to the culture and economy of the Inuit of Alaska, Canada, and Greenland. Although most hides are sold as is, some are still made into clothes in Greenland.

▲ In areas where bears are not hunted, they are unafraid of approaching cars. This makes them vulnerable to poaching in areas such as national parks, and to being run over, especially at night.

The Inuvialuit-Inupiat Management Agreement on Polar Bears in the southern Beaufort Sea

Article VII of the International Polar Bear Agreement states that "They [the Contracting Parties] shall… consult with other Parties on the management of [internationally] migrating polar bear populations…" However, actually doing so can be quite complicated. In the southern Beaufort Sea, the Inuvialuit of Canada and the Inupiat of Alaska both harvest polar bears from the same subpopulation. In Canada, seasons and annual quotas of polar bears were strictly controlled by law, and enforced. However, in Alaska, because of the United States Marine Mammal Protection Act of 1972, there was neither a limit to the number of bears that could be killed by native people for subsistence, nor any protection for females with cubs or bears in dens. Thus, it was perfectly legal to overharvest polar bears in Alaska and the Federal Government could not take any action until after the subpopulation had been declared depleted!

Although the kill in Canada was controlled, the recorded harvest in Alaska fluctuated widely and could not be regulated, leaving that subpopulation of polar bears vulnerable to overharvest. Negotiating a formal international agreement could have taken 10 or 20 years, by which time it might have been too late. Instead, the native hunters negotiated their own management agreement, patterned on the international agreement, and based on current scientific information. Although it has no formal basis in law and is therfore unenforceable, the fact that it has originated from the indigenous people themselves is a matter of pride and it is less likely to require enforcement. Admittedly, the Inuvialuit-Inupiat Agreement has not yet stood the test of time but, if successful, it will form a model for the resolution of similar problems with shared polar bear populations elsewhere.

▼ In a most unusual animal friendship, this polar bear near Churchill befriended a husky chained on a dog line. For several days, the bear visited the dog and they played together, with no sign of threat or fear.

BIBLIOGRAPHY

Bromley, M. 1989. Bear–People Conflicts: Proceedings of a Symposium on Management Strategies. Northwest Territories Department of Renewable Resources, Yellowknife, NWT. (Available from Publications Division, Department of Culture and Communications, Government of NWT, Yellowknife, NWT X1A 2L9, Canada.)

Bunnell, F.L. and Tait, D.E.N. 1981. "Population dynamics of bears—implications." Pages 75–98 in C.W. Fowler and T.D. Smith (eds), The Dynamics of Large Mammal Populations. John Wiley & Sons, New York, NY.

Craighead, F.C. 1979. *Track of the Grizzly*. Sierra Club Books, San Francisco, CA.

Elman, R. 1992. *Bears: Rulers of the Wilderness*. Todtri Productions Ltd, New York, NY.

Erdbrink, D.P. 1953. *A review of fossil and recent bears of the Old World*. Two volumes. Drukkerij Jan de Lange, Deventer, Holland.

Ewer, R.F. 1973. *The Carnivores*. Weidenfeld & Nicholson, London.

Gould, E. and McKay, G. (eds) 1990. Encyclopedia of Animals: Mammals. Malard Press, New York, NY.

Grzimek, B. 1990. *Encyclopedia of Mammals*. (English language edition; transl. S. P. Parker). Five Volumes. McGraw Hill, New York, NY.

Herrero, S. 1985. *Bear Attacks*. Winchester Press, Piscataway, NJ.

Jonkel, C. and Cowan, I. McT. 1971. "The black bear in the spruce-fir forest." Wildlife Monographs, 27.

Kurtén, B. 1966. "The Pleistocene bears of North America, I: *Genus Tremarctos*, spectacled bears." *Acta Zoologica Fennica*, 115: 1–120.

Kurtén, B. 1967. "The Pleistocence bears of North America, II: Genus *Arctodus*, short-faced bears." *Acta Zoologica Fennica*, 117: 1–60.

Kurtén, B. 1976. *The Cave Bear Story*. Columbia University Press, New York, NY.

Larsen, T. 1978. *The World of the Polar Bear*. Hamlyn Publishers, London.

Mills, J.A. and Servheen, C. 1991. *The Asian Trade in Bears and Bear Parts*. World Wildlife Fund. (Available from WWF Publications, PO Box 4866, Hampden Post Office, Baltimore, MD 21211, USA.)

Murie, A. 1981. The Grizzlies of Mount McKinley. US National Park Service Monograph Series, No. 14.

Pearson, A.M. 1975, The Northern Interior Grizzly Bear, *Ursus arctos* L. Canadian Wildlife Service Report Series, 34.

Proceedings of the International Association for Bear Research and Management. (The original research papers on the biology and management of bears, presented at nine international conferences held between 1968 and 1991. Copies of the Proceedings of the fourth to ninth conferences are available from Dr. M. Pelton, Department of Forestry, Fisheries and Wildlife, PO Box 1071, University of Tennessee, Knoxville, TN 37901, USA).

Rockwell, D. 1991. *Giving Voice to Bear: North American Indian Myths, Rituals, and Images of the Bear*. Rinehart Publishers, Niwot, CO.

Rogers, L.L. 1987. "Effects of food supply and kinship on social behavior, movements, and population growth of black bears in northeastern Minnesota." Wildlife Monographs, 97.

Rosenthal, M. 1989. *Proceedings of the First International Symposium on the Spectacled Bear*. Chicago Park District Press, Chicago, IL.

Schaller, G.B., Jinchu, H., Wenshi, P., and Jing, Z. 1985. *The Giant Pandas of Wolong*. University of Chicago Press, Chicago, IL.

Servheen, C. 1990. "The status and conservation of the bears of the world." International Conference on Bear Resources and Management. Monograph Series, No. 2.

Shepard, P. and Sanders, B. 1985. *The Sacred Paw: The Bear in Nature, Myth, and Literature*. Viking Penguin, Inc., New York, NY.

Stirling, I. 1988. *Polar Bears*. University of Michigan Press, Ann Arbor, MI.

Stirling, I. and Derocher, A.E. 1990. "Factors affecting the evolution and behavioral ecology of the modern bears." International Conference on Bear Research and Management, 8: 189–204.

Stock, C. 1972. Rancho La Brea, LA County. Science Series, No. 20. Museum of Natural History.

Storer, T.I. and Tevis, Jr., L.P. 1955. *California Grizzly*. University of California Press, Berkeley, CA.

Nowak, R.M. 1991. *Walker's Mammals of the World*. Fifth Edition. Two Volumes. Johns Hopkins University Press, Baltimore, MD.

FOR YOUNG READERS

Mathews, D. 1989. *Polar Bear Cubs*. Simon & Schuster, New York, NY.

Larsen, T. 1990. *The Polar Bear Family Book*. Verlag Neugebauer Press, Saltzburg, Austria.

Stirling, I. 1992. *Bears*. Sierra Club Books, San Francisco, CA.

Explorer Archives/AUSCAPE International

Ed. de Laplante, del.

ACKNOWLEDGMENTS

The publishers and the consulting editor would particularly like to thank the following people for their assistance in the preparation of this book: Sylvie Abecassis, Larry Agenbroad, Michelle Boustani, Julia Burke, Greg Campbell, Helen Cooney, Paul Geros, Selena Hand, Veronica Hilton, Arsen Kasbecki, Emilee Mead, Tristan Phillips, Andrew Rundle, Beverley Sharpe, Natalie Vellis, and Darren Ward.

We are also grateful to the following contributors for providing reference for and guidance with the production of illustrations: Fred Bunnell, Wendy Calvert, Shelley Cox, Valerius Geist, Robert S. Hoffmann, Judy Mills, Stephen O'Brien, Christopher Shaw, Kimberly Smith, Blaire Van Valkenburgh, Alasdair Veitch, and W. Chris Wozencraft.

Every effort has been made to acknowledge copyright holders of all material published in this book, but in the event of an omission please contact Weldon Owen.

ILLUSTRATIONS

Portrait illustrations on pages 20–21 and 38–49 are by David Kirshner; all other illustrations are by Frank Knight, unless otherwise indicated.

Skulls of polar bear and sea lion, p. 20
After Heptner and Sludskii, 1992.

Molecular phylogenetic family tree, p. 28
After diagram in *Scientific American*, Nov. 1987, "The Ancestry of the Giant Panda" by Stephen J. O'Brien, p. 107.

Skeletons of the left manus of a grizzly bear and a giant panda, and paws of a black bear and giant panda, p. 52
After D. D. Davis, 1964, "The Giant Panda". Fieldiana; *Zoology Memoirs* 3: 1–339.

Relative skull proportions of the grizzly bear and the giant panda, p. 56
After D. D. Davis, 1964, "The Giant Panda". Fieldiana; *Zoology Memoirs* 3: 1–339.

NOTES ON CONTRIBUTORS

ALISON AMES

Since graduating from Cambridge University in biological anthropology, Alison Ames has been studying the management and behavior of polar bears. She is currently a scientific officer for the Universities Federation for Animal Welfare in Britain. and is working on a project aimed at identifying the requirements of polar bears in captivity and meeting these requirements by means of environmental enrichment.

FRED L. BUNNELL

Professor Fred L. Bunnell teaches and conducts research at the Department of Forest Sciences at the University of British Columbia, Vancouver, Canada. He has received three national or international awards for contributions to science, including the gold medal for Scientific Achievement in Forestry in 1989, and has published over 140 scientific articles. He has acted as a consultant, frequently to governments, in 11 countries, and has served on over 70 provincial, national, and international committees dealing with resource management. A Registered Professional Biologist, Dr. Bunnell has held elected office in the Canadian Institute of Forestry, the Canadian Wildlife Society, the Wildlife Society, the International Union of Forest Research Organizations, and the B.C. Federation of Naturalist. For 12 years he was Associate Editor of *The Forestry Journal.*

WENDY CALVERT

Since 1974 Wendy Calvert has worked with the Canadian Goverment on polar bears. A biologist with the Canadian Wildlife Service, she has studied bear behavior, age-determination techniques, and computer-based data management.

JOSEPH D. CLARK

Dr. Joseph D. Clark gained a Ph.D. in zoology from the University of Arkansas in 1991. He served as Black Bear Project Leader at the Arkansas Game and Fish Commission from 1983 through 1990 and currently holds the post of Research Coordinator. His primary interests are carnivore ecology, population dynamics, and habitat modeling using Geographic Information Systems.

PETER L. CLARKSON

With a master's degree in environmental design, Peter L. Clarkson is a wolf and grizzly bear biologist with the Department of Renewable Resources, Government of Northwest Territories, Inuvik, Canada. He specializes in areas of conflict between wildlife and people.

SHELLEY M. COX

Shelley M. Cox is Curatorial Assistant and Laboratory Supervisor at the George C. Page Museum in California. As Laboratory Supervisor she trains and directs the activities of 50 volunteers in the cleaning, reconstruction, and identification of ice-age fossils recovered from the Rancho La Brea Tar Pits. Her current research involves defining size, range, and sexual dimorphism in the fossil ursid *Arctodus simus* from this site.

ANDREW E. DEROCHER

Dr. Andrew E. Derocher received his Ph.D. in zoology from the University of Alberta in 1991. His dissertation examined the population dynamics of polar bears and the factors that act to regulate their numbers. He is currently a Research Biologist on contract to the Canadian Wildlife Service and is continuing his research on polar bears.

DAVID L. GARSHELIS

After completing his master's degree studying the movements and activities of black bears, Dr. David L. Garshelis received his Ph.D. in wildlife from the University of Minnesota in 1983 with a dissertation concerning the ecology of sea otters in Alaska. Since that time he has conducted a long-term research project for the Minnesota Department of Natural Resources on the ecology and population of black bears. In 1990 he helped initiate a sloth bear study in Nepal. With Dr. J. David Smith of the University of Minnesota he co-advises Anup Joshi, a Ph.D. student investigating the factors limiting the distribution and abudance of the sloth bear.

VALERIUS GEIST

Dr. Valerius Geist is Professor of Environmental Sciences and Programme Director for Environmental Sciences at the University of Calgary, Canada. He has written six books, 106 technical papers, 130 general articles, various encyclopedia entries, and made seven films. He serves on two IUCN committees, is on the editorial boards of several technical and general journals and has been honored for his work by the Wildlife Society and the American Association for the Advancement of Science.

STEPHEN HERRERO

Professor of Environmental Science and Biology at the University of Calgary in Canada, Dr. Stephen Herrero teaches and undertakes research in wildlife ecology, conservation biology, and wildlife and environmental reserve planning and management. He is currently co-Chairperson of the IUCN/SSC Bear Specialist Group, and a member of Canada's Swift Fox Recovery Team. Author of the book *Bear Attacks: Their Causes and Avoidance*, he has also published over 100 articles on wildlife and environmental reserves. From 1986 to 1989 he was Chairperson of WWF Canada's Prairie Conservation Action Committee.

ROBERT S. HOFFMANN

Currently Assistant Secretary for Research at the Smithsonian Institution, Dr. Robert S. Hoffmann received his Ph.D. in zoology from Utah State University, and has worked as an instructor and professor in the Department of Zoology at the University of Montana. Before coming to the Smithsonian, he was Summerfield Distinguished Professor of Systematics and Ecology at the University of Kansas, and was Curator of Mammals at the university's Museum of Natural History. He is a world authority on the evolution of holarctic mammals, specializing in the Arctic and mountainous regions, as well as the mammals of the former Soviet Union, China, and Central Asia.

FRED W. HOVEY

Fred W. Hovey completed his master's degree in wildlife ecology at the University of British Colombia, Canada, and has been involved in the research and management of large mammals since 1984. He is currently working for his Ph.D. at Simon Fraser University, studying competition and resource partitioning between grizzly bears and black bears. He has radio-monitored 85 bears since 1988, and his bear research project is one of the largest in existence.

JACK W. LENTFER

Currently a wildlife consultant specializing in marine mammals, Jack W. Lentfer has worked for many years in Alaska as a wildlife biologist for the US Fish and Wildlife Service and the Alaska Department of Fish and Game. His areas of specialization include brown bear and polar bear research and management, and logging-wildlife relationships. He holds a governor's appointment to the Alaska Board of Game and is on the US Marine Mammal Commission.

ROBERT K. McCANN

Robert K. McCann has a master's degree in animal science from the University of British Columbia, Canada, his thesis centering on activity patterns and budgets of grizzly bears. He currently works as a contract biologist and has worked on a number of projects ranging from computer programming and simulation modeling to the writing of working plans for wildlife research projects.

JUDY A. MILLS

Judy A. Mills has a master's degree in resource conservation from the University of Montana, and is senior author of the 1991 World Wildlife Fund/TRAFFIC USA report "The Asian Trade in Bears and Bear Parts." She is a member of the IUCN/SSC Bear Specialist Group, her specialty being the Asian use of bear parts as medicine and the commercial trade in bears and bear parts for that purpose. She is currently writing a book about the bear trade.

STEPHEN J. O'BRIEN

Dr. Stephen J. O'Brien is Chief of the Laboratory of Viral Carcino-genesis of the National Cancer Institute at the Frederick Cancer Research Facility in Frederick, Maryland. He is co-Chairman of the International Committee on Comparative Gene Mapping and the Editor of *Genetic Maps*. His extensive studies in genetic analysis and molecular evolution have focused on the cat family and the giant panda and his present interests involve the co-evolution of genome organization in pathological viruses and in their mammalian host species.

MICHAEL R. PELTON

Professor of Wildlife Science at the Department of Forestry, Wildlife and Fisheries, the University of Tennessee, Dr. Michael R. Pelton has supervized research projects on wild animals in the Smoky Mountains since 1968, and his black bear study in Great Smoky Mountains National Park represents the longest continuous study of this species in North America. He and his students have conducted bear studies throughout the southeastern United States, as well as research on brown bears in Spain, on spectacled bears on in Colombia and on giant pandas in China. He and his students have received over US$1 million in research grants and contracts and have published over 140 articles.

MALCOLM A. RAMSAY

Dr. Malcolm A. Ramsay received his Ph.D. in zoology and is currently Associate Professor at the Department of Biology at Simon Fraser University, Canada. His research is directed at understanding the physiological and ecological implications of fasting on the life-histories of birds and mammals, and since 1988 he has been studying polar bears.

DONALD G. REID

Donald Reid is completing his Ph.D. on the role of predators, including the grizzly bear, in the regulation of collared lemming populations in the western Canadian Arctic, at the University of British Columbia. Since 1985 he has been working as a research biologist for the World Wildlife Fund and Wildlife Conservation International coordinating field studies of the giant panda, the Asiatic black bear, and the red panda with Chinese Ministry of Forestry scientists in Sichuan, China.

LYNN L. ROGERS

A wildlife research biologist with the US Forest Service's North Central Forest Experiment Station, Lynn Rogers has spent the past 25 years studying carnivores, especially black bears, in the forests of northern Minnesota. He spends long periods with the bears as they go about their lives, paying little attention to their observer close by. He has written many scientific papers on aspects of carnivore behavior and biology.

BARRY SANDERS

Dr. Barry Sanders occupies the Peter and Gloria Gold Chair in English and the History of Ideas at Pitzer College, California, and serves as a contributing editor for *The North American Review*. His most recent book, co-authored with Ivan Illich, is entitled *Alphabetization of the Popular Mind*, and he wrote, with Paul Shepard, *The Sacred Paw: The Bear in Nature, Myth and Literature*. He is currently completing *A is for Ox: A Case for Pre-Literacy*, and *Sudden Glory: Western Attitudes Toward Laughter*.

JOHN SEIDENSTICKER

Dr. John Seidensticker was one of the pioneers of the use of radiotelemetry in the study of large, solitary-living mammals. He was a student assistant in John and Frank Craighead's Yellowstone grizzly studies, and he studied puma social organization in Idaho for his Ph.D. He was founding principal investigator of the Smithsonian–Nepal Tiger Ecology Project, where he also studied sloth bears. As a wildlife ecologist and Curator of Mammals at the National Zoological Park, Smithsonian Institution, he studies the consequences of habitat insularization and change on populations of large and medium-sized mammals and their response to confined environments.

CHRISTOPHER SERVHEEN

Dr. Christopher Servheen received his Ph.D. in wildlife biology and forestry from the University of Montana, and has worked on grizzly bear conservation since 1975. He has a particular interest in international bear conservation and has undertaken research on bears in Spain, France, Taiwan, Malaysia, and Japan. In addition, his focus has been on the conservation of Asian bears, including habitat conservation and the development of research on the sun bear and the Asiatic black bear.

CHRISTOPHER A. SHAW

Christopher A. Shaw is Collection Manager of the George C. Page Museum, California, a job that entails identification, cataloguing, and storage of all fossils and archival material, totaling some 4 million items. He has been working in the field of vertebrate paleontology since 1967 and at Rancho La Brea since 1969.

SCOTT D. SHULL

Scott D. Shull is currently studying for his master's degree in the Arkansas Cooperative Fish and Wildlife Research Unit at the University of Arkansas. He is studying the movements and effects of negative conditioning on nuisance black bears in Arkansas.

KIMBERLY G. SMITH

Dr. Kimberly G. Smith received his Ph.D. in biology and ecology from Utah State University and since 1987 he has been directing research on the black bears of Arkansas. Currently at the University of Arkansas, his other research interests include community ecology, neotropical migratory birds, the tropical ecology of Belize, and periodical cicadas.

IAN STIRLING

Dr. Ian Stirling studied seals in Antarctica, New Zealand, and Australia for five years before returning to Canada to conduct long-term research on polar bears for the Canadian Wildlife Service. For the past 23 years he has studied the behavior, population ecology, and habitat use of polar bears, and how these factors are influenced by the distribution and abundance of seals. He has published over 100 scientific papers on polar bears, seals, and arctic marine conservation, as well as the authoritative book, *Polar Bears,* and a children's book, *Bears.* He is on a number of national and international committees which deal with the conservation of bears.

BLAIRE VAN VALKENBURGH

Dr. Blaire Van Valkenburgh is Associate Professor of Biology at the University of California and specializes in vertebrate morphology and evolution, especially in mammalian predators. Her current research projects focus on the feeding behavior of spotted hyenas, lions, wild dogs, and cheetahs in East Africa, and on the evolution of carnivore communities in the New and Old Worlds.

ALASDAIR M. VEITCH

Alasdair M. Veitch is working on his Ph.D. under the auspices of the Department of Zoology at the University of Alberta, researching the behavior and ecology of black bears living on the tundra of the Ungava Peninsula. He has been involved in wildlife research in Labrador, Canada since 1984, studying peregrine falcons, rough-legged hawks, caribou, moose, wolves, and black bears.

DIANA L. WEINHARDT

Ms. Diana L. Weinhardt is a zoologist at the Lincoln Park Zoological Gardens in Chicago, and has been involved in the captive management and conservation of spectacled bears since 1981. She is Editor of the International Spectacled Bear Studbook, Special Advisor to the Spectacled Bear SSP, and Secretary of the Spectacled Bear Specialist Group of the IUCN/SSC/Bear Specialist Group.

WENSHI PAN

Wenshi Pan began research on giant pandas in cooperation with the World Wildlife Fund in the Wolong Nature Reserve, China. Since 1985 he has been working as project leader with a group of experts under-taking research on giant pandas in the Qinling Mountains. His extensive ecological and conservation work in this field has resulted in him becoming the leading expert on giant pandas in China.

W. CHRIS WOZENCRAFT

Dr. W. Chris Wozencraft received his Ph.D. in systematics and ecology from the University of Kansas and is currently Zoologist at the Office of the Assistant Secretary for Science, Smithsonian Institution. His focus has been on the evolution and ecology of the mammalian order Carnivora and he has recently finished a long-term study of the evolution and comparative morphology of the family Viverridae—the civets, linsangs, and genets. He has also studied the phylogenetic relationships among the Ursidae (bears), Procyonidae (raccoons, coatis, and so on), and the Herpestidae (mongooses).

ZHI LÜ

Dr. Lü is a student of Wenshi Pan's and has taken part in research on giant pandas in the Qinling Mountains since 1985. Her studies focus on the adaptations, social behavior, and conservation of giant pandas.

Explorer Archives/AUSCAPE International

INDEX